'The supremacy of interruption-based advertising is over.
But what happens next? PJ Pereira and the other experts help us
to understand the consequences of the radical shift through
The Art of Branded Entertainment.'
– Dr Bjoern Asmussen
Senior Lecturer in Marketing, Oxford Brookes University

'A must-read in case you want to answer "senator,
we run great content" instead of "senator, we run ads
during a congressional hearing".'
– Fernando Machado
Global Chief Marketing Officer, Burger King

THE ART OF
BRANDED
ENTERTAINMENT

KAREN,

To a Creative
Partnership!

Jason X

THE ART OF BRANDED ENTERTAINMENT

Monica Chun, Jules Daly, Ricardo Dias,
Samantha Glynne, Carol Goll, Gabor Harrach,
Marissa Nance, Toan Nguyen, Luciana Olivares,
Marcelo Pascoa, PJ Pereira, Misha Sher,
Pelle Sjoenell, Tomoya Suzuki, Jason Xenopoulos

Edited by

PJ Pereira

Peter Owen
London and Chicago

Peter Owen Publishers
Conway Hall, 25 Red Lion Square, London WC1R 4RL, UK

Peter Owen books are distributed in the USA and Canada by
Independent Publishers Group/Trafalgar Square
814 North Franklin Street, Chicago, IL 60610, USA

Paperback ISBN   978-0-7206-2058-0
Epub ISBN   978-0-7206-2059-7
Mobipocket ISBN   978-0-7206-2060-3
PDF ISBN   978-0-7206-2061-0

A catalogue record for this book is available from the British Library.

Cover design: Moses Kelany
Typeset by Octavo Smith Publishing Services

Printed by CPI Group (UK) Ltd, Croydon, CR0 4YY

ACKNOWLEDGEMENTS

Left to right: Pelle Sjoenell, Marissa Nance, Jason Xenopoulos, Carol Goll, Gabor Harrach, Al MacCuish, Samantha Glynne, Luciana Olivares, Jules Daly, Monica Chun, Tim Ellis, PJ Pereira, Misha Sher, Amanda Hill, Steven Kalifowitz, Toan Nguyen, Tomoya Suzuki, Julian Jacobs, Marcelo Pascoa, Ricardo Dias

Cannes Lions actually started in Venice in 1954 as an advertising film festival with a single group of people looking at 187 entries from fourteen countries. Almost seventy years later the festival has grown somewhat. It moved to the French Riviera, incorporated new forms of advertising and increased the number of its juries to more than twenty groups of people from all over the world.

Yet, despite all the knowledge shared, the conclusions and perspectives developed in the judging rooms, this is the first book ever published by a Cannes jury.

My guess is that some may have thought about it before, but the amount of work it takes to organize the ideas from leaders scattered across the planet must have always discouraged our predecessors. In our case, the irresponsible bravery to overcome these obstacles came from a sense of responsibility. The field we discussed together is too important and our discussions way too inspiring to be left with us alone as we haunted the hallways of the Palais des Festivals et des Congrès. That's why not only the authors but everyone else around us who supported the plan deserves to be excited to see this tome out in the world.

Starting with the relentless team who wrote each of the individual chapters – some more than one. Those who endured my rain of emails, calls, messages and obsessive revision requests: Sam, Ricardo, Gabor, Marcelo, Monica, Carol, Misha, Jules, Toan, Tomo, Pelle, Jason, Luciana and Marissa, I hope in the end you are all as proud of the result as I am. Al MacCuish, Amanda Hill, Julian Jacobs, Tim Ellis, Steven Kalifowitz, as members of the jury who couldn't join us on the writing, I hope you feel your thoughts and contributions are represented, too.

Also, we have to thank Terry Savage, Phil Thomas, Jose Papa and Lisa Berlin from Cannes Lions for putting together this extraordinary group of people and Tiffany Spoden and her team for keeping us on track during our endless debates.

Getting the book produced also required the help of a lot of people. From Pereira O'Dell we have Moses Kelany, who designed the cover art with the support of Owen Bly, plus Denise Corazza, Russ Nadler and Christina Hadly, who helped manage the complex legalities of a book with so many authors. Jasmine Gothelf, from FremantleMedia, has put together the index of case studies at the end of the book, which the team at VML South Africa – Ernst Lass, Hans Liebenberg, Hayley Montgomery, Hannes Matthysen and Loki Magerman – have then turned into a website our readers can now visit to find all the work mentioned in these pages.

Finally, to the team at Peter Owen – Nick Kent, Antonia Owen, Sam Oates and Simon Smith – who kept the focus on the potential of this project and not on the challenges we would face to get it done, our sincere gratitude.

That's the full crowd behind the first book from a Cannes jury. People whose passion and enthusiasm compensated for our naive notion that maybe we could get this project off the ground, when no one else had dared before. To all of you, my most sincere thank you.

We are all firsts together.

PJ Pereira

FOREWORD

Imagine if none of us had ever seen a commercial break. Not one. They haven't been invented yet. Then someone comes with a pitch: 'So, Mrs CMO, we've had an idea. To get your message heard we will pay content channels to pause the series your audience is watching, play our ad then let them go back to the normal programming!'

Which brand in their right mind would ever want to associate themselves with such a terrible user experience?

The only reason why we still do it is because there are enough of us out there, old folks who haven't totally realized things don't have to be that way. The awakening is happening, though, and there is actually an entire generation who, like the fictional CMO above, has never seen an advertisement until recently.

It happened to me, actually.

It was like being shaken, literally. Living in the San Francisco Bay Area, the fear of a big earthquake is a real thing, so by the time my eyes were open the sheets were pulled over to the other side of the bed. Four inches from my nose was the face of my son Francisco. He's eleven, and that matters. He still had his hand on my shoulder from trying to wake me up with such urgency.

'Dad, you gotta get out of advertising.'

'Why?' I asked.

'Because it's so annoying,' he replied.

Kids have that ability to state the obvious with such candour and simplicity that it makes it impossible to ignore.

Which brings us to France, the Cannes Lions International Festival of Creativity, where I met the co-authors of this book.

Cannes Lions is arguably the largest and most prestigious competition of brand ideas in the world. In 2017 alone it received more than ten thousand paying delegates, including lots of chief marketing officers and advertising executives eager to refresh their ideas. In the halls and rooms of the Palais des Festivals we find them mixed with creative minds of all sorts, technologists and deal-makers of many nationalities, squeezing themselves in to watch the winners in twenty-three categories, including ours, Branded Entertainment. At five years old, and having had several name changes along the way – Branded Content, Branded Content and Entertainment and, finally, Branded Entertainment – this young category is considered by some to be the real future of the festival and the industry.

In the last ten years the evolution of marketing has been documented by the juries working at the Palais during the festival. A look at past winners will show when the industry started to incorporate technology, design, PR and media thinking into the work and the stories we tell, not just in the way they are distributed but also how they are conceived and told; it will show how we absorbed formerly alien techniques to generate new expressions of creativity and fresh ways of telling our stories. And that's always good – except it wasn't enough. That's what my son Francisco wanted me to understand with his seismic shake-up.

The most fundamental change in our business didn't come from our own hands, wasn't borne out of new formats or disciplines. It came not from what we have been doing within our field but from its upside-down, from consumers, tech-visionaries and the entertainment ecosystem who suddenly realized the cornerstone of our trade, buying people's time, doesn't make any sense if the owners of that time aren't the ones trying to sell it. According to Nielsen's 'State of Traditional TV', between 2012 and 2017 television viewing in the eighteen-to-twenty-four age group in the USA dropped by almost ten hours a week, reaching its lowest ever ratings. In the space of five years, close to half of this age group's traditional TV viewing time has migrated to other activities or streaming.[1]

Suddenly, the bizarro world is us.

Cue all the on-demand services out there: from YouTube to Netflix to Twitch to iTunes . . . As they expand and, in their gruesome march, eliminate the places where advertising used to exist, they also leave us with little choice other than to become the content ourselves. Our work is either worth pressing 'play' (instead of the newest show, video game or YouTuber video), or it will just disappear into the shrinking parts of the media where ads can still be bought.

And it's not only the audience that is shifting. The talent (and therefore the quality) is migrating, too. Look at the 2017 Emmys, for example. Of the twenty-six statues given that year, half went to platforms with no advertising support whatsoever, and, of the remaining thirteen, five went to Hulu, which is only partially supported by ads. If Hollywood ceases to need advertisers' money to justify their annoying breaks, brands will lose their voice, their most important opportunity to be heard; or, at least, the voice we got so used to being able to count on.

If Cannes is the frontline in the battle for advertising and its promotional warriors, the Branded Entertainment category is our resistance, our hope. The exploration of this new territory is where brands have to compete for an opportunity to be heard against all the 'unbranded' content on the planet, the highest creative bar we have ever had to face. A space that is not only difficult to inhabit but uncertain. A universe architected from the inside, developed as we explore it. Understood as we judged. What are the limits, the rules?

It was up to this group of twenty people to decide. Not because we are the wisest and most knowledgeable but because we were the ones in that room. Don't get me wrong; every individual in this group is highly accomplished, and combined we had accolades that would last for generations. But what made our choices important wasn't our pasts but the fact that we sat there and watched. Every single entry. In its entirety. For days, with quick breaks to eat and sleep. Then we let our guts and our brains tell us which ones stood out, and then we discussed.

It helped that from the start we agreed we weren't there to teach anyone but rather to listen, to learn on behalf of the industry so that we could share what we saw and felt as we browsed through thousands of ideas created by the best agencies in the world. That helped us to keep our goal in sight and pick a list of winners that inspire and teach us how to get better at what we do.

This book is the result of that experience, the essence of what we learned.

In order to outlive 2017, though, our conclusions couldn't just relate to the winners we picked that year. After the festival was over we took all we discussed, everything we absorbed and concluded during that week then applied them to winners from previous years and even to campaigns that had never won. We set ourselves a mission to adjust our insights so that they can apply to any work aiming to attract the time of the consumer; now, in the past or the future. A 'branded entertainment DeLorean'.

I hope you like it.

The book opens with **Part 1: The Need**, which focuses not on the emergency of experimenting and moving towards less intrusive ways of messaging but on what branded entertainment can do for a brand based on all the work we have seen. Starting with Ricardo Dias, CMO of Anheuser-Busch InBev's Grupo Modelo in Mexico, and Gabor Harrach, the New York-based film and television producer and former Head of Entertainment Content at Red Bull Media House who dive together into the definition of this space and what it adds to the marketing mix. Still in Part 1, Marcelo Pascoa, Head of Global Brand Marketing at Burger King, takes an in-depth look into what it means for the industry to have to *earn* time instead of simply buy it. Finally, Monica Chun, PMK•BNC's COO, shares her perspective of how branded entertainment isn't only the content itself but, often, the news it creates.

Part 2: The Art of Branded Entertainment addresses the core theme of this book, and it opens with challenging how brands have been thinking about their presence in entertainment experiences. Bartle Bogle Hegarty's Global Chief Creative Officer Pelle Sjoenell together with Jason Xenopoulos, Chief Vision Officer of VML and Chief Creative Officer of VML Europe, Middle East and Africa, share their observations of what happened when advertisers shifted from product placement to what they call 'brand placement' – a core idea that influences all the chapters that follow in this section of the book. Next we go back to basics with Tomoya Suzuki, CEO of STORIES, who looks at how branded entertainment needs to reincorporate the core principles of storytelling from Hollywood in order to have a better context surrounding their brand ideas. In fact, one of these principles was clearly so important that we decided to give it its own chapter,

'Amping the Tension', by Pelle Sjoenell. And if tension is important in scripted stories, it's even more fundamental in unscripted ones. Gabor Harrach tackles a desire expressed by so many marketing professionals who seem to believe that the only way to do it nowadays is to show the real world. Based on his personal experience as a documentarian, he shares his perspective on how a brand can stand out with reality-based stories. Finally, Luciana Olivares, CCO of Latina Media in Peru, shares her inspiring perspective on how the creators' motivations and emotions, especially anger, can become a way to turn brands and causes into content that changes the lives of the audience.

Part 3: Opportunities Ahead addresses the unexplored voids under-represented among the winners and the overall standouts in the industry, starting with Misha Sher, Vice-President at MediaCom Sport and Entertainment, who sprints into how, despite sports being the ultimate form of entertainment, brands don't seem to be chasing excellence in this field; or, if they are, then they don't participate in the competitions, which is also a missed opportunity that hurts the industry as a whole. This is followed by Toan Nguyen, partner at Jung von Matt/SPORTS, on how we not only need more sports but a greater variety of sports, notably eGames, a competition that currently attracts a massive audience and some sponsorship but still seems to lack the creativity invested in its older physical sibling. Then comes Marissa Nance, Managing Director for Multicultural Content Marketing and Strategic Partnerships at media superpower OMD, on how to add more research, media and distribution science to the art of branded entertainment.

Finally, **Part 4: The Business**, is dedicated to the business of branded entertainment. It opens with Jules Daly, President of RSA Films, dissecting the Hollywood way of making stories popular, followed by ICM Partners' Global Head of Branded Entertainment Carol Goll who asks what's in it for the stars. Brands have their needs, as do consumers, but it is when initiatives also take into consideration the needs of the artists involved that the partnerships can really flourish. The opportunity of scale, going from local to global, from campaigns to seasons, is the theme of the next chapter, in which Samantha Glynne raises important questions to help brands and agencies learn how to build their audiences in the same way that the entertainment businesses does. Jason Xenopoulos comes back on next for his encore, analysing how some of the biggest winners in our competition hail from hidden corners of bigger marketing operations or from marketers and countries that don't usually have the biggest budgets in the world – 'brand ninjutsu', as he calls it – only half a surprise, considering that boldness and innovation often comes from the most underscrutinized processes and the most focused groups of people.

And to round it all off, me, PJ Pereira, co-founder and Creative Chairman of Pereira O'Dell and President of the Cannes Lions 2017 Branded Entertainment jury. I will wrap it up with the backstage perspective of how some of this year's entries and previous winners adjusted their businesses to allow ideas that appear so much more expensive than they could theoretically afford.

Cut. Reset.

I know, it's a lot – of information, nuance, analysis, forecasting . . . Ideas generated after a week locked in a dark room watching brands trying to keep us entertained, then a few months digesting what we found. So, take it slowly. Look around. Think. These pages aren't meant to be read in one sitting, and many chapters mention the same case studies because they deserve to be analysed from multiple angles instead of just taking individual winners and looking in depth at every angle of each – there are other resources and better places to do that than in this book.

If our goal was to learn on behalf of the industry, then this is our homework, our project, dissected to allow ourselves and you, the reader, to have the widest perspective ever put together on paper on what's behind, beside and above the nascent idea of branded entertainment; an anthology of thoughts and questions to help guide you on your own enquiry. What is the right balance between my brand's message and the fun it's supposed to provide? How do I craft ideas that stand out in the entertainment landscape that has much more – I mean, *way* more – money than any brand? Or do we have to? Can we partner? Co-own? Pilot something that can grow by itself later? What can we do without the limitations of time or real estate but with the marketing responsibilities our 'competitors' in entertainment don't have to carry? Should we go long form, longer form or stay short where we can reign strong?

We, marketers and agency people, are living through the most profound reinvention of what we do in generations. We may not have all the answers yet, but if instead of trying to force our theories we let the best work speak, clarity will eventually happen.

This book presents the perspectives of this unlikely group of people who ended up locked in a dark room in France for a week in a relentless debate of what was great and what was just good, then trying to understand why. An experience that deeply changed the way we look at work, and we hope that it will impact on yours, too.

The chapters ahead belong to each author individually. They come from what we saw together but also from our own individual experiences as marketers, creatives, media, talent agents, publishers, networks, sports and games specialists and technologists. The opinions, therefore, are different, sometimes dissonant, but we believe that to be a good thing. By allowing the voices to stay independent we can have a more accurate depiction of the nuances of such a rich process – including the global aspect of it, since each contributor comes from a different place: South Africa, the UK, Brazil, the USA, Russia, Mexico, Peru, Japan and Germany.

The opinions here come out of work that has already been done, work that has been seen, judged and archived. They may teach, maybe even guide, but never fully apply to the next challenge landing on your desk. That is your job. We just hope what we learned and the work we picked, for the awards and the book, are a good warm-up to what you have to do next when it's your turn to push this industry forward.

Happy reading.

PJ Pereira
President of the Cannes Lions Entertainment Jury, 2017,
San Francisco, 2018

1. Nielsen's 'The State of Traditional TV: Updated With Q2 2017 Data' https://www.marketingcharts.com/featured-24817

CONTENTS

Branded entertainment is:

1. Entertainment produced by brands
2. Advertising you don't want to skip
3. Marketing made to be sought and not designed to interrupt entertainment
4. Advertisements that are both a good financial investment for brands and a good investment of time for audiences
5. Advertisements that attract their own audience instead of buying time to be watched or played

Part 1
THE NEED

DIGITALLY BORN KILLERS (OR WHAT BRANDED ENTERTAINMENT CAN DO FOR BRANDS)

Ricardo Dias, Anheuser-Busch InBev

Gabor Harrach, Consultant, formerly of Red Bull Media House

Call us brand detectives. As we began writing this chapter, something happened in the world (or in the skies above us) that might change the impact of branded entertainment for ever: Elon Musk's SpaceX Falcon Heavy rocket was launched from Kennedy Space Center in Florida; its payload Musk's personal red Roadster, an electric sports car built by his other brand, Tesla. Its humble mission, to orbit the sun (and Mars) for hundreds of millions of years. Strapped inside the Roadster is the so-called Starman, a mannequin in a branded SpaceX spacesuit.

It happened live on YouTube and everywhere else. It was a breathtaking demonstration of technological and marketing power. It was also beautiful (you know it, because you saw it). David Bowie's *Life on Mars?* played from the space car radio while our blue planet rotated slowly in the background. And it seemed that this song was written for exactly that magical moment. Days later we and countless others still watched the Starman live on YouTube. The images seemed to pick up where Red Bull's space jump left off in 2012. Was this a marketing film that would last millions of years? Was this a test flight or a real space mission? Or was it just a power demonstration by Elon Musk, because he could? It's probably all of the above. And it taught us a forceful lesson: not only is the threshold for marketing stunts now higher than ever (literally) but also the boundary between branded entertainment and the reality of a brand seems to have shifted to an extent that marketing itself becomes the brand. Only a day after the successful space car launch Tesla reported 'its biggest [quarterly] loss ever'.[1] However, Tesla's stock price continues to soar like Elon Musk's rockets. And only a few weeks later the energy-drink maker Red Bull announced a mission to the moon for 2019, featuring Audi lunar quattro rovers. The moon mission will be aired live across multiple devices and in various forms. Not even the sky seems to be the limit any more.

In this chapter we will look at the role branded entertainment plays as part of an increasingly complex and shifting marketing mix. We investigate a mysterious void that turns customers away from traditional advertising and commercials, and we try to identify the culprit behind the void.

Who or what kills advertising as we know it? Please buckle up. It's quite a ride.

Our detective story starts in Cannes. For most of the year, it is a sleepy resort town on the French Riviera with sandy beaches and palatial hotels, but once a year it becomes ground zero for all things (and everyone) advertising – our crime scene.

The need

'We decided we are not here to teach the world, to teach you guys, what we think branded entertainment was,' said jury president PJ Pereira at the 2017 Lions Entertainment award ceremony in Cannes while more than two thousand delegates anxiously focused on him. 'We didn't pick work that matched what we had been pitching to our clients and that we were trying to get sold during the last few years. We were here with a very humble attitude to learn on behalf of all of you and to try to understand not what branded entertainment is but what it is becoming.'

The two authors of this chapter were part of this journey, learning and investigating to get a grasp on the elusive yet fashionable but still evolving term 'branded entertainment'. Along with PJ and our co-jurors, we spent the better part of a week in a dark, windowless jury room deep in the bowels of the massive concrete structure known as the Palais des Festivals et des Congrès de Cannes – in the middle of June on the French Riviera! The jury rooms are notorious for their freezing air conditioning and even colder food. (Sorry, Cannes Lions, but both rumours are actually true.) At the very least it kept our heads cool and our minds sharp during the sometimes heated debates. When we left the jury room we had found a few hints and clues to the big question. But to fully understand what branded entertainment is becoming we had first to explain its need and answer two fundamental questions:

1. *Why* do people from all over the world and almost all demographics increasingly ignore content that is being forced upon them (be it by publishers, advertisers or traditional television)?
2. *What* does branded entertainment ultimately achieve for brands? (Having worked for content-loving brands like Anheuser-Busch and Red Bull, we might have some answers but even more surprises for you.)

At the end of this chapter we offer a few ideas on *how* to create great branded entertainment. For an in-depth blueprint, please look forward to Part 2 of this book, 'The Art of Branded Entertainment'. Or, to put it in the language of our detective story, it's all about the motive, the means and the opportunity.

Let's start by looking at why so many of us have a motive to avoid advertising.

On-demand lifestyles

The way we consume content is closely linked to our lifestyles. We live in an on-demand economy (or *shared society*). We move around town on demand (Uber, Lyft, Zipcar). We date (Tinder, Bumble, Raya) and listen to music on demand (Spotify, Apple Music). We have the house cleaned on demand (Handy, Hux, Whizz). We eat on demand (Uber Eats, Deliveroo, Caviar). We watch content on demand (YouTube, Netflix, Amazon Prime Video). There's a convenient app for almost everything. We rate services and value experiences and have less time for anything unwanted, random or coincidental. We're accustomed to paying for exactly what we want and when we want it and increasingly refuse to pay for anything (including TV channels) we don't need. We increasingly cut the cord from cable TV companies and use ad blockers, creating a void and leaving traditional advertising platforms behind. PJ is not the only industry professional who felt the seismic shake-up close to home, as he has described in the foreword to this book. Ricardo, one of the authors of this chapter, also experienced how the distaste for commercials has already engulfed his own family members, especially the younger ones, the ones who are 'digital natives' or, in an even stronger and more fashionable term, 'digitally born'.

What happened to my cartoon?

A few years ago Ricardo and his family went to his home country of Brazil for end-of-year festivities. They chose Trancoso as their destination, a beautiful yet remote beach in the northern part of the country, very close to where the Portuguese first settled a little over 500 years ago. Even though the hippie-turned-chic beach had progressed dramatically over the last two decades, their rental property did not have an internet connection, so his four-year-old's content craving had to be met in the good old local TV broadcast – a first for her.

On their first night, while Ricardo and his wife were having dinner with their friends, their daughter was enjoying her coconut ice cream and watching a Brazilian cartoon on TV in the family room next door. All of a sudden she shouted, 'Daddy!' He immediately ran over, thinking something must have happened, to find her looking at him, pointing at the TV in disgust. She then asked him, 'What happened to my cartoon?' He looked over to the TV and back at her and reluctantly broke the news: 'This is a commercial, sweetie.'

The void

Notable dictionaries describe a void as 'an emptiness caused by the loss of something'.

Let's translate this into marketing lingo. The void is 'the absence of an audience caused by the loss of interest of consumers in advertising'. This results in the audience leaving traditional distribution platforms such as cable TV, a process described as 'cord-cutting'. Others, like Ricardo's daughter, are too young and too 'digitally born' even to remember linear television. They are 'cord nevers'.

Both having worked for major brands in the past ten years, we had no choice other than to develop strategies on how to engage the developing void crisis.

Engaging the void

When thinking of brand communication, marketers have to keep in mind what their consumers – loyal and potential – want from them. It is now clear that people no longer want to be interrupted. They don't want to have products pushed at them while their time is being taken away. However, one thing has not changed over time: they do like being entertained.

Our logical conclusion: branded entertainment needs to fill the void. As with so many other recipes for success, this sounds much easier to do than actually getting it done.

With an abundance of entertainment options nowadays, consumers are still on the hunt for a product that resolves a specific need. Because people still like to hear from brands, there is opportunity in making their time valuable. However, consumer habits are changing faster than ever, leading to elusive audiences.

Let's try to paint a more detailed picture of this mysterious void. Since almost all marketers are now storytellers, we keep approaching it like a detective story. Changing lifestyles have created a motive for the void. But it is technology that provides the means and opportunity for the consumer to *kill* traditional advertising by avoidance.

Avoidance by technology

An entry from our detective's notebook: easy-to-obtain technology has enabled media avoidance owing to many factors, and some of the following are culprits:

- Shift to mobile across global markets
- Ad blockers
- Ad-free media platforms (Netflix, Hulu, Amazon Prime, Spotify)
- The DVR (digital video recorder) effect

The void in numbers

We didn't come to Cannes to judge creative work by the numbers. We watched the work as it is and then put its impact in context.

You didn't buy this book to get filibustered by statistics. You're looking for insights and clarity.

But this is a detective story. And we need to put two and two together. So let us measure how technology helped the consumer avoid advertising and extend the void.

The consumer-research platform eMarketer surveyed the growth of the void and cord-cutting. In 2017, before the year was even over, 22.2 million adults in the USA had already cut the cord on cable, satellite or telco TV services (that's up a frightening 33% from 16.7 million in 2016): 94% of consumers skip TV ads completely, and 236 million desktop browsers and 380 million mobile browsers were using ad-blocking software by the end of 2016 (up 38% from a year prior).[2]

Media fragmentation

If this testimony wasn't alarming enough for advertisers and publishers, let us take a look at the collateral damage that media fragmentation is bringing about to the traditional advertising model. Currently, there is an abundance of choices in entertainment and media, with weekly emergences of new distributors and content creators.

There used to be half-a-dozen major studios competing in Hollywood. Now several dozen streaming services and production entities have disrupted and fragmented the film business. The same fragmentation happened in the TV and music industry. Where a handful of serious competitors once dominated the market, a multitude of new competitors are now fighting over audience and revenue.

We wonder, is the newly emerged, easy-to-obtain technology the elusive, digitally born killer of the old advertising model, or does it merely play the part of an enabler for the real killer?

Overstimulated communities

Throughout the industry there has been a dramatic increase in the amount of content consumed as well as produced, with non-ad-supported platforms increasingly winning over more viewers. Reportedly, the video-streaming service Netflix will invest $8 billion in creating original content in 2018 and add to the total of more than 500 scripted shows already developed and produced in 2017.

Of the many millions who are watching the content (and this development) there is one group with a particularly keen interest in the fragmentation: the brands.

Brands don't want to fall victim to the overstimulated communities and have their messages lost in the void – too much is at stake.

Many brands believe that to remain relevant the move from an interruptive advertiser to one that attracts an audience is inevitable. There are quite a few examples of brands that became successful entertainers. The list starts to shine a light on *what* branded entertainment can do for brands.

Over the past twenty years LEGO has transformed itself from a traditional toymaker into a media powerhouse. Its beloved toy characters rival Disney's on the small, large and digital screens.

At the beginning of the century the German car-maker BMW

stunned the advertising world with a series of action-packed short films by notable directors such as Guy Ritchie, Tony Scott, John Frankenheimer, Alejandro G. Iñárritu, Ang Lee, Wong Kar-wai and Neill Blomkamp, which put high-performing BMW automobiles at the centre of the action. Fifteen years later the film series made a comeback starring Clive Owen.

Marriott International produces content for next-gen travellers, most of which is produced in-house. Not only do they produce social media content for about nineteen global hotel brands and a personalized online travel magazine (*Marriott Traveler*) but they also make TV shows (*The Navigator Live*), short movies (*Two Bellmen, French Kiss*), web series on YouTube and Instagram and a virtual reality (VR) experience in partnership with Facebook's Oculus Rift. One of Marriott's movies apparently resulted in $500,000 in hotel bookings in the first sixty days alone, the *Marriott Traveler* drove 7,200 room bookings in ninety days and the brand's interactive website is leveraging a built-in audience of 40 million visitors monthly.

Red Bull is not only known for its state-of-the-art movies, documentaries and digital content (the brand's YouTube channel currently has almost 7 million subscribers, more than 7,000 videos and more than 2 billion views), the energy-drink maker's media arm is also a successful publisher (*The Red Bulletin*) and has built its own digital content platform (Red Bull TV).

Digitally born (ad) killers

The further we investigate, the more likely it becomes that young digital natives' viewing habits and disruptive commercials aren't the only culprits to be blamed for the void and demise of traditional broadcast and cable TV. In the spirit of our detective story, let us look for other suspects.

The search starts with Gabor's first career in broadcast TV. Having worked as a television producer for more than ten years, he barely watches TV any more, with the exception of live sports. But it's not the commercials that annoy him – they can actually be quite fun. And as a Gen Xer, he's not digitally born – although, as kids, he and his friends had to create their own computer games because none was available or affordable. The main reason traditional TV has become disruptive and looks and sounds so dated to him is the fact that almost the entire content of today's TV is formatted so that it fits exactly into the spaces between commercial breaks – be it TV dramas, comedies, entertainment and reality shows, even made-for-television documentaries and news magazine shows. Everything is packaged like a kids' meal in a fast-food restaurant. Every act structure is basically the same and revolves around standardized commercial breaks. And if this isn't enough, there are endless recaps about what happened last time (or just before the commercial break) as well as countless, obnoxiously repetitive teasers to promote what else we must watch on this TV network. As a final assault, this already indigestible mix is frequently interrupted by local news breaks and severe weather warnings. It's the combination of these that is disruptive and makes the so-called linear TV experience more and more unbearable, especially in comparison to the smooth delivery of on-demand streaming platforms.

Nobody wants to be a suspect. Many stakeholders in the TV and production community, including some of Gabor's former colleagues and friends in broadcasting, may now cry out loudly in protest. They may point out their creative achievements in contemporary format development and successes in modernizing the TV experience for the twenty-first century. But the audience increasingly doesn't think so. And digital natives are disconnecting from linear TV altogether.

In our notebook the evidence and numbers keep adding up. Between 2012 and 2017 TV viewing by Americans aged between eighteen and twenty-four dropped by almost ten hours a week, or by roughly one hour and twenty-five minutes per day.[3] Instead, during the first quarter of 2017 the same demographic spent an average of 2,226 minutes consuming online videos via PC and 414 minutes watching mobile videos per month.[4]

Suddenly the group of suspects for causing the void has become a whole lot bigger. It's not only the people who cut their ties with the platforms or the ones who never engaged with them because they are too young and digitally born; it's not only the perceived annoying and disruptive commercials and display ads but also the people who create linear content and television experiences.

And, as in any classic detective story, the real killer might not only be among us, the killer might actually be us. By birth, behaviour or association – are we all digitally born killers?

Insult to our intelligence

Global leaders in branding and marketing have long understood the problem with the traditional TV experience. In a pitch meeting with the billionaire founder and chief executive of a major consumer packaged goods brand, TV executives were trying to educate him on how proper TV content is packaged. He emphatically countered by asking them not to insult his intelligence. We couldn't agree more. Sustainable businesses are not built on cookie-cutter solutions.

The TV industry and its current worldwide $178 billion advertising business have a much better chance of avoiding the void and ultimately surviving if traditional TV becomes less predictable, less annoying, less cookie-cutter-formatted, less trying-to-meet-the-audience-on-the-lowest-common-denominator and instead focuses more on the strengths of unrestricted storytelling, the power of new ideas and, most importantly, *empowering* their audience.[5]

In short, TV has a content problem not just an advertising one. Our colleague from TV production giant FremantleMedia, Samantha Glynne, shines her perspective on this in the chapter 'Ideas That Scale' in Part 4 of this book.

Navigating the void

If brands cannot come to the customer uninvited any more, they need to go where the customer prefers to spend his or her time, and they need to do more. As attention spans decrease and entertainment options increase, we need to transform from being a waster of time (and bandwidth) to a preferred choice. To put it succinctly, brands need to be entertainers not disrupters. And more and more brands and their agencies, especially the recent 2017 Lions Entertainment winners, do understand this need and earn the results – results don't necessarily mean a gold statue for that shelf in your office but measurable results that move the needle for your brand.

This list is more mounting evidence of what positive impact branded entertainment has for brands.

Gold winners score big returns

We're the Superhumans by 4Creative London for the Rio Paralympics features a cast of more than 140 disabled people doing everything from everyday activities to winning high-jump gold. It has achieved more than 40 million views and 1.8+ million social media shares.

Boost Your Voice by 180LA for Boost Mobile. During the last US presidential elections the phone company turned stores in underserved communities into voting stations – 766 million total campaign impressions, but, more importantly, in 'boost precincts' voter turnouts increased by 23%.

Evan by BBDO New York for Sandy Hook Promise. The story about the early warning signs of gun violence at schools reached 100 million people in less than a week, and it earned more than 2 billion impressions in 133 countries. Looking at recent real-life school shootings, where warning signs and suspicious behaviour by the future shooter, similar to those displayed in *Evan*, were ignored or not acted upon, this film can actually help save lives. The tragic events we never hear about (because they were prevented) make this and similar initiatives count.

Unlimited Stadium by BBH Singapore for Nike. During the 2016 Summer Olympics Nike opened the world's first full-sized LED running track in Manila, where athletes and brand enthusiasts could compete against their digital avatar. During the seventeen days of the games more than 26,000 people visited the LED track, and almost 6,000 actually ran, resulting in a 100% sell-through of Nike's LunarEpic shoe and contributing to Nike being the most mentioned brand on social media during the Olympics. *Unlimited Stadium* was broadcast on every major TV network in the Philippines and organically featured on *Mashable*, *DesignBoom Magazine*, the

Bleacher Report and many other publications, resulting in more than 100 million views of the wrap video across all online platforms. The successful campaign also contributed to the decision to name BBH Singapore *Ad Age*'s 2018 International Agency of the Year.

Lo and Behold: Reveries of the Connected World by Pereira O'Dell for NetScout, a provider of cyber security and network performance management products. The Werner Herzog-directed documentary about the beginning and future of the internet (and connectivity) was selected for the Sundance Film Festival, picked up by Netflix, received 94% fresh on Rotten Tomatoes and created countless articles and mentions in established entertainment (*Variety*), lifestyle (*Esquire*) and geek-friendly (*Wired*, *Mashable*) media, which drove NetScout searches from 2.5 billion to 25 billion, leading to the most new business enquiries in the company's thirty-year history. And, yes, because of its successful distribution, the film paid for itself. But it didn't stop there. According to NetScout's agency, the documentary helped lift the cyber-security topic from being a bland CTO conversation to a CEO conversation; it provided access to luminaries and stakeholders that were previously unreachable for the brand.

A Love Song Written by a Murderer by Circus Grey Peru for the women's charity Vida Mujer. Diego Dibos, a famous Peruvian songwriter, used a love letter by an abusive man who asks his wife for forgiveness for the lyrics of his new hit song. The song and its important message, not to forgive abusers, reached more than 8 million people; more importantly, it reached 3,000 abused Peruvian women who sought help in the first month alone.

Label of Love is an emotional short film by Rosapark Paris for the French supermarket chain Monoprix. It follows a young boy and girl whose destinies cross paths thanks to the words found on the iconic Monoprix packaging. The film delivered a total of 26.5 million views: 14 million on television, 350,000 in cinemas, 750,000 on display, 11.4 million social and 1.2 million views of a special digital experience on social media. It cemented Monoprix's position in French pop culture.

One Source is a campaign by VML Johannesburg. Absolut vodka may come from one source in Sweden, but hip-hop legend Khuli

Chana shows, with this audio-visual stunner, that Africa is the one source of all creation. Premiered on MTV's African Music Awards, the album topped the charts on iTunes in South Africa, turning Khuli's fans into Absolut fans: 1.75 billion media impressions, sales up 84% year-on-year, market share doubled from 14% to 28%, making Absolut the number one premium vodka in South Africa. The campaign also contributed to the growing perception of Absolut as a culture creator rather than just an advertiser and to the overall awareness of African art and creativity.

Home is a short film made by Black Sheep Studios (a unit of BBH London) for the United Nations Kosovo Team to address the refugee crisis when a comfortable English family experiences a life-changing journey. The film screened at more than fifty festivals and won eighteen prestigious awards, including the BAFTA award for Best British Short Film. During UK Refugee Week, Picturehouse Cinemas screened *Home* in all their cinemas across the UK, followed by more than seventy screenings by other chains and independent movie theatres. All in all, the film was discussed and debated in more than forty-six different countries, sparked 4 million impressions of the conversation and proved, with these numbers, that the refugee crisis is not a local phenomenon but a global one.

From the Start is a digital series and TV movie by OgilvyOne Worldwide for the Greek chocolate brand Lacta that compares its product to the sweetness of falling in love. This resulted in 2 million viewers in a country of just 5 million internet users, making it the number-one YouTube channel in Greece in views and subscribers. There were equally sweet results for Lacta, with a sales turnaround of more than 14% from -10% to +4.3%.

Ash to Art by J. Walter Thompson London. After a fire destroys the library of the Glasgow School of Art, twenty-five of Britain's leading artists create unique artwork from the ashes of the building. An auction of the artwork at Christie's raises £706,438 with bids from twenty-eight countries, not only bringing the school back into the national conversation but also helping the school rise – literally – from the ashes. The story reached 42% of the UK population.

And, finally, the 2017 Lions Entertainment Grand Prix winner,

Beyond Money, is a short sci-fi film starring Adriana Ugarte by MRM//McCann Spain for Santander Bank, which emphasizes that memories and experiences are more valuable than money (and the things you can buy with it). The bank claims that this message brought 12,426 attendees on the first day of the film's cinematic release and 7.5 million online views during the first week, which not only boosted the bank's image but also its 1|2|3 Smart Account with the fastest sign-up rate in Santander's 160-year history.

You are going to hear about all these Gold winners and more in this book. But we thought you should see this list now as part of the evidence of what impact branded entertainment can have.

The usual suspects

The same message that propelled Santander Bank to the Grand Prix (and to thousands of new personal accounts) has become popular on social media as well. There is a piece of inescapable wisdom on LinkedIn and Facebook about finding long-lasting happiness. This time it's not from a bank (or Sir Richard Branson, Deepak Chopra, Mark Cuban or the Dalai Lama, to name a few of the usual suspects) but from Dr Thomas Gilovich, a psychology professor at Cornell University. His research indicates that buying an experience (not material things) provides greater satisfaction and happiness because: (1) experiential purchases enhance social relations more readily and effectively than material goods; (2) they form a bigger part of a person's identity; and (3) they are evaluated more on their own terms and evoke fewer social comparisons than material purchases. In short, we should spend our money (and time) on experiences, not on things.[6]

We like to argue that branded content needs to be so strong that it becomes an experience as well, either from watching (for example, Red Bull's epic snowboarding movie *The Art of Flight*; just read the comment section on YouTube about how it changed the lives of the many who watched it) or actually experiencing it live and in person.

But for a fully immersive and highly successful consumer experience, which increased the love for a traditional beer brand, let's take a field trip to Mexico City and investigate a true house of horror.

Horror experience

While many brands try to establish themselves in the sports and music space, Anheuser-Busch InBev's Victoria beer took the bold step of putting its hook into the horror genre. This sounds less crazy if you consider the huge appetite for horror (and anything surreal) in Mexico and other parts of Latin America. The love of horror is not only deeply rooted in the local culture, the most famous example being the traditional Day of the Dead/Día de Muertos holiday, but also highly popular with millennials both within Mexico and elsewhere – six of the Top Ten most profitable films of all time are horror films.

Starting in 2016 the brand took over an abandoned hotel in Mexico City and established the 'Hotel de Leyendas Victoria' experience, celebrating modern and traditional Mexican myths. 'Hotel Victoria' has reshaped Mexican culture through entertainment. How? Consumers embraced the Day of the Dead in a different and meaningful way, while the Victoria brand transformed an immersive horror experience into a successful entertainment franchise. Think of Punchdrunk's *Sleep No More* meeting a haunted house on steroids. In both theatrical experiences the audiences decide what to watch and where to go in the performance space.

At the Hotel Victoria seventy-five actors in fifteen scary rooms (in which you would never want to spend a single night) create a fantastic 'horrible' experience that instantly ignites Mexican culture:

- More than 50,000 visitors
- All performances sold out
- All merchandise sold out
- 92% of the national media covered the experience
- Mentions in high-profile international publications such as the *Guardian* and *National Geographic*
- Accompanying original web series filmed on location at Hotel Victoria
- More than 100,000 impressions on mobile

- Successful multimedia consumer experiences: TV, Snap-chat filters, trade shows
- An immersive VR experience at multiple retail locations entertains more than 15,000 horror fans
- Activations in more than 13,000 bars around Mexico
- Victoria becomes the number one alcohol brand related to the Day of the Dead
- Number one among millennials (aged over eighteen)

All of this was done not by hiding the brand but by putting it at the *dead centre* of the experience, from naming it 'Hotel de Leyendas Victoria' to ending the horror trip through the hotel in a Victoria-branded bar, where the shaken visitor could cool off with a tasty – what else? – Victoria.

The 'Hotel Victoria' experience is not a random success. A process called POV (purpose, ownership and vision), created by the advertising executive Joah Santos, links efforts to desired results. He believes that the greatest opportunity lies in creating entertainment for the people who already like a particular brand, inspiring them to become the voice of the brand. The key to this process is to increase their love of the brand, which means allowing them to live a brand's purpose through the experience.

'Hotel Victoria' meets its fans on familiar grounds – their love of local mythology, horror stories and the surreal – and extends this longing through the experience into true love of the brand.

Call it Goofy

No brand is probably more successful in inspiring its fans than Disney. Think of Disneyland, Disney World, Disney cruises, Disney stores and so on, which are examples of Disney entertainment that increases the love people feel for Disney movies, TV shows and experiences. It allows people to go deeper into the Disney brand. Furthermore, their digital ecosystem offers the opportunity to continue the journey as a fan. You can even get Goofy to call you.

The goal is to entertain fans across multiple channels with one cohesive experience by pulling them into the brand instead of pushing messages at them. Ultimately, their experience must be unique, so they share it with others.

Now that we have an objective and a clear path we can begin to answer the difficult questions. How do we become like Disney? How do we entertain fans across multiple channels with one cohesive experience? How do we pull fans into our brand instead of pushing our message at them? How do we make their experience unique so that they share it with others? Essentially, how do we use entertainment to increase the love people feel for the brand?

Let's turn our detective story into a quick recipe for great branded entertainment.

Let me entertain you

Making work (partnering or original creation) that attracts – and does not interrupt your audience – adds value to the brand, business and consumers.

Brands must be present in creating culture, and the way to do it is through entertainment. However, a major shift is required, focusing on developing messages that people want to watch for their own sake.

Marketers must be ready to accept giving up a measure of control of the content and/or distribution in an effort to create work to which people will pay attention, with planning based on a creative idea that is free of the form it may take or how it finds its way into the world. This non-linear process can lead to unexpected and, it is to be hoped, more impactful outcomes. Finally, a non-linear budgeting routine must be adopted, part of an advanced planning process, while allowing the flexibility for impromptu opportunities.

Don't bury the brand

Branded entertainment might not always be the answer to all your marketing needs, especially if you are engaged in a brand war where frequency still wins or when you have to adapt quickly and require instant communication. You can't ask your customer to watch your epic snowboarding movie twenty times over, but if your film or experience has scale and true event character then you can multiply the ways you communicate about it. It helps when your brand name is actually part of the event title, which will not only help the event *become* the brand but also get your brand name into any media reporting independently about the event. **Red Bull** Stratos, **Corona** Sunsets, **Red Bull** Crashed Ice, **Bud Light** Dive Bar Tour, **Red Bull** Air Race, **Hotel Victoria** . . . get it?

Young journalists learn early on in their careers not to bury the story. Young detectives are being instructed by their more experienced and street-smart colleagues not to bury their lead. We say, don't bury the brand. Our colleagues Pelle Sjoenell and Jason Xenopoulos have more insights on such unapologetic brands in Part 2 of this book with their appeal to 'Replace Product Placement with Idea Placement'.

The right marketing mix

Using your sharpened detective senses, you will have noticed that the successful 'Hotel Victoria' experience in Mexico City was built by more than one entertainment and marketing component. There were live performances, a digital web series, Snapchat filters, VR experiences, TV and media reports, merchandising, a trade show and so-called on-premise activations (that is, product introductions in bars, nightclubs and restaurants).

Earlier we concluded that there isn't a single culprit causing the void. But there isn't a single solution (or secret sauce) either to reconnect the consumer with our message. We need the right marketing mix.

In 2018 we're still watching traditional car commercials, not only short action movies starring cars (or space cars in orbit). We still come across BMW and Marriott print ads, and, usually, digital content doesn't replace traditional advertising but complements it. Even content powerhouse Red Bull does billboards and TV commercials (in the form of humorous cartoons). Marketing is just too complex and complicated to succeed using one strategy alone. Specific needs in local markets, short-term product activations, immediate responses to cultural conversations or crises . . . Not every need can be addressed with entertainment. And the customer is not always ready to watch something on demand, especially when you need to communicate an urgent message. Sometimes you still have to bring the message to the customer, sometimes even uninvited.

Branded entertainment is usually most effective when the customer already understands the brand and your intention is to deepen and extend this understanding. Earlier in this chapter we called this process 'POV'. There are many examples proving that it actually works.

Did it say Red Bull?

Gabor was living in Salzburg in Austria, near Red Bull's global headquarters, when he received a phone call from a friend visiting Switzerland who claimed that she had just seen one of his 'Red Bull shows' on Swiss television. He asked her if it said 'Red Bull' or if she had noticed any brand logos? She answered saying not really, 'but it just looked so amazing and Red Bull'.

This is not only a huge compliment for the makers of this film but it might also be evidence that many people and customers have a preconceived idea of a brand. This can provide a solid basis for brand-produced content and entertainment, as some marketing detectives have already suspected.

And yes, after investigating the Swiss TV listings, it was confirmed that Gabor's friend actually did watch a Red Bull Media House-produced show on that particular day.

Rules of engagement

Entertainment works to its own calendar and has its own set of rules. We need to understand that brands are welcome and creators are open to new opportunities. But we have to be more than trans-actional: a long-term investment in relationships usually yields results. But investments into entertainment could take anything from six months to two years to materialize, such is the nature of the business, making most branded entertainment a long-term investment for a deeper impression.

Entertainment fallout

How does our detective story end? With a sequel, of course! Many sequels. As more and more brands invest in content studios and produce branded and on-demand entertainment, it won't be a battle between brands any more but a battle over the consumer's time.

And come the day when the very last brand has become an entertainer, all of us will most likely miss those shiny old-fashioned print ads in magazines. Because disruptive is not what really disrupts but what we perceive as disruptive.

Who is the true hero of this story, and who determines what makes marketing successful? Creativity, access to top talent and distribution platforms, scale or money? Or, again, is it Elon Musk? Conventional wisdom is that money can buy the world. In 2018 this wisdom converted to zero money.

Of all the significant (car) brands, only Tesla reportedly has an ad budget of exactly $0. That's zero dollars generating maximum marketing impact and brand gravity. With stunts such as shooting his car into orbit (or promoting a flamethrower on Instagram), Tesla founder and CEO Elon Musk manages to get the entire planet talking about his brands, and he hovers like his space car above the void that so many others in marketing are struggling with. This brings us back to the beginning of this chapter.

It wouldn't be a solid detective story without a little twist at the end. Three centuries ago Sir Isaac Newton, the *godfather* of all things gravity (and space travel), discovered an indisputable law of nature: what goes up must come down.

1. https://www.cnbc.com/2018/02/07/tesla-q4-2017-earnings.html
2. https://www.emarketer.com/Article/eMarketer-Lowers-US-TV-Ad-Spend-Estimate-Cord-Cutting-Accelerates/1016463
3. https://www.marketingcharts.com/featured-24817

4. https://www.statista.com/statistics/323867/
us-weekly-minutes-online-video-age/

5. https://www.recode.net/2017/12/4/16733460/2017-digital-ad-spend-
advertising-beat-tv

6. https://static1.squarespace.com/static/5394dfa6e4b0d7fc44700a04/t/547d5
89ee4b04b0980670fee/1417500830665/Gilovich+Kumar+Jampol+%28in+p
ress%29+A+Wonderful+Life+JCP.pdf

THE BATTLE OF TIME AND THE FALLACY OF THE SHORT ATTENTION SPAN

Marcelo Pascoa, Burger King

Let me start by saying that had our editor deleted one word from this chapter's title I would have asked him to delete the entire chapter. Allow me to explain. For more than ten years now, the advertising industry has been talking about how the fragmentation of media has turned getting people's attention into a Herculean challenge, one that has been intensified by the relationship between content and a new generation of consumers, particularly millennials, a target group whose aversion to advertising is allegedly matched only by their inability to focus on anything longer than the time it takes to like an Instagram picture.

Honestly, if I have to attend one more seminar on the subject of time and attention span I will probably kill myself. So when asked to write about what appeared at first glance to be this very subject, my initial reaction was not exactly a joyous one.

Upon closer examination, however, I realized that our jury president PJ Pereira wasn't asking me to discourse on time and attention span at all but, rather, on the fallacy our industry has created around the topic. The idea of attention as the new Holy Grail of advertising and the subsequent need to treat time as an unavoidable limit on creativity is, indeed, nothing short of a fallacy, a gross simplification used by those constantly looking for a new subjective theory capable of excusing the objective mediocrity of their work.

The real crisis that advertising faces today is a much more complex equation, in which time is but one of many variables. Time might exert a powerful influence on the success of a marketing campaign, but its value is relative; it is ultimately a function with a set of numerous inputs and countless permissible outputs, the predominant factor being, today as it has always been, the quality of the message and its inherent ability to touch people's hearts.

Freud, Buddha and the perenniality of first impressions

At a recent meeting at Google I was exposed to global numbers on how people watch YouTube videos. It will probably come as no surprise to anyone, but looking at the facts made it hard to avoid: in an environment where the next video is always calling at the corner of your eye, the first five seconds are the most critical for securing attention. Guess what? With the exception of cinema and theatre, because you're there, locked in a dark room so you have no other stimuli to distract you, most forms of storytelling have always been like this. Own the eyeballs in the opening or you're done.

Take books, for example. Ask any novelist what's the part they sweat over the most, and they will all say the first line. An example: '"Where's Papa going with that axe?" said Fern to her mother as they were setting the table for breakfast.' That thrilling opening doesn't come from Stephen King or George R.R. Martin. It is the opening of E.B. White's *Charlotte's Web*. A children's book!

In any form of story, as in advertising or in life, once you raise your hand before an audience you'd better have a good story to tell. Unfortunately, more often than not, that is just not the case. Whether it is a pick-up line at a bar, the opening statement of an agency pitch or the initial five seconds of an advertising film, the odds are not in our favour. Most frequently, these well-intended beginnings result in a lukewarm, unsatisfying exchange, with the receiving end of the message searching desperately for a way out.

No one will give you their time unless they are getting something valuable in return. And the more time one is requesting, the more valuable that return should be. This is who we are as humans, regardless of our individual or generational attention spans. And it has been so for millennia, long before the invention of the internet and social media. As Freud first put it in 1895 (not unlike the Buddha many centuries before him), human actions are driven by the instinctive seeking of pleasure and avoiding of pain in order to satisfy biological and psychological needs.

As a result, whether you choose to believe Freud or in the Buddha, it is fair to assume that what drives our attention is not the length of a story but its ability to engage the audience, giving them some kind of pleasure in return for their time. The battle of time is less about time itself but, rather, about what we can give consumers in return for this most precious asset.

Turning thirty and the death of time

Something awful happens when you turn thirty. And I am not talking about wrinkles and love handles or the fading of that magical glow that seems to cover the young as some sort of natural Facetune filter. Don't get me wrong; those are all indeed part of the painful process of the so-called second adolescence – thank you, millennials! The most terrifying element of turning thirty, in fact, has nothing to do with such narcissistic obsessions. It is all about time. Once you turn thirty you come to the inexorable realization that time is finite. At least when it comes to our passage through this world. We are born, we grow up, we reproduce (or not) and, eventually, we die. And although we've been hearing about it for the past thirty years it is not until sometime around our thirtieth birthday that this most obvious of truths will finally sink in.

You will not live for ever.

You will not travel the entire world.

You will not read all the books, watch all the films, acquire all the knowledge you once aspired to possess. The clock starts ticking anticlockwise, and there is now a timer on God's iPhone Z Plus counting down to your inevitable death. Depressed? Hey, this is a book of essays; feel free to skip to the next chapter.

But, for someone working in advertising, the full realization of the inevitability of death and the finite nature of time, however depressing it might be, also comes as a precious gift, a new-found appreciation for the value of time. Advertising is a craft constrained by time. Sure, an artist such as Richard Wagner can indulge himself, giving his operatic masterpiece *Der Ring des Nibelungen* an astonishing fifteen-hour running time and still be hailed as one of the greatest composers of all time.

But we are not Wagner, are we? Please, tell me you understand we are not Wagner. We are not geniuses. And we are definitely not artists. In the preface to *The Picture of Dorian Gray,* Oscar Wilde writes:

> We can forgive a man for making a useful thing as long as he does not admire it. The only excuse for making a useless thing is that one admires it intensely.
>
> All art is quite useless.

So, we are not Wagner, we are not Wilde. And what we do is definitely not art. Advertising is meant to serve a purpose, to be useful. It is like solving a mathematical problem with a painting or a song. The painting might be beautiful, the song entrancing, but they will always be constrained by their purpose – the purpose of a brand. And they will always be constrained by time. Because time is expensive. It is something we, as advertisers, will always have to pay for. Or won't we?

If you search for 'Doritos Roulette Challenge' on YouTube, Google's video website will display almost 60,000 results. It is reasonable to assume that if you were to scroll down the entire list the connection between the videos and the product mentioned in the search might start to fade. However, if you sort them by view count and watch the top ten videos you will realize that all of them follow the exact same formula: a bunch of YouTubers of various ages and nationalities gather around bags of Doritos, each picking a crisp from the bag and cautiously gobbling it down before revealing to the audience whether they have picked a regular cheesy Dorito or one of the few ridiculously highly spiced ones that come in each pack.

The idea might sound silly to you, but together these ten videos have a combined audience of almost 70 million views. None of them seems to have been produced or sponsored by the brand. Some of the creators, in fact, specifically point out that they were uploaded in response to a massive request coming straight from their online followers. Add up the length of the same ten videos and you have more than two hours of advertising that cost the tortilla-chip brand virtually nothing,

The point being? While many of us lament the challenge of audience fragmentation and limited attention span in the digital age, others celebrate the success of truly engaging ideas that are able to earn huge amounts of people's time – instead of having to pay for it in costly instalments of a measly fifteen seconds.

The agonies of a failed actor and the struggling writer

As a child I never dreamed of working in advertising. Sure, there was no *Mad Men* when I was growing up. No Don Draper to populate my dreams, professionally or otherwise. I took up classical piano when I was five. I walked up and down with a portable turntable that I used to listen to records that ranged from Michael's Jackson's *Thriller* to Verdi's *La Traviata*. I produced a new show every weekend, tyrannizing my poor friends and forcing our parents to sit and watch – my father used to offer me money not to do this. In short, I was a hopeless, shameless, unapologetic geek who didn't differentiate fine art from popular culture – which, by the way, I still don't.

I dreamed of being an actor, a pianist, a conductor. Then my teen years came and my artistic aspirations were squashed by the bourgeois idea that those were not practical life choices. So when the time came to choose a career I did what any lover of the arts would: I became a lawyer. During those five long years of law school I tried to convince myself that I was on the right path. It didn't work. Fulfilling my mother's (mostly) unspoken hopes, I did get my degree, passed the bar and even worked for a while at a prestigious Brazilian law firm. But I knew I wouldn't find happiness in that environment. On the other hand, I was conscious that a life of travelling, concerts and museums doesn't come cheap and, without any trust funds to my name, I had to find a way to balance my passions with the need to make ends meet.

I started in advertising school without any real understanding of what advertising was. I had absolutely no idea what an ad person actually did. But this time my ignorance paid off. I immediately felt I had stumbled upon a world that could be fulfilling and exciting, while also providing me with a somewhat decent pay cheque. As a copywriter I found that my years of dabbling in theatre, music, literature and movies could actually be a valuable asset to my professional career. In every job I got I tried to look for inspiration in art and entertainment, more than in advertising itself. And, to my surprise, it worked. The digital revolution was in full bloom and my long-term interest in anything tech compelled me to experiment with new communications formats. But it was the advent of the now legendary *BMW Films* campaign in 2001 that really struck a chord with me.

The Hire, a collection of short films starring Clive Owen and directed by some of the most talented film-makers alive, ranging from Guy Ritchie to Ang Lee, took the world of advertising by storm, generating as much confusion as excitement. Created specifically for the internet, the series of shorts by the iconic German car brand subverted one of the most sacred rules of advertising: the working vs non-working split in marketing spending. Blindly followed by a legion of prominent executives, it postulates that the production budget of any given campaign, regardless of the idea, should be a fraction of the corresponding media budget, certainly no greater than between 10% and 20% of the media spend.

The vice of replacing critical thinking with dogmatic general-izations greatly troubles the advertising industry. But its effects on the work it produces are among the most damaging to creativity today. What BMW bravely proposed was nothing short of a complete inversion of this so-called principle. Its approach was to invest most of its marketing budget into production, believing that the quality of the content would lead consumers to the campaign without the usual massive media effort to reach them. The brand put its money where its mouth was and changed the relationship between entertainment and advertising for ever. In 2004, unable to define *The Hire* within the limits of its existing categories, the Cannes Lions

Festival of Creativity introduced a new kind of award to recognize BMW's groundbreaking campaign. It was the birth of the Titanium Lion, which would go on to become the festival's most coveted prize, reserved solely for 'provocative, boundary-busting, envy-inspiring work that marks a new direction for the industry and moves it forward'.

Before *BMW Films* I had been happy to be able to use art and entertainment as inspiration for traditional advertising campaigns. But the idea that I could actually be producing short films, documentaries, reality shows and web series for brands completely blew my mind. By using content formats to build brands and sell products I was finally able to merge advertising and entertainment, bringing my work closer than ever to what had led me to it in the first place.

Suddenly the constraints of advertising did not feel like constraints any more. Matching a product with an entertainment format that could advance the brand's mission and generate significant business results seemed like an exciting new adventure. Advertising was no longer a compromise that allowed me to make a living but something I felt truly privileged to be a part of. I finally felt free of the idea that I had somehow settled for a less noble, derivative version of what I had dreamed of as a kid. And, on a more practical level, there was something else I was finally free from: the constraints of time.

Pied Piper of Silicon Valley

One of the most enticing opportunities presented by the rise of branded content was that idea of freeing creativity from the restraints of time. Creatives everywhere rejoiced in the possibility of telling stories that went beyond the castrating limits of a thirty-second TV spot. We could finally enjoy some of the same liberties once reserved solely for such geniuses as Wagner, Wilde, Spielberg and their peers. The explosion of the internet as a mass media channel reinforced this promise, as brands rushed to create their proprietary digital platforms on which content could air for free regardless of its duration. Suddenly we were teenagers again, inebriated by the revival of time as an endless resource. Our stories would now be able to run their natural courses, their time determined by nothing but the proper unfolding of their plots.

As we toasted and waltzed in the lavish ballroom of our newly refurbished dreamboat, we failed to see the iceberg coming. In urgent need of monetizing their platforms, the captains of Silicon Valley crashed our party, announcing the end of the internet as a media free-for-all. Truth be told, the exponential growth of available online content was equally devastating for brands who had until then believed that they could gather huge audiences by following the once successful strategy of BMW's collection of short films: if you build it, they will come; produce content that is truly great and consumers will find their way to it, like the children of Hamelin following the irresistible tune of the Pied Piper's magic flute.

Long story short, we were catapulted right back to where we'd started. The idea of telling relevant stories that could bring advertising closer to entertainment and pop culture became sort of a trade unicorn, terrific in theory but, like my childhood artistic aspirations, simply not a practical choice. Brands that had invested heavily in branded content were taken over by new marketers who criticized their predecessors for being easily seduced by a frivolous fad invented by creatives avid for awards but ignorant about their business. Big agencies rushed to agree with the conservatism of their clients in the undying hope of returning to the golden era of print and television – a simpler time when commissions were higher and the answer to most problems lay at the bottom of a good bottle of Scotch.

There is no denying that, following the success of seminal entertainment campaigns such as *BMW Films* and Coca-Cola's *Happiness Factory*, many similar attempts by good-willed brands and talented creatives resulted in failure. Even successful examples like *Happiness Factory* somewhat failed to fully live up to the great expectations they raised. The campaign, created in 2006 by Wieden + Kennedy Amsterdam in partnership with animation and design studio Psyop, played with the idea of Coke's secret formula by portraying the inside of a vending machine as a magical universe where elf-like creatures worked merrily together to deliver each customer a perfect ice-cold bottle of Coca-Cola.

It was as entertaining as it was effective, drawing from Coca-Cola's intrinsic benefits of great taste and refreshment as much as it drew from the hero's journey, a timeless storytelling approach that serves as the architectural foundation of masterpieces ranging from Homer's *Odyssey* to George Lucas's *Star Wars*.

The campaign successfully experimented with various communication formats, from TV spots to online games, including a six-and-a-half-minute animated short film. There were some, however – myself included – who believed the idea was destined to achieve even greater goals, particularly in the form of the first commercially launched, animated branded feature film – cut to 2014 and the triumphant release of *The Lego Movie*, which some of my fellow jurors will explore further during their own chapters of this book.

Adding insult to injury, these failed attempts had typically consumed an amount of effort, time and money significantly greater than the usual TV-centric campaign.

Digital platforms boosted their media sales and, as their commercial strategies became closer and closer to those of traditional media, so did the content they encouraged advertisers to produce. The principle of advertising as an unavoidable interruption of the content experience rose from the ashes stronger than ever and was now applicable not only to traditional media but also to the most disruptive of digital platforms. The separation between editorial and advertising was reclaimed as both inevitable and necessary, much to the satisfaction of idealistic journalists who failed to realize that, as the advertorials faded, so would many of the publications they so righteously defended. Under the least original of headlines many essays were written proclaiming the death of branded content.

Take me *Back to the Start*

So, after a few bumps in the road, all was lost in the realm of branded entertainment. Or was it? You see, the thing about passion is that it is hard to kill. While the idea of fusing content and advertising was being bombarded by naysayers around the world, entertainment campaigns continued to win the hearts of consumers everywhere.

In 2012 American Chipotle Mexican Grill was awarded the Grands Prix for both Film and Branded Content at the Cannes Lions International Festival of Creativity. In contrast to an abundance of YouTube videos depicting graphic images of enslaved chickens and other horrifying farm practices, the restaurant chain produced a heartfelt, beautiful animated short film, *Back to the Start*, portraying the story of a family farmer who turns his farm into a factory only to find out that he could only thrive by sticking to his faith in sustainable practices. An original rendition of Coldplay's 'The Scientist' by Willie Nelson, one of the founders of the outlaw country-music genre, accompanied the farmer's tale, inviting the world to take us *back to the start*.

It was a remarkable piece of work, and only the most cynical of critics could deny its rightful place in the advertising canon. It also skyrocketed Chipotle to superbrand status overnight, and in subsequent years the brand would go on to produce other equally charming animated shorts. But among the increasing controversy surrounding branded content and entertainment, Chipotle's double Grands Prix gave room to some dangerous interpretations. Chipotle's first ever national ad was officially launched as a short film on YouTube and, more than 4 million views later, aired in full during the live TV broadcast of the Grammy Awards. While many celebrated the campaign as an outstanding piece of branded entertainment, others argued that *Back to the Start* was, in essence, a typical TV spot, despite the video's length of two minutes and twenty seconds.

In the same year a partnership between Intel and Toshiba gave birth to the web series *The Beauty Inside*, created by long-time content enthusiast agency Pereira O'Dell. The heartbreaking story of a man who woke up every day in a different body, while remaining the same person inside, became an instant hit, especially among a highly coveted but extremely elusive target: millennials.

The entire series totalled more than forty minutes of content divided into six episodes – all of which forced me to sink into my chair in an attempt to hide my uncontrollable tears. What moved me was not only the delicate beauty of the hero's ordeal but the perfection of the piece, its undeniable evidence of the power of branded entertainment. The greatest challenge of creating content for a brand is finding a single premise that is equally strong from an entertainment and marketing perspective. Most attempts tend to prioritize one to the detriment of the other: they are either a compelling story that resonates with viewers but fails to deliver the brand's objectives or they compromise the narrative's appeal by unnecessarily subjugating it to the need of convincing consumers to buy the product they advertise.

The real beauty inside Pereira O'Dell's campaign (pun intended) was its ability to combine equal measures of enchantment and persuasion, creating content that could rival any award-winning Netflix show in production quality while also delivering a challenging brand message – that what is inside a computer should matter more than the carcass that envelopes it.

What many don't know, however, is that *The Beauty Inside* was not the first attempt by Intel and Toshiba at appealing to young consumers through an entertainment project. In the previous year the two brands had aired a different web series by the same agency. Titled simply *Inside*, it told the story of a girl who awakes to find herself trapped in a dark room with nothing but a laptop to find her way out. Presented as Hollywood's first social film, the series was also an impressive piece of content but didn't achieve the same level of success as its sequel. Faced with growing criticism of entertainment as a new way to reach consumers, both brands and agency stuck to their belief that this new approach would pay off, a bold move that eventually benefited not only them but also the entire advertising industry. *The Beauty Inside* went on to win several Cannes Lions, including the 2012 Cyber Grand Prix, as well as an Emmy for Outstanding New Approaches in an Original Daytime Program or Series. More importantly, it proved that millennials were willing to give brands a considerable amount of their time, as long as the content they were provided in return was good enough to justify their attention.

The fallacy of the short attention span

Despite the achievements of long-format campaigns such as *The Beauty Inside*, many in advertising currently advocate that the key to a successful connection, especially among new generations, is all about time. Particularly in the digital space, brands are encouraged to convey their messages in the shortest possible time, reflecting the behaviour of consumers who, making no distinction between their online and offline lives, long for snackable content and instant gratification.

These rules, however, do not seem to apply to the relationship between young audiences and entertainment in general. It is a known fact that many millennials would rather stay at home on a Friday binge-watching their favourite shows than go out for a night of drinking with their friends. And while many might say they don't really care about TV, the impact of TV in today's popular culture could be described as stronger than ever, with TV shows such as *Game of Thrones* dominating conversations among young people all over the world, not to mention the Netflix phenomenon, which, by making entire new seasons available at once, is able to hypnotize consumers with original content for hours on end. Even YouTube's top creators, such as gamer PewDiePie and comedy duo Smosh, seem oblivious to the constraints of time and attention, collecting millions of views with videos in which they often talk for between ten and twenty minutes on a single subject. Sure, other social media giants, such as Facebook and Instagram, may be characterized by briefer interactions between content and their users, but to say that younger generations cannot hold their attention on anything for more than a few seconds is a gross generalization that simply does not tally with the facts.

It seems more reasonable to infer that, given the abundance of content these consumers grew up with at the tips of their fingers, their attention has become highly selective and cannot be bought as easily as before. If you want it, you better be prepared to give something in return. And that something, dear reader, is high-quality, deeply interesting, truly entertaining content. It might have cost millions or nothing to produce. It might star a big Hollywood celebrity or an old lady with a cat. It might be editorial or even advertising. It might last less than fifteen seconds or more than fifteen hours. They don't really care. But it better be good.

If there is one lesson I have learned during the long and laborious process of judging the 2017 Entertainment Lions, it is the value of time in advertising – and, more especially, in entertainment campaigns. More so than any other categories, the Entertainment Lions confront the jurors with the challenge of time. We were faced with the arduous task of evaluating entries that put our own attention span to the test, judging pieces that ranged from twenty-second vignettes to ninety-minute feature films. And yes, we did watch them all in full, in case you are wondering. It was, at the same time, one of the most inspiring and sometimes maddening experiences of my career. In the end, the winners proved that there truly is no precise correlation between the strength and the length of a great content idea.

In full transparency, I confess I began this experience with a different mindset. Perhaps influenced by the same dogmas I am now trying to dispute, I entered the jury room convinced that a piece of branded content would ideally last between two and three minutes, enough time to set it apart from traditional advertising formats yet still be respectful of the average consumer's predisposition to engage with content produced by a brand. As the week of judging went by, though, I came to realize that the question of length was not as absolute as I believed. If a content idea is truly good, if it tells an engaging story and effectively communicates the message of the brand, time becomes a relative factor, albeit still one we cannot afford to ignore. That is true not only for branded content but also for content in general. How many times have you left a cinema, thinking that if only the director hadn't indulged himself in those extra twenty minutes the film could have been a much more vigorous experience?

Among the winning entries, on the short-length end of the spectrum, I would highlight the hilarious *Batman Continuity* vignettes. The campaign created by PHD UK consisted of a collection of vignettes of a mere twenty seconds each advertising *The Lego Batman Movie* in between programmes on Channel 4 in the UK, all of which made me laugh harder than the actual animated film ever could. In contrast, Werner Herzog's theatrical documentary *Lo and Behold: Reveries of the Connected World* lasted precisely one hour and thirty-eight minutes. Created by Pereira O'Dell for cyber security firm NetScout, it is a frightening and eye-opening journey into a dangerous reality in which we are constantly immersed, despite rarely noticing how deeply it affects us in our daily lives. The film opened at Sundance 2016 and eventually found its way on to Netflix, an unprecedented feat for a production originated by a brand.

Maybe the most surprising of all entries, particularly in the matter of time, was *From the Start*. This Greek campaign created by OgilvyOne Worldwide for chocolate brand Lacta consisted of five episodes with a total length of approximately seventy-five minutes. The idea of spending more than an hour watching the story of a man falling in love with a woman he would see in his dreams after eating a piece of chocolate seemed at first a bit too sweet for my taste (and, as you will see in other chapters, most of my co-authors felt the same). But, compelled by my sense of duty as a juror, I sat down one afternoon to watch the first episode hoping it would be enough to dismiss the campaign as a serious contender. One hour and fifteen minutes later I was humbled by the realization that I couldn't have been more wrong. Time actually flew by as I moved from one episode to the next, unable to shut down my computer until the final credits had rolled up my screen. Once again, the combination of a story inspired as much by the product as by timeless human truths had produced an exceptional content campaign.

Apart from the three-minute rule, another preconception I once had about branded entertainment was that it must differ from advertising in every possible way. Like a rebellious sibling trying to assert his individuality, I believed that my mission, as an enthusiast of the craft, was to convince the world that one had nothing to do with the other. In this misguided crusade I often used time as a differentiating factor. I was happy to be writing scripts that were several pages long and even happier to commission them from entertainment writers with no advertising background, for whom a thirty-second story made as much sense as dropping an apple and expecting it to rise up to the sky.

Ultimately, I came to realize that there was no glory to be found in a longer production if it wasn't able to touch people's hearts. Meanwhile, other copywriters I had pretentiously judged for being too traditional elevated their work to new heights by creating extended versions of thirty-second TV spots specifically crafted for the digital world. There are a few laudable examples of this kind of film among the 2017 Entertainment winners. For instance, you would have to be a black-hearted Grinch not to fall in love with *Ostrich*, the captivating, one-minute-fifty-second story of an ostrich who dreams of learning to fly, created for Samsung by Leo Burnett Chicago. Yes, if I had a gun to my head (which is how I sometimes felt locked in the dark room of the jury) I might say that I do not consider it to be the most perfect definition of a branded content campaign. But outside of the small, relatively insignificant world where these definitions matter, who cares, really?

People loved it. My mum loved it – actually I'm not sure whether she saw it, but I can guarantee she would if she did. I could easily see it as a successful Pixar short film, and if that is not a commendable achievement from an entertainment perspective then I don't know what is.

French retail chain Monoprix took a similar route with *Label of Love*. The story of a young boy who uses labels from Monoprix products to send anonymous messages to his first crush lasts four minutes and fourteen seconds. It is closer than *Ostrich* to what a purist would deem to be entertainment, and, despite the short length and the lack of dialogue, evokes the same tenderness one would feel during the less sombre moments of Netflix's *13 Reasons Why*. Still in the realm of first loves and coming-of-age tales, the most striking piece among the 2017 Entertainment winners, treading a less definable line between content and traditional advertising, was *Evan*, created by BBDO New York for Sandy Hook Promise. It draws from both branded content and traditional advertising, seamlessly combining elements from both worlds into one of my favourite pieces across all categories of the festival that year. I will purposefully refrain from revealing any details about its plot to offer the reader the chance of experiencing the story in its full, devastating glory. Just search the title on YouTube, and you will certainly find it. Go on, I'll wait. It will only take two minutes and twenty-nine seconds of your precious time.

Need I say anything more?

Reveries of the content world

In attempting to be a good student and follow the teachings of (actual) kung fu master PJ Pereira, I have written this essay with the most humble intention of sharing what I, during my ongoing, insignificant passage through this world, have been able to learn so far, particularly during those long days when I was kept hostage with my fellow jurors, while my other friends watched seminars, drank and strolled up and down La Croisette – not necessarily in that order. I do not presume anything I say to be more than my own limited perceptions of a story whose end I will never myself witness. But, however worthless these thoughts might be (I'll let you be the judge of that), they come from a place of sincere fondness and curiosity for what I believe to be the most exciting time in the history of advertising.

Never before have we had so many tools to create work that people might actually want to see. In a world where time is the ultimate luxury, the combination of talented agencies and brave advertisers still produces work that is able to captivate consumers' attention and hearts, including from new generations, regardless of the condescending misconception that they all suffer from attention deficit disorder. Yes, it is difficult to sustain someone's attention for longer than thirty seconds, three minutes or whatever length you may feel an ad or entertainment piece should not dare to exceed, but the same challenge applies to all human interactions. Try talking about how much you love your mother at the beginning of a first date and see if you can make it last for more than thirty seconds.

Trust me, you can't.

As a rule of thumb, time has to be respected not feared. In advertising, however, we've got used to buying time instead of earning it. And although it is possible to buy media this no longer guarantees that consumers will give us their time. We know how to pay for media, but we are still learning how to pay for time. And this is a lesson we will always be learning, because time is even more mysterious as a currency than bitcoin. It is a capricious, volatile asset that requires ever-changing techniques to be conquered. But we are intrinsically an inventive industry, and if we can apply our creativity to the pursuit of time with the same enthusiasm with which we pursue ideas, we might even be surprised at how much of it we may get from consumers.

Farewell, Don Draper

On 17 May 2015 I was among the millions of viewers anxiously watching the finale of *Mad Men* on AMC. Few TV shows in history have had such a profound impact in popular culture, its broad influence ranging from fashion and design to personal grooming and, of course, advertising. In a reversed product placement, 'Pass the Heinz', created by agency David Miami for the iconic ketchup brand, brought to life a fictional campaign pitched by Sterling Cooper's team in Episode 4 of the show's sixth season. In pitching the campaign, David proved to be more successful than Don Draper's associates, convincing Heinz to air in 2016 the exact pieces that had been rejected by their fictional colleagues five decades earlier.

One of the big questions surrounding *Mad Men*'s last episode was whether it would succeed in escaping the curse that looms over every hit-show finale. Suffice to say, given the legal opportunity, I would punch J.J. Abrams in the face for what he did to *Lost*'s final episode. To my joyous relief, the end of *Mad Men* was, at least for me, a truly satisfying conclusion to the saga of Don Draper, Peggy Olson and the rest of the *Mad Men* gang. But what actually had me jumping up and down, literally screaming like a child who just got everything he asked Santa for at Christmas, had nothing to do with the outcome of these characters I had grown so fond of over the course of the past seven years.

For the last sixty seconds of his acclaimed masterpiece, show-runner, writer and director Matthew Weiner chose not to write or direct any of the footage. Instead, he decided to air, in full, a historic Coca-Cola commercial from the 1970s titled *Hilltop*. As someone who was then working for Coca-Cola as a creative director, I would be more than happy to claim this unparalleled partnership as the ultimate product placement. It wasn't the case, though. The idea came not from the brand or any of its brilliant agencies but rather from the show's producers themselves, who got in touch with Coke requesting to use what is deemed by many as the best TV spot of all time as part of the series' last episode. I will not go into the merits of Coca-Cola's *Hilltop* as a major milestone of advertising – that would require a whole other essay – but the fact that a piece of advertising was used as the last sequence of such a landmark of popular culture is, in itself, proof of how relevant advertising still is and how powerful it can be in promoting meaningful connections between people and brands, regardless of how long that connection might last.

The timelessness of time and the beauty of a worthy instant

From *Dorian Gray* to *Back to the Future* to *13 Reasons Why*, time has long been an obsession of our kind. We dread the little we waste, the chunks we spend aimlessly, the moments we miss. That's exactly why, long or short, we need to respect each second the audience agrees to grant us. The time they spend watching our stories. The time taking a peek (which still counts if the brand is clear enough, as Gabor and Ricardo mentioned in the first chapter). The time discussing and participating – if an idea is lucky enough to deserve such a treat. But also the short yet still precious time people spend hearing about it on social media and in the press, one of the most underrated forms of counting your earnings in this field. Not only are they great concepts that can be told in a tweet they also have the brand so seamlessly and inherently ingrained it simply can't be taken out.

Most of the stories in this chapter (and probably the entire book) achieve this: Coca-Cola's *Happiness Factory*, the fantastical journey of a bottle inside a vending machine; *BMW Films*, a series of thrilling car rides so deserving of being watched, some of the biggest stars in entertainment agreed to ride along; Intel's *The Beauty Inside*, a heartfelt celebration of 'it's what's inside that counts'. Projects like these are such great achievements they would have served a purpose even without an audience. They produce results just by existing.

But that thought is so important that it deserves a chapter of its own – and a better writer.

Turn the page and say hello to Monica.

THE NEWS IT CREATES

Monica Chun, PMK·BNC

As I write this, the offices of PMK·BNC are abuzz with chatter and excitement. Several of my colleagues on the Entertainment side have just come back from a Time's Up meeting. Launched just two weeks ago at the Golden Globes, Time's Up was founded by several women in the entertainment industry as a response to Me Too and what has been called the 'Weinstein effect'. Their mission is to create a safe working environment and promote equality in the workplace – no matter what industry you are in. The gathering was especially important and informative for our talent publicists, who attended because every one of our clients doing press these days is being asked about harassment, equality and their point of view on what seems to be an endless list of powerful men being accused of sexual misconduct.

The meeting inspired those in attendance to do more and motivated those who weren't to get involved. If you sit back and really think about the massive cultural impact and absolute-zero tolerance for any type of harassment that the Me Too and Time's Up movements have created (both of which, no doubt, will be dominant themes in the 2018 Cannes Lions), it's pretty mind-blowing. It made me wonder at what point does a moment become a movement? For the above, you can arguably say that while the jaw-dropping *New York Times* article on Harvey Weinstein was definitely a catalyst, the momentum that we are seeing now really started long before with a gradual but consistent stream of prominent, courageous women finally going on record about their traumatic experiences, women whose voices became a collective scream demanding change. Their stories were, and still are, all of us.

Which brings me to the topic of this chapter, 'The News It Creates'. While branded entertainment is technically content advertising meant to entertain the audience in a creative way – at the heart of all branded content is storytelling – its key is the ability to reach your target and emotionally connect and relate with them, whether your story is about a cause, a product, a person or a purpose. Great storytelling is the foundation of great (branded) entertainment, and if your story resonates enough, people will share it and help make it into news. While it's certainly not a requirement for a branded entertainment programme or piece to make news in order to be considered successful, what it does do is generate visibility and help propel your programme/initiative into the mainstream. News creates buzz. Buzz creates awareness. Awareness creates conversation, and it's that conversation that can make you feel like you are part of something bigger. That conversation can also significantly expand your reach.

Think about it. When great content is created, the audience is typically considered to be those who view, enjoy and are entertained by it – 'fanboys', if you will. But if the story you are telling is able to transcend that audience thanks to widespread news and conversation created on owned, earned, social or paid media outlets, this allows you to reach a limitless number of people that you might not otherwise have been able to get to. These days it's not enough to create great content or a great experience; you want people to talk about it, share it, praise it, validate it, to reinforce the message you are trying to communicate. And if you are really successful you might even be able to effect or promote change, whether it's a change in perception, public opinion and/or policy.

A good example of this is *A Love Song Written by a Murderer*, created by Circus Grey Peru for Vida Mujer. This campaign really spoke to me. What starts out as a beautiful but melancholy love song by Diego Dibos, one of Peru's most popular and widely admired romantic songwriters, as he launches his new single on the radio, turns out to be something much darker and more terrifying – which people realize later on. After the song became popular in Peru, Diego revealed that the lyrics of the song were actually pulled from a letter of apology written by a man who abused and eventually murdered his wife six days after she received the letter. Once the public realized this truth, it not only propelled a dialogue around domestic violence in a way that really forced people to stop and pay attention it also reinforced the simple but extremely important message that people should never give an abuser a second chance. Especially in a country like Peru, where sexual violence against women is widespread (statistics show that on average ten women a month are murdered), a campaign such as this can have a profound effect in helping to protect vulnerable women when their own government or society doesn't do it.

I should probably mention that while this campaign did create significant news coverage around the topic of domestic abuse, *A Love Song Written by a Murderer* was not without its own controversy. In 2017 an article written by Juliana Oxenford on Altavoz.pe questioned the authenticity of the 'letter'. After launching an investigation and on a quest to verify the actual letter behind the song, Oxenford discovered that the lyrics were actually based on more than one letter. The writer questioned the integrity of the programme if some of the facts were manipulated and exaggerated (such as Diego Dibos being touted as the most important romantic songwriter in Peru) in order to have a greater impact because 'femicide is not a game'.

In an unrelated article in *Adweek* Charlie Tolmos, creative director at Circus Grey Peru, the agency that created the campaign, wrote: 'The brief was to do something big that shows women it is absolutely dangerous to give a second chance to an abuser. The main objective was to start a conversation about this problem and to explain to people that behind beautiful words there are sometimes ugly intentions.'[1]

In a country in which violence against women is so prevalent and an accompanying despicable sexist attitude towards women widely pervasive, does it really matter if certain facts were exaggerated to get people to pay attention and help get the message across in a meaningful way? In Peru it's not just about changing behaviour, it's about changing the overall mindset of men who still think of their spouses, girlfriends and partners as property. Regardless of whether the love song was written by a murderer or partly written by an abuser, you cannot deny that it was an extremely effective campaign that shocked a country in denial about the exceptionally high rates of violence against women. It didn't just create news, it incited people to act and seek help.

Thanks to this campaign Vida Mujer was able to help more than 3,000 women.

Another example of a campaign that was so powerful it actually persuaded a government to change the law was *#Undress522* created by H&C Leo Burnett Beirut for a women's-rights non-governmental organization (NGO) called Abaad. This programme won three PR Silver Cannes Lions, an Entertainment Bronze Cannes Lion and a Glass Silver Cannes Lion. In Lebanon rape and sexual assault against women is unfortunately extremely common. To make matters worse, if a rapist marries his victim there is an unknown law that says his crimes can be dismissed. That law is article 522 of the Lebanese penal code. *#Undress522* sought to have that law overturned. To help raise awareness *#Undress522* launched with a disturbing video of a woman being sexually assaulted. Then, bruised and beaten, she is forcefully wrapped in medical gauze tape that looks like a wedding dress. The following words flash on the screen: 'Article 522 of the Lebanese Penal Code exonerates rapists if they marry their victim. A white dress doesn't cover the rape.' The video ignited anger and disbelief in Lebanon. News outlets reported on Article 522 with incredulous repudiation. To have an actual law that protects rapists if they marry their victim (especially a law that only 1% of the population even knew existed) seemed so preposterous that people's immediate reactions were of shock, awe and outrage. People flooded social media screaming about the hypocrisy of the law. The public demanded change. Prominent politicians demanded change. People not just in Lebanon but around the world called for Article 522 to be abolished.

#Undress522 then executed a stunt that really drove the message the home: thirteen women, standing in unison in front of the parliament in Beirut, wearing bloodied wedding dresses and veils in silent protest of the law that protects rapists. Then another dramatic stunt followed, in which thirty-one torn wedding dresses were hung in the air on the Corniche of Beirut. The images taken at these two protests were captured and shared around the world, and *#Undress522* received news coverage not just in Lebanon but globally, and the campaign shamed the Lebanese Parliament into repealing

the law and finally protecting the rights of rape victims. Because the news that covered this went far beyond the Lebanese audience it was intended for, reaching global proportions, #Undress522 was a motion that became a movement that became a government mandate.

Information is power, and the key to that power is spreading it. But in today's fragmented and unpredictable landscape it is becoming increasingly difficult to do that when you have an audience that is so constantly overfed with information. This oversaturation can create indifference. You start to hear the same type of story all the time and soon, without realizing it, you begin to ignore it. That is what made the programmes here so special. They both found a way to incite conversation through meaningful experiences and then created an intense audience engagement along the way. They both found a way to shock the audience, whether through the element of surprise (*A Love Song Written by a Murderer*) or through provocative and disturbing images (*#Undress522*). A good news story needs to be able to travel seamlessly across multiple channels – earned and owned media, social feeds, video players and newswires – and in various formats including photos, videos, headlines, bite-sized content and so on. And these examples do exactly that.

The above two programmes were specific to movements tied to women's rights. However, not every famous branded entertainment piece has such purpose. Sometimes it's just about finding a way to help your product break through the clutter. This was the case with 'Pass the Heinz' (mentioned in the previous chapter by my esteemed colleague Marcelo Pascoa), created by the agency David Miami for Kraft Heinz, a completely different example of a campaign that ended up generating significant news coverage – for ketchup of all things. The campaign used the popular TV show *Mad Men*, which celebrated the tenth anniversary of its premiere last year, the fictional advertising agency Sterling Cooper Draper Pryce and the TV show's main character Don Draper as inspiration for a ketchup ad. In one of the past episodes, in Season 6 of the show, Don Draper pitched a simple but sleek idea to the Heinz marketing team (which, by the way, he doesn't win because the ads didn't feature the actual bottle of ketchup, which is comical). What follows, fifty years later in

2017, is that the actual ads Don Draper created in the show are run in real life as a series of traditional print ads and outdoor billboards, with credits to both the real agency David Miami and the fictional ad agency Sterling Cooper Draper Pryce– proof that Don Draper's words a half-century later still ring true.

Touted as the first 'reverse product placement' in advertising, this clever concept was so popular it earned a whopping 2.6 billion media impressions and more than $55 million in earned media value – for ketchup . . . product placement. That is pretty incredible. 'Pass the Heinz' became the brand's most successful ad campaign ever.

So what was it about this that generated so much buzz, interest and coverage? Well, first and foremost it integrated an iconic and widely loved TV series into a real-world campaign. By the time 'Pass the Heinz' debuted the TV series had actually ended almost two years before. However, there was still a lot of love and nostalgia for the show and its characters. By partnering with the show you already had a built-in audience that would pay attention, be emotionally connected and want to talk about anything *Mad Men*-related. 'Pass the Heinz' helped reignite people's passion for *Mad Men* and allowed them to feel part of something bigger. Plus, the campaign was truly authentic to what the characters actually did on the show. Finally, bringing the campaign full circle by tying it to the present day was something that had never been done before. People (and the press) ate it up. It's ironic, because most brands partner with different entertainment properties to make them relevant, but in this case the reverse happened. The 'Pass the Heinz' ads helped generate new discussion around a show that had gone off the air back in 2015. And in a mobile-first era, in which everyone looks at content on their phones, Heinz got people to pay attention and appreciate the simplicity of a print ad. The campaign was obviously covered by all the industry and entertainment trades, major print and online publications, consumer-lifestyle outlets, but its reach was really pretty much everyone, everywhere. I mean who doesn't use ketchup?

I think I need to take a break now. All of a sudden I'm hungry.

The evolving news landscape

What constitutes news today, and how do you create it? We all know we live in the era of the 24/7 news cycle. There is a new news ecosystem and distribution model as it pertains to 'coverage'. The world of media has changed as 'me as media' continues to grow in influence and a new generation has redefined the media landscape. Today everyone is their own medium, and consumers discover and discuss news wherever they are. Influencers and experts have a growing voice as they gain equal footing with traditional news sources. In the eyes of the consumers all sources are seen as equal. As the 'news for you' becomes more targeted, the source of news becomes less important, which can result in the fake news we currently have all around us. With so much noise, how do you get people to hear what you have to say?

To really cut through the clutter and make something meaningful, something that will not only make news but incite discussion and ongoing dialogue, you have to create a defining moment or experience that stands the test of time. This is when your idea becomes part of culture itself. But what is a defining moment today? It's a shareable experience, rooted in the cultural jet streams, linking people and evoking a personal connection or emotion. In order to optimize storytelling today marketers feel the pressure to have mastery across all areas of content distribution, whether it is a traditional news source, social media platform, content farm, aggregator service or digital influencer. But in the end what is trending is really about understanding the simple truth that consumers want a story with heart, a story that is relevant and engaging. If you have this, your audience will find a way to share it.

One of my favourite entries from 2017 was *Real Color Stories with Tracey Norman* created by the Grey Group for Clairol Nice'n Easy. It won a Silver Lion for Excellence in Partnerships with Talent. The entry told the story of Tracey Norman, the first African-American transgender model. In the late 1970s, when Norman was a young model, she was working with Clairol and featured on their hair colour box Born Beautiful, the first African American ever to do so. Her work with Clairol led to several additional lucrative modelling jobs, including Italian *Vogue* and *Essence*. However, as times were different back then, Norman was not yet out about being transgender. Eventually, at a photo shoot, her gender identity was discovered, and, just like that, her career as a model was over. Fast forward to 2016, after a story about Norman was published in *New York Magazine*'s digital fashion site 'The Cut', Norman was approached by Clairol to be the face of their *Nice'n Easy Color As Real As You Are* campaign. The campaign highlighted the confidence that comes from self-acceptance, living your truth and creatively expressing yourself through things like hair colour. In fact, Clairol's tagline for the campaign was 'Color as real as you are'.

As mentioned, this entry was for Excellence in Partnerships with Talent, which is a difficult category to stand out in, much less win. Since partnering with talent – whether it is with a celebrity, actor, musician, sports athlete or social influencer – honestly is nothing really new (and there were tons of entries in this category) we really held the entrants in this category to a higher standard. It's not enough to have a cool idea or programme with talent, you really have to do something that has never been done before. What was special about this campaign was the simplicity and honesty of the story. It's a tale of prejudice, history, redemption, truth and empowerment all rolled into one. *Real Color Stories with Tracey Norman* is an incredibly moving comeback story – and who doesn't love a comeback? – and the news created by the campaign helped promote the message of living your truth, no matter what that truth means to you, and not being afraid to live your truth at a time when transgender acceptance is starting to become more widespread. To have a major brand such as Clairol show its support for transgender was inspiring and a major step in the right direction for equal rights for all. Kudos to them for creating this moving campaign.

How to tell your story: think like an editor

At a time when everyone is creating content, how do you ensure yours breaks through and reaches your audience? As new tools for content creation and distribution continue to develop rapidly, we look back to the old-school world of the 'editor' for inspiration on how to curate relevant content. Good editors not only understand what their audience wants but the importance of editorial planning, taking into consideration that their coverage and story can be disrupted by breaking news at any time. Editors imagine the storyline from the start and anticipate what visual assets they need in order to tell the story. Editors are also constantly analysing the direction of cultural conversation, ongoing events and the ever-changing news curves. They wait for just the right moment to publish a story to create the greatest impact, and they prepare additional content to keep the conversation going. Even though news happens in real time all the time, you can still, believe it or not, plan ahead.

If a story is designed to be discussed, and the brand involved can be organically and authentically included, it becomes impossible not to have the brand mentioned – and that in itself is a big win. If the initiative goes beyond its audience to become news, the brand starts being able to enter spaces where it wouldn't be allowed otherwise.

The most obvious example of this is probably *Fearless Girl Arrives* by McCann Worldgroup for State Street Global Advisors. While *Fearless Girl* was not entered in the Entertainment Category at the 2017 Cannes Lions you couldn't escape its tremendous impact and the dialogue it generated. The concept for *Fearless Girl* is one of the simplest yet most brilliant ideas brought to life. *Fearless Girl* is a statue of a young girl with her hands on her hips in defiance, created to promote the power of women in leadership and encourage companies to have greater gender diversity. Launched on International Women's Day, and strategically placed in front of the iconic *Charging Bull* on Wall Street, New York, *Fearless Girl* became an immediate global sensation and symbol of female empowerment. It garnered an astounding 4.6 billion impressions on Twitter and 745 million Instagram impressions in just twelve weeks. It's pretty incredible to see how a statue that doesn't actually say anything can say so much. As writer Gail Collins so eloquently puts it in her op-ed in the *New York Times*: 'She reminds you that while marching is important, sometimes you can make a difference by standing still.'[2]

Another excellent example is *Survival Billboard* by McCann

Worldgroup UK (McCann London, Momentum, MRM/Meteorite and Craft) for the Microsoft Xbox game 'Rise of the Tomb Raider' from 2016. *Survival Billboard* picked up a whopping six Entertainment Lions, including Gold. Keep in mind that those six Entertainment Lions won were on top of the eleven Lions it won in the Outdoor, Direct, Integrated, Media, and Promotion and Activation categories.

I am not a gamer and have zero interest in video games – zero. I am only slightly aware of game release dates, and that is because my twelve-year-old son loves a bit of 'Call of Duty'. Most video-game launches clearly target those folks who actually play the games, since it is a very specific audience. Back in 2000 (yep, Y2K), when my company represented Sony PlayStation, I remember we held a glitzy Hollywood party to launch PlayStation 2 like a blockbuster film with celebrities such as Michelle Rodriguez, Luke Wilson, Vin Diesel and Carmen Electra in attendance (before celebrities and influencers had to be paid to attend an event). At the time (a much simpler time), the goal was to broaden the PlayStation 2 audience beyond hardcore gamers and have people view PlayStation 2 as an entertainment system rather than just a video-game console. The launch was very successful. We received a ton of entertainment and lifestyle press and a slew of new Hollywood gamers addicted to the various titles available on the PlayStation 2. However, those days are (sadly) long gone, and since then game publishers and console manufacturers have had constantly to raise the bar and fight to get attention for their games with everything from sophisticated content that tells the backstory of game characters to live-action trailers or crazy stunts where you get the game for life if you have a baby the day of the game's release and then name him or her after one of the characters (The Elder Scrolls V: Skyrim, I'm talking to you).

But, in my humble opinion, *Survival Billboard* was definitely a game-changer (no pun intended) and raised the bar on how to create an idea that appealed to a mass audience and also couldn't be talked about without mentioning the brand (or, in this case, the game). 'Rise of the Tomb Raider' is an action-adventure game that follows Lara Croft through various environments with a focus on survival and combat. To celebrate the launch McCann London created a live 'survival of the grittiest' billboard in the middle of London where eight brave people (who were recruited weeks before via a print and outdoor campaign that solicited those willing to submit themselves to 'horrible, horrible conditions') literally stood on the ledge of a billboard and were exposed to various extremely harsh weather conditions. The goal was to outlast your opponents and be the last person standing. Do this and win a grand prize to somewhere spectacular inspired by the game.

Again, I am definitely not the target, but I remember this campaign very clearly, and I remember talking about it with people because it allowed the public to be part of the programme. To make the stunt more interactive and engaging, consumers were able to vote on exactly what conditions the eight participants would experience: biting snow, pouring rain, intense heat, strong winds, all while standing in place. The insane stunt was streamed online and on Twitch and quickly caught the attention of the public. There was tremendous social chatter – 32,000 comments in one day and 3.5 million views in just twenty-two hours. What was it about this campaign that made it so appealing to so many different people? Was it because it played into our love of reality TV and sensationalism (this was, after all, a mini outdoor version of the *Survivor* TV series) or our obsession with extreme physical challenges or that feeling of power you get when you have someone's destiny in your control? Whatever it was, this idea gave new meaning to Xbox Live.

There is no such thing as bad publicity

As I mentioned earlier, creating news is not a prerequisite for a great branded entertainment programme, but it certainly helps. However, what happens if the news created isn't exactly positive?

Let's look at HBO's *Game of Thrones: Ice & Fire* created by 360i digital marketing agency for HBO and entered in the Live Broadcast/ Live Streaming category. This entry did not win a Cannes Lion, but it was shortlisted. In March 2017 HBO wanted to leverage the incredible fandom, obsession and anticipation around their hit show. Season 7 was set to begin some time in 2017, and people were patiently and anxiously waiting for the official announcement of exactly when it would return. To announce the release date HBO executed a stunt on Facebook Live where the release date was hidden inside a huge block of ice. (The name of the series of books that the TV series is based on is 'A Song of Ice and Fire', hence the theme for the stunt.) Since fire melts ice, viewers were asked to write 'fire' in the comments, and every time they did the block of ice was torched with fire.

There were technical difficulties that caused the live stream to be interrupted twice. In the end more than 160,000 viewers watched the live stream, and it took over an hour for the ice to melt and for fans to learn the release date (which was 16 July 2017). Let me repeat that again, more than 160,000 people spent over an hour watching ice melt . . . watching . . . ice . . . melt. It should, therefore, be no surprise that this stunt did receive quite a backlash. Most of the news coverage talked about how even the show's creators didn't like it, with headlines including: 'The People Making Game of Thrones Also Found that Block of Ice Stunt Pretty Embarrassing' (vulture. com);[3] 'The Game of Thrones Showrunners Hated That Ice Block Stunt Too' (mashable.com);[4] and 'HBO Made Game of Thrones Fans Watch Ice Melt for a Painfully Long Time, and They Went Nuts' (businessinsider.com).[5]

The idea in itself is extremely creative, simple and cost-effective to execute, and honestly hilarious if you really think about how people paid attention to melting ice. It shows you the power of *Game of Thrones* and reinforces how much hype there was (and still is) around the show. We ended up giving this the shortlist acknowledgement because it was a clever and creative shareable moment that connected people, but the emotion you would normally feel participating in an experience around a show you loved was the wrong emotion. There was so much negativity, both from fans and the press, that it made what should have been a bonding moment something people became annoyed about. We ended up not awarding a Cannes Lions in this category at all, but *Game of Thrones: Ice & Fire* Season 7 announcement live stream, however, was the only entry that was actually shortlisted. So, did the news coverage affect the outcome? You be the judge.

The great debate

Recently I was driving my son to go and check out the new hyper-reality VR experience called 'The Void' in Downtown Disney in Disneyland. Unlike regular VR, which brings you into a simulated realistic experience, 'The Void' also allows you to touch, feel and even smell that experience, making it one of the most immersive and realistic experiences in existence. There was a lot of traffic on the way (as per usual in LA), and since my electric car has a (semi-)auto driving feature I took advantage of it so I could sit back and listen to the news (which was about bitcoin dropping below $10,000) while my son played around with Snapchat on his phone in the back. There is nothing really unusual about my day, right? However, if you start to break it down – VR, self-driving cars, cryptocurrency and social media – I realized that I'm drowning in technology. Today, no doubt about it, we live in a world dependent on technology. Few would argue that we are in the middle of a technological evolution – or is it a revolution? I guess it depends on how you look at it.

As a marketer, one question I often hear from my tech clients is, how can we humanize technology so we can show how that innovation makes people's everyday lives better? The word 'humanize' has actually been a big marketing buzzword over the last couple of years: 'humanize your brand'; 'humanize the experience'; 'humanize technology'.

But what about the reverse? What happens when technology is used to make humans more, well, high-tech? Remember the 1980s movies *RoboCop* or *Blade Runner* – both films set in a dystopian future with bioengineered cyborgs? What once seemed so advanced and far away is here now and has been for a while.

Anyone who has a prosthetic limb, a pacemaker, a hearing aid, a hip replacement, a bionic eye, a mechanical hand or any artificial part can technically be considered a cyborg since they are humans who have been augmented by technology. This technology has enriched the lives of those with disabilities who would otherwise be at a disadvantage physically. In fact, in many cases, these augmented humans actually now *have* the advantages thanks to their enhanced abilities. At what point does it become fallacious or perverse? Should there be a clear limit to how far we can bioengineer human beings? Just because we can doesn't mean we *should*.

These questions are explored in 'Deus Ex: Mankind Divided', a role-playing game set in 2029 after an event where mechanically augmented humans were unknowingly implanted with technology designed to control them but instead became uncontrollable, lawless and violent. To launch the game, Square Enix and agency Turner International created an integrated campaign called *Human by Design*, which tapped into the hot topic of the ethics of human augmentation to help raise awareness and reach beyond the average gamer. The campaign centred on the first ever summit of cyborgs, which featured industry panellists, game developers and actual augmented cyborgs from around the world to show how technology has enhanced their lives. The conference was accompanied by a half-hour documentary on the subject premiered by Amazon Prime. They even published the first bill of rights for cyborgs. By taking this approach the programme sparked a larger debate and conversation around human augmentation and its ramifications in the future. The campaign received widespread publicity with one media outlet (IGN) even declaring that '*Human by Design* redefines the future of mankind'.[6] That is a pretty big statement

Again, this is an example of a programme scaled beyond the brand to create news, or, in this case, public debate and discussion on a topic far more important than the product being promoted.

When no news really can be good news

As creative as an idea may be, it still has to be measurable in some way to know that it was effective. But news coverage is not the only metric taken into consideration. One of the best examples of a programme that had large impact but not massive news coverage around it was the *Penguin Frozen Storybook* created by TBWA China for Penguin Books. The book told the story of an ordinary penguin that had to leave its home because the environment around it was melting because of global warming. But this was no ordinary book.

The actual book was made using a special ink that would react and disappear to increasing temperature: the world's first frozen storybook. As the story progresses and the reader accompanies the penguin on his journey in search of a new place to live, the images of his homeland, the places he visited and the friends he made along the way gradually disappear. The book could only be read for fifteen minutes at a time before everything inside would fade away – but it was enough time to tell the story of how global warming greatly impacts on the environment and all those who live in it in a purposeful and memorable way.

The concept of the book, as well as the story it told, was daring, charming and captivating. The case film stated that 16,500 books were pre-ordered in a month, 85.6% beyond sales expectations. The *Penguin Frozen Storybook* was also selected as an environmentally friendly book by several pre-school organizations – ensuring that a new generation of readers will be educated on the devastating effects of global warming. So while there weren't billions of media impressions around this programme as there were on 'Pass the Heinz', there was impact and a meaningful story that could live on for generations (even if only for fifteen minutes at a time).

When creating branded entertainment, don't start with whether your concept is newsworthy, start with the story. This may seem obvious, yet in a world where everyone is telling stories on any number of channels pretty much every minute of the day, having a purposeful story that resonates with anyone is getting harder and harder to achieve.

Not everything can make the news. But then again, not everything should. Just because you are able to get PR, even its significant coverage doesn't make your programme a standout. It's the story that is within the news coverage that can help make your content shine through. Does it have purpose? Does it have a larger goal? Is it part of a bigger conversation? Does the audience understand your message? Are people helping spread whatever it is you are promoting?

All of the examples mentioned in this chapter share common denominators – they were designed to be watched, shared and discussed and to provoke a raw emotion or reaction from the intended audience in a way that was relatable, relevant, engaging and authentic to the brand involved in it. They all tapped into the zeitgeist – whether entertainment, politics or women's rights – and because the story being told resonated so broadly (far beyond its intended audience) these entries were able to create defining moments that will undoubtedly stand the test of time. Additionally, each of the programmes mentioned had the ability to scale up with storytelling that went above and beyond the initial intent.

Don't be afraid to take that risk, get out of your comfort zone and utilize branded entertainment as a vehicle to connect with consumers and tell your story in an effective and thought-provoking way. Even the simplest idea can have a huge impact. If you do it right, you have the opportunity not just to be part of culture but actually to create it, making the return on your initial investment priceless.

1. http://www.adweek.com/creativity/this-seemingly-lovely-pop-song-is-winning-big-in-cannes-for-hiding-a-terrible-secret/

2. https://www.nytimes.com/2017/03/08/opinion/little-girl-statue-wall-street-bull.html

3. http://www.vulture.com/2017/03/got-team-found-that-block-of-ice-stunt-pretty-embarrassing.html

4. https://mashable.com/2017/03/25/game-of-thrones-ice-block-showrunners/#sofnXycAdZqd

5. http://www.businessinsider.com/game-of-thrones-season-7-ice-video-facebook-hbo-2017-3

6. http://www.ign.com/videos/2016/08/01/human-by-design-documentary-redefining-the-future-of-mankind

Part 2
THE ART OF BRANDED ENTERTAINMENT

FROM PRODUCT PLACEMENT TO IDEA PLACEMENT

Pelle Sjoenell, Bartle Bogle Hegarty

Jason Xenopoulos, VML South Africa

The best pieces of work that we saw this year in Cannes Entertainment were the ones that made us think; stories that made us think about something that matters to the brands behind the work.

A bank made us rethink our relationship with money. A Swedish vodka reminded us that we are all from Africa. An internet security company made us worry about the future of the internet. A grocery chain reminded us of the need for romance in everyday life. An NGO gave us some understanding of what it is like to be refugees.

None of these stories was really centred on a product or a service; they all focused on a value, a belief or a point of view. It is that point of view that makes the product look very attractive. Done right it becomes synonymous with the brand and its product.

In this chapter we will try to break down why ideas are necessary and how touching an audience is key. Our thesis is that we think the audience out there is more interested and moved by idea placement than product placement. It makes for better stories and better sales.

Make the idea bigger, not the logo

In the early 2000s Jason Xenopoulos, one of the authors of this chapter, directed a feature film called *Critical Assignment*. It was an action movie about a suave African James Bond-type hero called Michael Power. It was the opening-night film at the New York African Film Festival at the Lincoln Center, New York, and went on to enjoy mainstream distribution around the world. But what made *Critical Assignment* such a special film is that it was funded by Guinness in the UK.

To our knowledge, *Critical Assignment* is one of the first feature films ever to be fully funded by a brand. Despite the fact that the film has many faults and limitations, it was a massive success in Nigeria and across the African continent, where it drove huge awareness and positive sentiment. But what makes it truly remarkable is that the Guinness brand is largely invisible in the film. There is almost no product placement, maybe one or two drinking shots in the entire ninety minutes, and yet it managed to achieve awareness levels of 89% in Nigeria and 81% in Ghana.

The reason for this exceptional attribution is the fact that Michael Power, the lead character in the film, had already become the personification of the brand. For five years before *Critical Assignment* went into production Guinness ran a television and outdoor campaign featuring the Michael Power character. The television commercials were so popular that TV stations began to play them for free as programming. One of the ads began with a shot of Michael Power, standing strong and proud, accompanied by a voice-over that said something like *If Guinness was any man . . . it would be this man!* From that moment on Michael Power became the living, breathing embodiment of the brand. By the time the feature film was released Michael Power was so well-established across the continent that when people saw him they saw Guinness.

In the case of *Critical Assignment* the Power character *was* the idea. He was the physical embodiment of the Guinness brand. His strength, courage and integrity personified the brand values and served as a compelling demonstration of what it meant to be a Guinness man. But he was also the hero of the film, and so everything he said and did to amplify the brand message also helped to drive the story forward. *Critical Assignment* was a massive commercial success for Guinness and an early example of the fact that idea placement can be more effective than product placement.

The feeling is the message

The Canadian academic and intellectual Marshall McLuhan famously said that the medium is the message; but, as human beings, the only medium that really counts is the way we feel. Emotion is our primary conduit for communication because it opens us up to receiving deeper messages. The brain can understand things, but the heart is where they resonate. This notion is central to our thesis because when done properly idea placement can transcend the superficiality of product placement and deliver a much deeper and more resonant message. There were two great examples of this at Cannes 2017: a moving and important short film called *Home* and a feature-length documentary called *Lo and Behold: Reveries of the Connected World* directed by the legendary film-maker Werner Herzog.

Home tells the familiar story of a young family of refugees, driven from their home and forced to endure endless hardships and humiliation as they fight their way across the border to freedom. What makes *Home* so different, so unexpected and so personally moving is the fact that the family portrayed in this film is the antithesis of what we have come to expect. These are not refugees from Syria or Somalia or the Congo or Myanmar. They are not African or Middle-Eastern or Asian, and they don't speak in a language that we can't understand. This family is British. They are from a normal suburban home. Their lives look familiar. They could be your neighbours or your friends. When you watch them being bundled helplessly into the boot of a car, and when you hear them crying feebly and grasping for their dignity, you understand (perhaps for the very first time) what being a refugee might really be like. According to Ant Austin, co-founder of Black Sheep Studios, co-producers of the film: 'This role reversal was designed to create empathy, to help the audience feel the situation as if it was happening to them and to bring it much closer to *Home*'.

The strategy worked. The twenty-minute film (which does not mention the United Nations or the specifics of their cause until the very end) has helped to persuade millions of people to sign the UN's #withrefugees petition. In addition to winning Gold at Cannes Lions, the film has been screened at more than fifty festivals and won many awards, including the BAFTA for Best British Short Film.

Home is a perfect example of idea placement, and it is proof that 'the feeling is the message'. The creators might not have been trying to sell a product or build a commercial brand, but their objective was still to persuade an audience to shift its point of view. They could have tried to do that with statistics, making an information-laden corporate ad or releasing a White Paper, but instead they used branded entertainment and the power of emotion to deliver the message in a way that facts and figures never could. 'Home made people empathize and feel the problem for themselves,' says Black Sheep Studios. 'It added a new and powerful perspective to the conversation.'

As jurors at an advertising festival we were not expecting to be moved by anything to this extent. Admittedly, to call Cannes an advertising festival is unfair – it is so much more – but the creative work on display is often limited by the constraints of having to persuade an audience to buy something. Cannes is where we discover the best creative ideas from around the world, but the cinema is still the place where we go to be moved and entertained. Home, however, blurred those boundaries in an inspiring way. From the first frame to the last we knew that we were watching a piece of art. The impressive part of it, though, is that this art film was actually shifting our perspective on an important issue, and, by the time it ended Home had fulfilled its mandate to persuade better than traditional advertising ever could.

People are moved by great stories. They are swayed by the way something makes them feel, not necessarily by what they are told. This is the reason why idea placement is so powerful. It doesn't just enhance the audience's experience of the brand, it is also a more effective way of delivering on a brand's communication objectives.

Another branded film that set out to make people feel the problem for themselves and change the conversation was Lo and Behold, a brilliant documentary film for NetScout directed by Werner Herzog. Lo and Behold is an excellent example of a brand using idea placement rather than product placement to achieve its business objectives. The NetScout brand doesn't feature anywhere in this film, and yet, after ninety minutes of superb film-making, they managed to create a tangible need for their products and services.

NetScout is an internet security company that has traditionally focused on B2B marketing. Their services are designed for large corporates, and fees can sometimes run into hundreds of thousands of dollars per month. To secure these mega-contracts, NetScout needs to communicate with the C-Suite, the CEOs and other high-level executives. They have to convince these prospective clients of the need for sophisticated and costly security solutions. The most obvious route might have been to produce a series of PowerPoint charts outlining the risks involved in running a large-scale network. While this might have conveyed the necessary information, it wouldn't have had the emotional impact they needed. It wouldn't have sparked a conversation or inspired executives to think more deeply about the problems that NetScout is trying to solve. The brand needed something more impactful, something that could live beyond the boardroom and capture its audience's imagination; something that would persuade customers to prioritize these issues and create new demand for NetScout's products and services. To achieve this, NetScout and its agency, Pereira O'Dell, decided to make a feature-length documentary that would expose the power and fragility of the internet. But to do this in a credible way required them to go beyond advertising.

Enter Werner Herzog

Unless you have been living under a rock for the past fifty years you've probably heard of the Oscar-nominated film director and seen at least one of his films. If not, we suggest that you add them to your list. Werner Herzog's skill as a film-maker is only one of the reasons why he was such an inspired choice for this project. According to film critic Roger Ebert, Herzog 'has never created a single film that is compromised, shameful, made for pragmatic reasons, or uninteresting. Even his failures are spectacular.'[1] Attaching Werner Herzog's name to this branded film ensured its credibility and marketability beyond the boardroom. Having said that, Herzog's reputation precedes him for a reason. He is not a gun-for-hire. He won't say or do anything he doesn't believe in. Herzog is a visionary film-maker who puts himself into every picture, and *Lo and Behold* is no exception. The genius of this project is the fact that Herzog's dystopian vision of our evolving technocracy intersects perfectly with the cautionary tale that NetScout set out to tell. The ideas and themes that Herzog uses to drive *Lo and Behold*'s compelling narrative are the very ideas that NetScout wanted to seed into their audience's consciousness. This is idea placement at its most sophisticated.

Some might argue that the NetScout brand is too 'shy' in this film, that people might watch the entire movie without ever realizing that the brand is involved. Indeed, this is something that the jury debated quite extensively – especially when it came time to select our Grand Prix. *Lo and Behold* was a firm favourite to win the big prize because the jury unanimously agreed that it was the best film in the festival. But when measured alongside other great pieces (especially *Beyond Money* for Santander Bank, which eventually won the Grand Prix) the jury decided that the excessively subtle treatment of the brand was a limiting factor. The truth, though, is that without this level of subtlety *Lo and Behold* wouldn't exist. Werner Herzog would not have agreed to make the film, and without Herzog's singular vision the film would not have had the same kind of impact. It would not have been sold to Magnolia Pictures and thousands of prospective clients would never have been exposed to these ideas. In 2017, when branded entertainment was still seen as an extension of the ad industry and separate from mainstream entertainment, *Lo and Behold* could be criticized for taking such a stealthy approach to brand integration. But in the future, when idea placement finally replaces product placement as the *de facto* approach to brand building, we believe that *Lo and Behold* will be viewed as a true trailblazer.

Make the brand part of the story

Critical Assignment was Jason's first foray into branded entertainment, and it changed his perspective for ever. Like the great films described above, *Critical Assignment* proved that brands can achieve their objectives without being overt. He became quite militant in his resistance to product placement in any form of entertainment – whether it be a can of Coke on the table during a talk show or James Bond wearing his Tag Heuer watch; to him it was all brash and inauthentic, no less irritating than other forms of interruption marketing.

But as a judge at Cannes Lions in 2017 Jason saw several pieces of work in which the brand played a powerful and unapologetic role in the content and realized that, when executed well, a brand and even a product can be a powerful addition to the entertainment itself. We have discussed this phenomenon at length, trying to unpack why the 'unapologetic' placement of a product or brand works so brilliantly in some instances but becomes a fatal distraction in others. After much analysis we realized that the brand is a red herring. It's not about the prominence of the brand, it's about the depth of meaning that it represents. In other words, it's less about how well the product placement is handled and more about how well the idea placement is executed.

Branded love stories that fuel brand love

Romantic films don't appeal to everyone, so you can imagine how surprised the jury was when we all found ourselves moved to tears by two heavily branded love stories. The first was *From the Start*, the five-part web series made for Lacta chocolate in Greece. This wonderful campaign has been described in detail by our co-authors in other chapters ('The Battle of Time and the Fallacy of the Short Attention Span' and 'Back to Basics'), so we won't describe the story here again in detail. Suffice to say that, while the film may have been funded by a brand, it is a great piece of entertainment that can easily compete with anything else on TV. This is an awesome achievement in itself (as demonstrated by Samantha Glynne in the chapter 'Ideas That Scale'), but it is an even bigger deal when you consider the central role that the product plays in the story.

Ogilvy Worldwide in Athens, the agency responsible for this campaign, describes *From the Start* in their Cannes entry as 'a web series that tells the story of a man who doesn't believe in love falling for the girl he sees in a dream that he has each time he eats a piece of Lacta chocolate'. That short synopsis makes it sound like the brand plays an important role in the narrative – and indeed it does. It also makes it sound like a glorified TV advert, but nothing could be further from the truth.

From the Start is an excellent film, and the product plays a valid role in the story. In some ways it reminds us of the golden ticket in *Charlie and the Chocolate Factory*. No one would accuse Roald Dahl of trying to drive sales of Wonka Bars. He was simply using a chocolate bar as a narrative device. *From the Start* does the same thing. The use of Lacta chocolate is shameless and unapologetic, but it's never an imposition. It doesn't get in the way of the story. It doesn't dilute the emotion. It enhances because it both serves as a narrative trigger and is done in such a way that it fits seamlessly into the world of the film. Ironically, if the brand had a more subtle presence in the film (perhaps lying on a counter somewhere like common product placement) it would have done more harm to the piece than this very purposeful use of the product in the story.

There was lots of passionate discussion in the jury room about whether or not this overt product placement added to the value of the content or detracted from it. In the end the supporters won through and the film was awarded Gold. The judges believed that the product played an authentic role in the story and added to its overall entertainment value. The brand is there, proud and unapologetic, but it doesn't simply represent a bar of chocolate, it symbolizes the magic of falling in love – an idea that sits at the heart of both the narrative and the brand.

Finding the intersection between your story and your brand is the ultimate goal of branded entertainment. It's not necessarily about giving your brand a physical presence in the content but, rather, finding a way to encapsulate and communicate what the brand is really about. It's not about pasting a logo on to the surface of the content; it is about weaving meaning into its very core. In *From the Start* the agency managed to do both simultaneously.

Panos Sambrakos, the Executive Creative Director of OgilvyOne Worldwide in Athens, explains why they approached the film in this way. 'The previous branded film we'd done for Lacta moved audiences to tears, but the product wasn't present in the drama at all. We gained a lot of viewers, but we didn't sell much chocolate. So we took a conscious decision to make the product more integral to the story; to really embrace it. We decided to turn Lacta into our very own Aladdin's Lamp. You eat the chocolate . . . and the magic happens! Not only did the audience not mind when the product appeared – they were actually looking forward to it.' This beautifully symbiotic relationship between the product and the story elevates the use of Lacta chocolate from common product placement to sophisticated idea placement and ensures the film's success as both entertainment and advertising.

The second love story that made us cry and forced us to rethink our position on branded entertainment was the beautiful little film for Monoprix called *Label of Love*. If you think the storyline for *From the Start* sounded far-fetched and gratuitously tilted towards a brand message, wait till you hear this one!

Label of Love is a sweet romance that spans ten years. It tells the story of a young boy who secretly passes love letters to the girl he likes by cutting out labels from Monoprix packs and slipping them into her locker. One day he arrives at school to discover that the girl has moved away. He is devastated. Cut to ten years later. The boy is now at university where he eyes a beautiful young woman in the hallway. She opens her locker and a shoebox falls on to the ground, spilling a collection of cut-out labels. It's her . . . and she has obviously saved all of his letters! He runs to a supermarket and finds one final label. He cuts it out and gives it to her. It reads: 'Better "latte" than never.'

Label of Love might also sound like a glorified TV ad, but by the time we reached the end of the four-minute film there wasn't a dry eye in the jury room. The performances were wonderful, the music was spectacular and in the end *Label of Love* managed to deliver more emotion in four minutes than many feature films do in ninety. One could accuse the film of being a bit sentimental, but what love story isn't?

Like the team behind *From the Start*, the creators of this project found a way to embed the brand into the film without detracting from the content. Indeed, in this instance the product is even more than a narrative device – it is a character in the film. It is essential to the telling of the story, and it ultimately becomes the vehicle through which the film's emotional payload is delivered. Without the Monoprix brand this little love story would not exist. In this case the product is actually the idea. As a result, by the end of the film the audience doesn't just know what Monoprix stands for, it knows how the brand wants them to feel.

We believe that creators of branded entertainment should strive to substitute product placement with idea placement, but *Label of Love* and *From the Start* are proof that if handled correctly you can accommodate both.

Let's move on to another background story. Pelle Sjoenell hasn't been as cool as Jason and made an African Bond film for beer, but like his esteemed colleague he has a valuable tale to share from long before he sat down with the rest of the great jury of geniuses in a dark room on the sunny French Riviera. Back in 2011 he had the honour to work on a campaign for Google Chrome, the internet browser, together with Google Creative Lab. The campaign was *The Web Is What You Make of It*. One commercial from that campaign, specifically, became one of the biggest things that had happened in his career so far. The film was called *Dear Sophie*. Bartle Bogle Hegarty had worked on Google Chrome for years and had done some great work and won several Cannes Lions doing so, but this one was different. It was bigger. It became a phenomenon. When it is shown in meetings, even today, people cry almost every time. The reason that happens is because it digs deep; it makes us feel.

The story was quite simple. It was basically a product demo made up of screen grabs of someone on the internet using Chrome, Gmail and YouTube among other things. It told the story of a clever father who writes emails to his young daughter as she is growing up in order to share the emails with her one day.

It was all based on the insight that people do not surf or browse the internet. We use it more to plan and organize our lives. It's become an important tool for *doing*, getting things done. That was the opinion Google had, and that was what made Chrome special. The story itself was told in a way that touched people. *Dear Sophie* went on to be named the number-one ad of the year in 2011 by *Time* magazine, and Chrome became, and still is according to various online polls, the number-one browser.

Now that is all great, but that was an ad, a commercial, and you might ask what the hell does that have to do with entertainment? Well, the reason we are bringing this up in this chapter about idea placement is that the exact same formula is true when you set out to create great entertainment for a brand. Same as it is to create regular advertising. Have an opinion, an idea, and then make people feel it to believe it. The idea in this case is the opinion. The idea is not the product, but the product is used to clarify the opinion.

When it comes to creating feelings, the medium itself is obviously important, and film or video has been the most successful format in the entertainment business to date. It is by far the biggest format on the internet, with more than 300 hours of video uploaded to YouTube every minute and almost 5 billion videos watched on YouTube every single day. Crazy, but it makes perfect sense. It is because it makes us feel more than, say, a picture can. It is also why video killed the radio star. The saying runs that 'a picture is worth a thousand words'. Well, film is usually twenty-four frames – that is, pictures – per second, and that adds up to 24,000 words per second for film. That's a lot of feeling.

Will VR kill the video star?

One new format that has enormous potential in this sense and can make us feel more than was technically possible before is VR. It uses even more of our senses than film. It manages to do that through deeper immersion and is therefore able to transport us and to feel what it is like to be other people or to go to places we haven't been. It is different from a film because we are not looking at it, we are looking *with* it. This obviously lends itself to colossal gains for brands who are seeking to entertain and captivate an audience, and brands today should definitely consider starting to explore more VR.

One big Entertainment Lions winner from 2016, winner of the Entertainment Grand Prix, did just that. It used VR to make us feel what it was like to go to places and feel like other people as we had never done before. It was *The Displaced* from the *New York Times*. It used VR to make people feel they had been transported to other parts of the world and to experience, almost at first hand, what it was like to be a refugee. Only VR could do that so profoundly and accurately. And there was not a single *New York Times* newspaper planted anywhere in the experience, as that would have made it less accurate and truthful. It was the journalistic integrity that the *New York Times* demonstrated that was the idea in this case. It was idea placement, not product placement, and the medium of VR made it even more powerful, because the audience got to feel like a refugee, to go to a place we had only read about before.

As mentioned earlier, *Home* did a similar thing for the exact same cause. It also made us feel what it is like to be a refugee, only it wasn't using VR but a storytelling technique – flipping the script on the audience. Both are ways to create a relationship with others and make us feel more. It forced us to relate.

Bringing people together and helping them relate to one another are two of the most important and necessary things brands can do to help the state of the world today. Done well they can make the brands and their products look very good while doing good. A divided world needs unifiers, and brands are very well set up to fill this role. If you think about it, there are no global governments, but there are many global brands, brands that have the ear of the people and the means to unite. In our opinion that is not only a privilege but also a huge responsibility.

Media and news organizations are questioned across the world in today's political environment, and it is not only the *New York Times* that has seen the need to communicate its belief in truth and understanding. The agency ... & Co. with TV2 in Denmark did this as well with *All That We Share*, another big winner in 2017. It won Silver in our Entertainment category, but it also went on to win a Gold Lion for Social Video in the Cyber Lions category. If this film did one thing it was to unite us. The idea is brilliant in its simplicity. It puts a lot of people in a room and divides them into their respective groups, groups that seem obvious at first glance: the bikers, the yogis, the high earners, the nurses, the immigrants, the Danes who were born in Denmark. Then all were asked to step forward if they, for instance, liked to dance. People from different groups joined new groups, groups that had things in common. Brilliant.

This film experiment helped us see and feel what it is like to change our perspective and start understanding others more. It united us. The idea placement in this case was that TV2 believes we all have more in common than divides us. There was no need to show any product with such a powerful message, and at the time we saw it in that dark room on the sunny French Riviera it had more than 284 million views. Bear in mind that the population of Denmark is just shy of 6 million . . .

Products cannot have opinions, but brands do, and they certainly should have one

We'd like to take some time now to talk about the need for brands to have an opinion. Why what matters to them makes them clear to the audience and makes for great stories and how we can use that to create great entertainment. We'll stick our heads out and say that a product cannot have an opinion. Products or services don't think. That would be silly. They do not possess emotions. A brand, on the other hand, can, because a brand is the people behind a product. These people can have an opinion. Sometimes the opinion is about how we see others and the world, as we saw in the case of TV2 or the *New York Times*. Santander Bank, whose project *Beyond Money* is mentioned in a number of chapters in this book, believes we need to make sure we value life over money. These are opinions, and they come from brands and not from products. That's why it is important we make the stories about the opinion and not about the product. Yes, *The Lego Movie* has product in it, even all over it, but the movie is not about that. As mentioned in Pelle's chapter about conflict, 'Amping the Tension', the movie is about those who build LEGO following the instructions (relying on education) and those who ignore the instructions and build whatever comes to mind (using their imagination). That's a story worth one and a half hours and millions of box-office dollars.

One opinion that all brands have is that they like their own products. It is a given. There is no need to tell that story, as we already know it. But, at the end of the day, the reason why brands would go and invest money in advertising in the form of entertainment is to sell more product, so how the hell do we know how much product is OK then?

What is right for one brand is not necessarily right for another

What is 100% certain to us is that each case is different. It all depends. As always. Boring but true. If we take Red Bull and *The Art of Flight*, something you can read more about in Gabor Harrach's chapter 'Everybody Wants a Documentary', this is a perfect example of a brand that has created branded-content history around the belief that the energy drink gives you wings without having any cans in the content itself. That's right for them. If you're the audience you'd buy it. You'd go: 'They, Red Bull, think an active lifestyle calls for an energy drink.' Makes sense. But you'd also rather watch videos of people having an active lifestyle than watch people drinking an energy drink.

Another energy-drink campaign that won big at Cannes was Gatorade's *Replay* idea back in 2010, which scored a Promo Lion and PR Grand Prix, a Gold Lion in Integrated and a Silver Lion in Media. This was before there was an Entertainment category.

TBWA\Chiat\Day and Gatorade brought back two arch rival high-school American-football teams, whose members are now in their mid-thirties, to replay a game that ended in a tie way back when. For us this is still one of the best branded entertainment campaigns or ideas ever. But in this one, as opposed to in Red Bull's work, they drink Gatorade, and there is nothing weird in that at all. It's right for them. Energy drink, and lots of it, is what the thirty-somethings need to bring back their game. So what is right for one energy drink is not necessarily right for another.

When Sweden went to Africa

Finally, it's important to shine a light on another favourite from the 2017 Lions. In VML's work *One Source* for Absolut Vodka we have a brilliant example of idea placement that made us feel. It is also a great example of just enough product.

A little background first. Every drop of Absolut Vodka is manufactured using ingredients from the area surrounding their distillery in Åhus, a tiny medieval village in the county of Skåne, Sweden. They call this process 'one source'.

Now Skåne is pretty far away from the continent of Africa, but the link is there. The idea of 'one source' connects them. What worked brilliantly for Absolut in Africa was that they used that Swedish concept and made it utterly relevant to Africa by acknowledging that the same thing is true for humanity. We all come from the same source, Africa.

The *One Source* campaign for Absolut is a celebration of African culture in the form of a concept album by hip-hop artist Khuli Chana. It had ten artists collaborating to make eight original tracks, a documentary series, a stunning music video and live performances, all celebrating the one source of all human origin: Africa. Brilliant.

Now, this could have all been done without any product in the content at all. Absolut was behind it, and it had been crystal clear to the audience 'whodunnit'. But one thing that we found to be exceptionally well done was how seamlessly and sometimes unapologetically the Absolut brand and vodka product was present throughout. The album art used Absolut's famous typeface on the cover, all shots of fire in the videos and pictures have a tint of blue just like when you light a shot of vodka and, heck, Khuli Chana even drops an occasional 'Absolut' and 'vodka' in the lyrics! Should be blasphemy. But we don't mind. Quite the opposite. We loved how they managed to put it in there as part of the whole amazing Absolut African vibe.

So, when it comes to how much product is the right amount of product in branded content, the rule is: it still depends. Every case is different, and that's how it should be. But if you don't have an opinion as a brand, there is no idea and no story worth telling. And that is true for every single Cannes Lion that we awarded in Entertainment this year.

1. Ebert, Rover, *Awake in the Dark: The Best of Roger Ebert* (2nd edn), Chicago: University of Chicago Press, 2017

BACK TO BASICS: PRINCIPLES OF STORYTELLING APPLIED TO BRANDED ENTERTAINMENT

Tomoya Suzuki, CEO and Creative Producer,
STORIES® / STORIES® INTERNATIONAL

When I was in elementary school my father took me to the city library every Saturday morning for six years, with not a single week off. Each time we spent a few hours reading books there. In the afternoon my father borrowed fifteen books using his own, my mother's and my little brother's library cards. Yes – fifteen books every week. As I remember, he did not have many hobbies, but he loved reading. He was a literary junkie. Thanks to him I borrowed five books with my card every week. The stories have fascinated me ever since. Like my father, I became addicted to literature and fell in love with stories. I still remember the tales from Greek and Egyptian mythology and the Three Kingdoms of China and many others, even though I read them several decades ago. Stories have a magical power to engage and inspire people. Despite the fact that those Saturdays in the library made me a socially awkward literature addict, I thank my father for them because they inspired me to become a film-maker and storyteller, which I love.

Stories matter

I believe the world is built on stories not science. Around 17,000 years ago our ancestors depicted stories of hunting in the mural paintings of Lascaux, southwestern France. Nearer to the present day, the ancient Greeks looked up at the stars and created mesmerizing narratives of gods and goddesses, heroes and heroines. These were passed down from generation to generation – eventually reaching me in Japan about three millennia later. Yes, those stories survived more than 3,000 years. What is more, stories have powered history, which is driven by people's decisions based on desire, love, sadness, rage and other emotions. The French mathematician Blaise Pascal said of Cleopatra's nose that 'had it been shorter, the whole face of the world would have been changed'. In other words, a different romance would have changed an entire history. Many of the scriptures that have profoundly influenced our culture are built on stories. Stories are important today, too. Politicians tell stories to gain votes. A boy tells his mother a story to get himself a new toy. People watch *Star Wars*, Beyoncé's concerts, *American Idol* and sports in order to enjoy stories.

You can create entertainments in which narratives are not the most important element, but, nevertheless, stories should still be at their foundation. Without stories, movies, TV and theatre wouldn't exist. People find stories to follow and celebrate even in unscripted shows when they feel empathy for characters' inner transformations and in sports where they follow the ups and downs of teams, managers and individual athletes.

As the world of branding and marketing puts the spotlight on branded entertainment, the power of stories is becoming more important than ever in the communication business.

Entertainment audience vs advertising targeted consumer

Two main shifts have facilitated the expansion of branded entertainment in the past ten years: one in media and another in the advertising format. Traditional mass-media models have been able to convey messages effectively using standardized formats such as the thirty-second spot or the four-colour single-page ad in which creative focus is on grabbing attention more than telling a story, but the format is changing. On the internet, media and brands are beginning to use long-form content such as short films without the limitations of traditional formats. As our co-author Marcelo Pascoa pointed out in 'The Battle of Time and the Fallacy of the Short Attention Span', we are being freed from time constraints.

An audience-first approach rather than a target consumer-based approach is important in brand communication today. Brands' competitors are not only other advertisers' messages but all the information and entertainment content available on-screen. In this cluttered environment it has become difficult to ensure that your product will be watched, read and enjoyed by an audience that has the freedom to choose. The story is the key element in creating branded entertainment to attract the audience's attention.

For brands and marketers I believe that it is important to focus on an audience that wants to be entertained rather than send messages to a group of target consumers in the way that we have for the past fifty years in the traditional mass-media model.

Storytelling and craft (production values) in the era of branded entertainment

Long-form brand communication needs to be established as entertainment, otherwise we may find that the audience does not care. It is difficult to force viewers to watch thirty minutes of advertisers' announcements. That is why it is important to use storytelling techniques and immerse audience members in a narrative while achieving a high level of craft. This keeps the audience within the world of the content. What we call 'craft' in advertising is often referred to as 'production values' in the film and television industry. In this chapter I will try to explain the basics of storytelling formats and filmed entertainment craft and outline how these techniques are used in some of the 2017 Cannes Lions Entertainment-winning projects in the following section.

What is storytelling and what are production values (craft)?

Storytelling techniques are explained in popular screenwriting books by writers such as Syd Field. In the hundred-year history of film and centuries-long history of plays and novels, basic story formats with fundamental structures and key elements to create emotion and empathy have been established. Not all stories follow these basic formats and there are good stories without them, but the most entertaining content tends to benefit from utilizing these basic formats.

The basis of a story is plot and character. The plot is the series of events – in other words, what happens in the story and the order in which it happens. The plot follows a principal character who seeks something and is transformed in some way. This process of transformation is called 'the hero's journey', and the audience sympathizes with this. Many widely acclaimed entertainments – and old myths – are composed of three acts. Within the structure of three acts there are about ten to twenty detailed plot points. The three acts simply consist of a beginning, a middle and an end. These are also referred to as the 'departure for adventure', the 'adventure to tackle obstacles' and the 'completion and return'. It's possible to rearrange the chronological order of the three acts or deconstruct the acts, a method called 'fractured narrative' (examples of which are movies such as *Run Lola Run* and *Pulp Fiction*), but the three-act structure remains the basic one.

The main character's objective is sometimes called 'the want', and the awareness that drives the main character to grow is called 'the need'. The objective of the story is often called 'the central question'. It is also important to set the stakes high. Higher stakes enhance the tension of the story and make the audience more excited. Tension is generated by conflict. Creating intriguing conflict and moments of tension are the keys to enhancing the audience experience. For example, will Luke become a Jedi Knight and destroy the Empire's massive Death Star? If it's a love story, a central question would be will the man and the woman get together? If it's horror, then the question would be will the main character survive?

Again, most plots have a three-act structure. In the first the main character usually faces events that trigger him/her to go into the new world. In the second act the main character goes through various initiations and makes several efforts to achieve the objective, but by the end of the second act loses all that he/she has gained. In the third act he/she will solve problems and will achieve the objective. These are the basic components of a plot. If the plot is too simple it's easy to predict, so a few modifications are added while maintaining the basic components. For example, in the film *La La Land* the answer to the central question is not revealed until the last minute. This builds up to a well-constructed third act in the film.

Another important element in the story is character. A main character is called the 'protagonist' or 'hero/heroine'. A protagonist seeks something and changes to achieve his/her own destiny. In the original *Star Wars* trilogy, Luke Skywalker is the protagonist. His character arc is to become a true Jedi. Not every protagonist will be the character with the most screen time. *The Shawshank Redemption* is a good example of this: Andy, a major character played by Tim Robbins, is not the protagonist; Red, played by Morgan Freeman, is the protagonist because he transforms over the course of his journey. If there is a protagonist then there will often be an antagonist, a mentor, an ally, an anti-hero and a sidekick who brings comic relief. Through interactions with these characters, the main character grows and transforms in the course of his/her journey. In the original *Star Wars* films, for example, Luke is the protagonist, Darth Vader is the antagonist, Obi-Wan Kenobi is the mentor/guide, Han Solo is the anti-hero and R2-D2 and C-3PO are comic relief.

In addition to plot and character, many stories have another important element: 'high-concept'. High-concept is generally considered to be a story that features an intriguing world, an interesting setting, unique characters and so on. This is an important factor in attracting a wider audience for film and TV. In entertainment, creating interesting yet relatable characters and settings is important. In the late 1970s *Star Wars* was definitely a 'high-concept' project since telling a 'space war saga' through the eyes of a protagonist possessing a mystical power known as 'the Force' was a unique concept. Other great examples of high-concept projects, where character and setting are used to attract and engage the audience, are the TV series *Dexter*, about a forensic technician who has a double life as a vigilante serial killer, and *Breaking Bad*, featuring a high-school chemistry teacher who becomes a drug lord.

To maintain the audience's engagement it's important to design and implement 'set-ups' and 'pay-offs'. A story needs to plant set-ups that will later be paid off. Shonda Rhimes, a showrunner of *Grey's Anatomy* and *Scandal*, has said that 'planting and pay-off' are what stories are all about. It is particularly important to use this technique in the mystery and thriller genres; however, others, such as drama and rom-com, use set-ups and pay-offs effectively. Elements include dialogue, scenes, locations, subplots, props, music and so on to create an emotional, funny or satisfactory moment. The great use of set-ups and pay-offs in *Star Wars* establishes that the reason the Force is strong with Luke is because of his relationship with Darth Vader, revealed much later to be because he is Vader's son. Of course, the signature line 'May the force be with you' is used repeatedly in the important scenes. To target the global market, it should also be noted that film and TV should focus on visual storytelling rather than explaining everything through dialogue.

Last but not least the stories that are celebrated as great are those that have a universal theme or are in tune with the zeitgeist. They hit a nerve in contemporary audiences and inspire viewers despite differences of culture and language. Zeitgeist issues include gender, diversity, stress, social media problems and any topics about which people hesitate to speak. The elephant-in-the-room theme tends to hit a nerve with people. Typically, people won't talk about prominent negative issues that concern them in the early twenty-first century, such as murder, never-ending war and discrimination. Immature adults, matchmaking, divorce and dysfunctional families are examples of issues often highlighted in contemporary stories. Universal themes deal with topics such as issues between children and parents, romantic relationships and social-dynamic issues in schools, offices and communities. These two elements are most important because it has to do with 'the reason why' someone wants to tell his/her story. A story can inspire people when a storyteller has true passion and deep reasons to tell it. If you don't have a reason to tell your story you don't have to tell it. 'Audacity' is another way of describing this element: we really engage audiences only when we have the true passion or audacity to tell our stories, when we don't compromise and we keep our artistic integrity.

Craft (production values)

There are two important reasons why craft can reinforce the world of the story and make it even stronger:

1. **Capturing the audience and keeping them in the world of the story**
   Craft is essential when giving the world of a story reality and making everything believable. Although the audience is in the fictional world, everything is ruined if they spot something strange or inauthentic. It's like waking up from an intriguing dream. To keep the audience engaged, there should be no compromise. Just one mistake in the dialogue, cinematography, lighting, production design, VFX, music, sound effects or editing could ruin it all. Even in a documentary, reality matters. Audience members can easily smell a fake. Authenticity stemming from high production values in fiction or sincerity in non-fiction are the keys to capturing the audience.

2. **Astonishing artistically**
   Artistically superior visuals, sound, acting and composition can hook and impress the audience. The audience members are inspired by a visual they have never seen or by intriguing acting, overwhelming sound or compelling music. Endorphins are released in the brain as they experience a moment they will never forget. The scenes and sounds from the film *The Ten Commandments* (the 1956 version) and *2001: A Space Odyssey* astonished audiences when first released. In recent years the opening scenes of *La La Land* and *The Dark Knight* were just as astonishing – brilliantly integrated scenes with excellent craft. Integration of each of the elements as well as calculated directing, editing, grading, sound mix, music

and other elements are necessary to achieve this reality and artistic astonishment.

Different skillsets are needed to create a thirty-second spot or a thirty-minute TV drama successfully. That is why in producing long-form content it is important to collaborate with people who can take responsibility for delivering the production values needed for this type of content. To create successful branded entertainment the quality of the project must meet the standards of regular entertainment, such as movies and TV shows. Only then can branded entertainment have a chance of being distributed via regular entertainment channels on TV and SVOD, including Netflix, Hulu, Amazon Video and so on, instead of buying advertising space. Without question, the success of the project also relies significantly on this distribution.

Successful storytelling cases from Cannes

I would now like to analyse how storytelling and production values were used in some of the Entertainment winners from Cannes Lions 2017. I was fortunate enough to review more than a thousand projects as a member of the jury and saw that many relatable projects used story and craft creatively and effectively. Projects using visual storytelling to convey a universal theme were evaluated highly by the jury. Important evaluation points were as follows:

- Does the project demonstrate visual storytelling along with a strong universal theme that is in touch with the zeitgeist?
- Is it easy to understand the central question of the story?
- Is the project high-concept and does it have a great pay-off?
- Note that well-executed craft = high production values.
- Does the project integrate a solution for the brand's problem into a story organically and effectively?

Beyond Money – Santander Bank, Spain: Cannes Lions Entertainment Grand Prix 2017

Definitely a Grand Prix-worthy project, this has a theme with a strong core insight, great storytelling and high production values. The story and production values are powerfully immersive while the audience can enjoy it as entertainment and as a thought-provoking project. Its genre is sci-fi/psychological thriller.

As expressed in its title, *Beyond Money*, it is a high-concept narrative set in a world in the near future where you can sell your memories. The story follows a wealthy woman who is a shopping addict and who has begun to sell her key memories. As a protagonist she is a victim of the material world, and her predicament suggests the question: 'What is more important? Money or experience?' The story has a well-established universal theme that is in touch with the zeitgeist and deals with the notion that life experience is more important than money as well as the issues of materialism and shopping addiction. A very insightful treatment. How much would you sell your memory for?

The central questions posed in this story are how far she will go to sell her important memories and whether she can stop herself from doing so. She starts by selling a memory of her first boyfriend and eventually sells her memory of her wedding, leading her to struggle to remember her husband and her own child. The plot line, with the stakes increasing as the story advances, is highly effective. The protagonist's best friend works as a guide character and helps to introduce the world to the audience. In the story materialism is an antagonistic force for the protagonist; it leads her away from her destiny, which is to stop selling her memories and embrace her family and real life. As for set-up and pay-off and planting the set-up, the opening scene, where the protagonist has a dream of not being able to remember her husband's face at her own wedding, is well paid off when it is revealed in the second act what it is she has sold. And the project title itself – *Beyond Money* – is paid off as an answer to the audience in the end.

The project's production values are extremely high. Thanks to the quality of the acting and cinematography and exceptional colour grading, the story is well-explained and organically produced for the audience with a visual story basis. It contains great VFX, which is especially important for sci-fi. The high-quality production design catches the audience's attention and creates an authentic world.

The concept of how much you would sell your memories for is inspired by a universal question: how important is money in your life? It could be paraphrased as 'money vs love'. For a bank to create a branded entertainment on this theme is a bold choice – and that's part of why it was successful as a campaign. This project is producing great results in solving the brand's problem – to change a young audience's attitude towards the bank from negative to positive. The quality of brand integration is high from the scriptwriting stage onwards, since the script incorporates insightful themes within an entertaining story. The bank works as an important character

Beyond Money, created by MRM//McCann for Santander Bank, 2017

as well. The project's success derives from its insightful themes, high-concept setting, multiple set-ups and pay-offs, a clear central question, an intriguing protagonist's journey, an overwhelming yet understandable antagonistic force and solid characters who help facilitate the story. In addition, great craft – including the acting, cinematography, VFX, production design and editing – definitely helped enhance the project as entertainment content.

From the Start – Lacta Chocolate, Greece

This is a five-episode web series of approximately fifteen minutes per episode that was later re-edited as a feature-length TV movie and broadcast on Valentine's Day on network TV in Greece. It's a love story with a sci-fi element: the tale of an immature bachelor who falls in love with a girl at a party. He sees her in his dreams every time he eats a piece of Lacta chocolate but wakes up from his dream every time he gets closer to her. Each dream starts again from the beginning, the point at which he enters the party. The plot uses a repeating loop as a fractured narrative plot in which the protagonist relives a specific event, as in films like *Groundhog Day*, *Run Lola Run* and *Edge of Tomorrow*, although it still has a simple three-act structure as a whole, with beginning, middle and end. In addition, each episode has its own three acts, which helps to keep the audience engaged.

The questions are 'Why does he dream?' and 'Who is the girl in a dream?', but the central or most important one is 'Will he find this girl in real life and get together with her?' At the end of the second act he can no longer go back to the dream even if he eats the chocolate. That is the worst moment and key to getting the audience to relate to his final decision. He is about to give up until a Skype call with his friend makes him realize that the party he sees in the dream is an actual future event rather than a make-believe one. The key set-up, or planting, is when he notices a wedding-party poster shown in his first dream. Later, the poster will become a key trigger to reveal that in his dream he was looking forward in time. People cannot stop binge-watching this content because it is such a well-executed project as entertainment with a high level of storytelling and craft.

The love story deals with universal, zeitgeist-based themes that are about an immature person who cannot commit to a relationship (a zeitgeist issue) and who is trying to find the love of his life (a universal theme). In terms of character development the protagonist is depicted as a playboy but is also really charming, so the audience can easily connect with him, while high production values successfully capture the viewers and never lets them leave the world of the story. Acting, cinematography, grading, editing and music composition are excellent. Examples include a shot of the beautiful coastline of Greece, the night-time sea, a romantic scene or a party scene during the evening golden hour. The great score and music also contribute to expressing the characters' journeys, with the lyrics from the theme song working as a set-up as well. Regarding the value of the branded entertainment, 'Eating a piece of Lacta chocolate gives

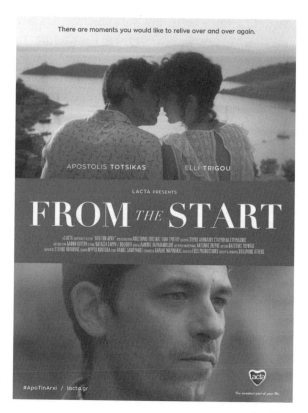

From the Start,
created by
OgilvyOne Athens
for Mondelez
International, 2017

the world sweet dreams' is effective and organic as brand integration. Lacta chocolate is not just used as a prop; it plays an important role as a character to advance the story.

Label of Love – **Monoprix, France**

This project combines great storytelling and high production values. In terms of plot it is a simple love story with a three-act structure. Boy meets girl, she leaves and he reunites with her. Yet the surprise and the worst moment at the end of the second act work effectively. It is a story about a boy at elementary school who has a crush on his classmate. He is shy, so he decides to put notes in her locker. He makes these by cutting out words from boxes of biscuits, crackers and tea. One example is 'Totally "crackers" for you'. He keeps sending messages

Still from *Label of Love*, created by Rosapark for Monoprix, 2017

this way but eventually finds that she has left town suddenly at the end of the second act. Finally, during the third act, he is reunited with the girl in college and they share a tender moment when he gives her a note from a package that says 'Better "latte" than never'.

What is wonderful about this project is that it uses the most iconic characteristic of the brand: Monoprix's own-brand packaging labels. These labels act as a character to help drive the love story, and this is one of the cleverest and most organic examples of brand integration.

How the main characters reunite may be a little too convenient, but this is the ending the audience wants. The worst moment, as the second act closes, provides audience disquiet and works well to enhance audience satisfaction at the end.

Production values are also high. There are many great elements that make this story believable and attractive, while keeping the audience engaged for the full four-minute running time. Key elements are the cinematic direction, detailed visual storytelling, solid sound design, sympathetic music and great performances by the two child actors. Although there is almost no dialogue, the story and the boy's emotions are beautifully depicted in a visual way that the audience clearly understands without the need for language. This is exceptional entertainment but also a great online brand campaign that audiences sometimes watch without sound. In sum, the project is very successful because it uses clever and organic brand integration along with a solid storytelling format and high production values.

Evan – Sandy Hook Promise, USA

This is another Gold Lion-winning campaign. The structure maximizes the effect of its major plot twist by planting unexpected set-ups. The project is a web-based short film for a not-for-profit advocating the need to raise awareness around the prevention of gun violence in schools. In the story, Evan, a high-school student, is trying to find a girl with whom he has been communicating by carving messages into a desk in the school library. Evan scribbles 'I AM BORED' and receives the response 'Hi Bored, nice to meet you' the following day. At the end of the second act Evan tries to find his mystery girl but notices that the library is closed for the summer, which means he cannot find her, at least for now. In the third act a girl recognizes his handwriting from a signature in her friend's yearbook, and finally boy and girl get together. However, this project has an extra layer/extra act in addition to the simple three-act love story. The moment that Evan gets together with the girl at the school gym we see the door open and hear the screams of other students as another student enters with a machine-gun. Then the video gives us an unexpected pay-off by showing us the same story from the beginning but from a different perspective – a victim of bullying who begins to prepare to carry out a school shooting – with different sound and lighting focus. The surprise gives the audience the important message that to prevent gun violence we should all know the signs of at-risk behaviour in high-school students.

The project's success relies heavily on its high production values. The cute, realistic acting of high-school kids, including all the extras, solid cinematography and tight editing work very well. The pay-off is a huge surprise, and along with excellent music and sound design deliver an experience that gives us goosebumps. Great storytelling and solid production values draw the audience into the world of the story while not allowing them to guess the surprise. The trick is simple but unexpected. Most importantly, as branded entertainment it is great integration of the message 'know the signs' into a story-based communication.

East vs West

Are there differences between Western and Eastern storytelling formats? Certainly. But there are many similarities, too. Western mythologies, plays and movies tend to use the three-act structure, with the format aiming to create empathy via the protagonist's growth during his/her journey. In Asia, for as long as I've been aware, most major entertainment, film and TV projects follow the same three-act structure. In fact, the old stories and myths have almost the same structure even in Japan, where I was born and raised.

I believe the reason we share similar structures for stories is because it is universally easy to follow and engaging. 起・承・転・結, or *Ki sho ten ketsu* in Japanese, is the traditional Asian style of arranging a narrative composed of four parts: introduction, development, twist or turn and conclusion. This four-part structure stems from Chinese poetry. The twist at the end of the second act is more emphasized, but it is basically the same as the Western three-act structure. Thus, I believe that the format for storytelling is essentially universal, regardless of region or culture. However, cultural context varies by region and time: there are gendered differences in language use and cultural differences in clothing, as well as family structures and relationship dynamics sometimes being different according to culture or religion. So in telling a story these cultural and contextual elements need to be considered. In Asian stories the slice-of-life storytelling format seems to be more widely accepted than in Western ones. A slice-of-life story sometimes does not have clear plot points or character arcs and leaves the ultimate conclusion up to an audience's imagination.

For example, a Silver Lion-winning project from Taiwan, Volvo's *Alice's Wedding* and The Glenlivet's *Single Belief* both begin with vague central questions whose answers are revealed later in the story. Both projects worked effectively in different regions because they were able to catch an audience's attention regardless of this unique use of story format. Sony's *Gravity Cat* project from Japan, which won a Silver Lion, has a very long first act, but eventually the project gains a great level of engagement when the world it's created starts spinning around. It works well because it also waits a long time to reveal the pay-off. My co-author Pelle Sjoenell will talk more about this surprising piece in the next chapter, 'Amping the Tension'.

Storytelling formats can transfer across cultures, but projects need to adjust to a target audience's region, time and cultural context. However, many successful projects, including Gold Lion-winners at Cannes, effectively use a universal format and visual story that works in any cultural context.

Creating effective branded entertainment

Looking back over the course of six days as a member of the jury, it didn't take long for the importance of storytelling elements and production values to become evident. Successful projects, as we have seen, recognized their target consumers as an 'audience' seeking entertainment over mere 'target consumer', because brands and their marketers know that in the era of multiple screens in front of an audience information and content are now competitors fighting for audiences' time and attention. In other words, without a strong and entertaining project audiences wouldn't bother to view branded entertainment at all. The successful projects highlighted in this chapter focused on entertainment and artistic integrity, and this enabled the projects to deliver the brand message.

I learned that an audience-first approach is important in creating successful branded entertainment projects and that high-concept ideas must be based on insightful and universal themes. If an entertainment can hit the nerves of people today, they will watch it and share it to discuss what they watched with their friends, as discussed in Monica Chun's chapter 'The News It Creates'. Powerful storytelling and entertainment can earn a large media purchase, as we saw with *Beyond Money*.

In addition, successful projects were able to integrate the brands' messages into the entertainment content by giving the brand a key role as a character that moves a story forward – as in the case of Lacta chocolate – instead of just placing the brand in the narrative without a significant role. What brands want to avoid at all costs is simple product placement in long-form content.

As discussed above, I learned as a jury member that to create a great branded entertainment campaign and a story-driven project the following elements need to be taken into account: the three-act narrative structure is key – although it can be modified; it's important to present an interesting yet easily comprehensible central question; the protagonist's character should transform through his/her journey; the audience's expectation should be subverted at the end of the second act (the worst moment); visual storytelling is important; and the audience derives satisfaction from multiple set-ups and pay-offs and a theme that has universality and taps into the zeitgeist.

Regarding production values, it is important to create an authentic world that draws the audience in and keeps them engaged by ensuring you have great casting, direction, cinematography, production design, VFX, editing, grading, music and sound effects. Production values should be as high as in the filmed entertainment industry.

If a branded entertainment project addresses storytelling techniques and production values to high standards I believe it will be

113

highly regarded as regular entertainment as well and could be distributed through regular entertainment channels. Successful cases include *Beyond Money*, which is distributed on SVOD along with other regular entertainment contents, and *From the Start*, which was re-edited and broadcast on network TV. Being distributed as regular entertainment is proof of success as branded entertainment because it shows that the audience will watch and enjoy it as a regular entertainment. It's important that all stakeholders – including the brand manager, creative director, director and screenwriter – work together towards the same goal and share the notion that 'the audience should come first' as entertainment to avoid a product placement that is no more than boring long-form advertising.

On the jury we all knew before we began our journey that branded entertainment is an ever-changing, evolving category in marketing communication. But that is why getting involved in the area is exciting. Thanks to fellow jurors and PJ – a great leader as jury president – I was able to enjoy insightful discussions and absorb diverse perspectives from around the world. Thanks to the whole experience, as a story-teller I was able to create stories that make an audience feel lucky to be spending their time watching content regardless of whether it is branded or regular entertainment.

AMPING THE TENSION

Pelle Sjoenell, Bartle Bogle Hegarty

As I'm writing this my family and I are being evacuated from the roaring Los Angeles fires (picture below). I hope I'll be able to finish this chapter and also hope that the home we built for our kids will still be there when (or if) we are allowed back home again.

Early morning, Los Angeles, 6 December 2017. The roof of our home is the white structure in the lower right corner. (Pelle Sjoenell, 2017)

There it is: the conflict, the tension. The most essential part of any story. The reason to stick around and see how something plays out. Without conflict there are no great stories, no great heroes or tales worth retelling. I'll spend this chapter breaking down why embracing conflict is the key to success if brands want to compete against the best stories ever told. And then I'll tell you if our house is still there . . .

Any great story relies on tension because without tension there is no attention.

There are no comics, films, TV shows or books about what goes on in Gotham City when there is no villain in town. Not one. I mean, imagine it. Batman and Robin hanging out in the cave just digging their gear, while Alfred is out shopping for groceries and running errands. Perhaps later that day they enjoy a nice dinner, then they all gather in the library for a quiet round of gin rummy before bedtime. Not much of a movie. But what if we cut back to the library and we see there is one single card left on the table, the joker. Then we have a movie.

Brands, and advertising agencies for that matter, are not brought up to embrace conflict; quite the opposite. We are shaped to avoid it, and there are a number of logical reasons for that.

The first is about choice. We spend most of our careers picking or generating ideas that are more or less forced upon our audience. They have to see what we make as we invade the public space with our messages and stories. In traditional advertising we do not have to hook them in, so to speak. We don't need an interesting conflict to make them stay. Pre-roll (online video advertisements that play before the start of a video that has been selected for viewing), when it came around, taught us otherwise and was probably the first sign that we needed to recalibrate the way we tell stories if people can opt out of them. We know that the last five seconds is the most important on TV; and now it's the first five seconds online. We used to tell stories on TV that had the explanation, or 'rug pull', and the brand at the end as gratification for having watched the story. Now we have to put something interesting up front to give the viewer a reason to see how it will play out or they'll just 'Skip Ad'. Great writers have always known this. Many great screenplays and novels start with the ending, so we get curious about how it all ended up like that. A couple of chapters back Marcelo Pascoa offered you a great first line from a book. So here is my favourite, the opening line of *The Trial* by Franz Kafka (1925): 'Someone must have slandered Josef K., because one morning, even though he knew he had done nothing wrong, he was arrested.'

The second reason for conflict avoidance is the idea that negativity doesn't sell. To advertise something means to have some kind of an offer to sell or suggest to someone else. One dictionary definition of 'advertise' is: 'describe or draw attention to (a product, service or event) in a public medium in order to promote sales or attendance'.[1] Very rarely is that offer something really bad or threatening, as that wouldn't be worth buying and not much of a promotion. It's got to be something good, something positive or new, that the brand wants to say about itself or its product. We are taught to advertise the positive and avoid the negative. But even advertising history tells us that's a lazy way of looking at it. There are great examples of campaigns that didn't follow that rule and have thus become some of the greatest successes of all time: 'Avis – We're only number two so we try harder', VW's 'Lemon' or 'With a name like Schmucker's – it has to be good'. Al Ries and Jack Trout clocked this in their *22 Immutable Laws of Marketing*. 'Law 15: the Law of Candor' explains that when you admit a negative the prospect will give you a positive.[2] This is especially true in the case of entertainment. I'd call it the first commandment of branded entertainment – the Commandment of Conflict: if you avoid showing the negative, you won't see much of the prospect.

The third reason for avoiding conflict concerns time. If you have a short amount of time, say thirty seconds short, you have to prioritize what to say. More often than not what needs to be said is already prioritized in the brief or assignment itself. But there is usually more information than there is time to fit it in. The same goes for billboards that need to be read quickly from far away. There simply hasn't been room for conflict in ads because we haven't had time for it. This changes completely with long-form content and entertainment. Not only is there room for it, it's absolutely necessary if we want to keep our audience interested.

The winning formula to create successful stories is to embrace conflict, which has been clear in the winning work for Cannes Lions Entertainment for as long as the category has been around. The Grand Prix winner in 2017, by unanimous decision, was *Beyond Money* from Santander Bank (yes, a bank won in entertainment!) created by MRM//McCann Spain and directed by Kike Maíllo.

At the very heart of this amazing piece of work is conflict and tension. This work needs to be seen in the context of the harsh economic times experienced in Spain during the latest recession, which provoked in people a negative attitude to money and banks. Instead of avoiding the issue, Santander ran straight at this tension and made sure that Spaniards knew that Santander understood how they felt about it. The plot is deeply rooted in conflict, as well. This Hollywood-calibre short sci-fi film is asking what is worth doing for money. It tells the story of a woman named Lucia who sells her memories. This creates a wealth of problems, as Tomoya Suzuki explains in detail in his chapter on 'Back to Basics'. It's a brilliant plot and really worth watching to the very end.

The family in *Lo and Behold* who saw the photograph of the almost decapitated fourth sister go viral on the web: 'The internet is the Antichrist'. (A still from *Lo and Behold*, advertisement for NetScout created by Pereira O'Dell, 2016)

Another big winner this year was *Lo and Behold: Reveries of the Connected World*, Pereira O'Dell's Werner Herzog-directed documentary made for the cyber-security brand NetScout. One of the Gold winners that was in the running for the Grand Prix, this 98-minute documentary is about the past, present and future of the internet. One thing is for sure: it certainly does not avoid the tension and conflict the internet has brought upon humanity. It tackles hacking, web addiction and the rise of artificial intelligence. Some parts are light-hearted, others brutal. 'There's a moment where Werner interviews a family whose daughter had a tragic accident,' PJ Pereira said about the film in an interview with *Adweek*. 'The police didn't let the family see what happened to her. But one of the officers or first responders took a photo and sent it to a friend, and it started to spread. And someone sent the photo of the girl, nearly decapitated, to the family. It was a horrible thing. At one point, the mother looks at the camera and says: "I think the internet is the Antichrist."'[3]

A third example from 2017's winners in Entertainment is *Home* for the United Nations High Commissioner for Refugees. To quote Tim Nudd, former editor of *Adweek*, 'one of the most celebrated agency projects of the past year hasn't been that easy to see'.[4] Now, before I continue, I need to mention that this one is produced by Black Sheep Studios,[5] the production arm of BBH, so I'm biased – I have a conflict of interest! I wasn't allowed to vote on it for that very reason (and rightly so), but my fellow jury members and authors of this book did,

The family in *Home* arrives in their new temporary sanctuary, a refugee camp, after being forced to leave the safety of their former home. (A still from *Home*, created, written and directed by Daniel Mulloy; a co-production of DokuFest, Black Sheep Studios and Somesuch, 2016)

and BBH is very grateful that it won a Cannes Gold Lion. It was never in the running for a Grand Prix, though, as the rules state that work for good causes cannot win a Grand Prix. Fair enough.

Home is about one of the largest and most difficult issues we have encountered in recent history: the refugee crisis. The difficulty in tackling it is that even though people in the West, who can help, see refugees on TV and in the media every day, we still have a hard time relating to others in danger. The story aims to bridge that gap by flipping the script and having a British family leave its home and become refugees in another country in a quest to find a new home somewhere else. This allows us to experience what it is like to leave the safety of home, to lose control, to put children and loved ones in severe danger. It *is* hard to watch, but it's also deeply relatable, and it is for this reason that it was referenced by the United Nations in discussions of the crisis. Try doing that during a thirty-second slot between segments of *The Voice*.

Conflict doesn't have to be all gloom and doom, however; it can also be very funny. Most comedy is, in fact, based on some kind of conflict or misunderstanding. Take *Dumb and Dumber*, *The Hangover*, *Curb Your Enthusiasm*, *Home Alone*, *The Jerk*, *Meet the Parents* and *The 40-Year-Old Virgin* to name a few. That last one even has tension in the title itself.

That conflict and humour is a winner was proven at the 2017 Cannes Lions Entertainment category by my own personal favourite, *Gravity Cat* for Sony Interactive Entertainment by Hakuhodo Japan and the Tohokushinsha Film Corporation. When I say personal favourite it's because this was one that I kept bringing back and trying to get the whole jury to love as much as I do. It ended up with a Cannes Bronze Lion, which isn't cat shit, to coin a Swedish phrase.

Gravity Cat and its genius is born out of what should be a tragic event but turns out to be a hilarious one, when two young Japanese sisters and their beloved cat are introduced to unearthly gravity. At first gravity is 'messing with' their cat, then it upsets their apartment and eventually the whole world. The apartment burns and gets totally trashed, and all three of them fall out of a window to certain death – except now that gravity is wack perhaps they'll survive and have a more exciting life because of it. A brilliant example of highly entertaining long-form video, worth sharing for Sony PlayStation's new gaming title 'Gravity Rush 2'. All thanks to the (you guessed it) conflict that it is built upon.

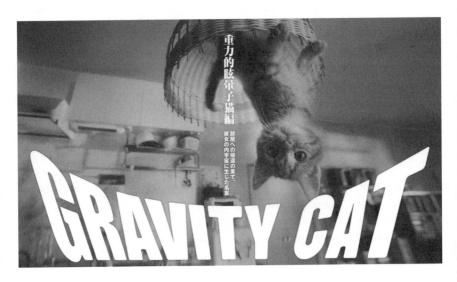

This little cat, along with messed-up gravity and brilliant film-making, completely destroys two cat-loving sisters' apartment. (A still from *Gravity Cat*, advertisement for Sony Interactive Entertainment created by Hakuhodo, 2017)

The cat theme is one that the entertainment world has been aware of for a long time. Besides cat videos ruling the internet (try a web search for 'cat videos' and you'll get close to 161 million hits with nearly 85 million on YouTube alone), ask most screenwriters and they'll know of the best-selling book *Save the Cat! The Last Book on Screenwriting You'll Ever Need* by Blake Snyder.[6] The book begins by telling people to start their script by writing a logline: a short description that explains what the story is by describing the conflict in it. It's that conflict that makes someone want to watch; it's that conflict that keeps people watching. We as marketers just need to take that little format and find a way to make the brand an irreplaceable part of that plot.

Creating conflict doesn't necessarily mean unfavourably polarizing your audience. These days, when the world is as divided as it is, big brands have a huge opportunity, or rather responsibility, to bring us together with unifying ideas. A successful example from the past year is 180LA's *Boost Your Voice*, a voting campaign for Boost Mobile that won the Integrated Grand Prix – the campaign's second Grand Prix after winning the top prize for Promo and Activation. This brilliant campaign was incredibly powerful and important, as Boost Mobile's customer base is centred in underserved, low-income and minority communities. 'Last election, millions of lower income and minority voters faced long lines and inconvenient locations,' said William Gelner, Chief Creative Officer, in a statement to Creativity/ Adage. 'With Boost Mobile stores in these areas, why not offer them up as places to vote and allow all voices to be heard?'[7] Boost's initiative was not a gimmick but entirely credible and relevant for both the brand and its users. It was an idea that didn't choose to pick sides but served both sides of the political spectrum. It dived straight into a conflict without polarizing the audience.

OK, so in case it isn't really clear by now, I'll say it again: without conflict you'll have no winning formula in entertainment as a brand. But how do you find your conflict or story? I'd like to conclude with some great examples that might help you to find yours. My only request is that we try to use and begin to see the word 'conflict' as a positive one from now on, as something we want to find in order to uncover a great story.

The conflict (that is, the 'Great Story') can be in the product itself

The one example that always pops up here and that should, in my opinion, have won a Cannes Entertainment Grand Prix (or five), is LEGO. The brand has become one of the leading entertainment brands in the world, with multiple titles making millions at the box office worldwide. It all started with *The Lego Movie* and how a conflict in the product was the key to a fantastic story.

The plot is propelled by two ways of looking at how to play with

LEGO. There are those who follow the instructions (education) and those who see a coloured pile of wonderful possibilities (imagination). Because of that conflict in the product they managed to make a hugely successful ninety-minute film that's essentially a highly entertaining, feature-length product demo. If it were a TV commercial assignment for an advertising agency I swear we would have said: 'You can't stand for both education and imagination – pick one!' And we would have been right, if it was for a TV spot, but not for a movie, one that people would pay to go and see.

The conflict can be found in the history of the brand

The Tale of Thomas Burberry, made by Burberry, written by Academy Award-nominated Matt Charman and directed by Academy Award-winning Asif Kapadia, depicts the challenges faced by the company's founder, Thomas Burberry, who was a pioneer in fashion. It describes how Thomas invented a fabric that could withstand water and how he outfitted, but almost lost, the explorer Ernest Shackleton in Antarctica. It tells us how British soldiers during the First World War were forced to struggle and die in the trenches wearing the legendary Burberry trench coats. It tells us how Thomas cheated on his wife with the record-breaking pilot Betty Kirby-Green. It's not the usual 'good-times' lifestyle fashion we are used to from brands such as Burberry. Instead, they manage to make us empathize with the founder and respect the brand's success even more because of all that he, and they, have been through.

The conflict can be brought to you by the brand; the brand doesn't have to be in it

This year at the Academy Awards, history was made when an e-commerce site won Best Original Screenplay for *Manchester by the Sea*. Amazon is that site. When they set out to create entertainment, undoubtedly they weren't thinking: what are the great stories we have to tell about the delivery of boxes with a smile on or about great customer service? Instead they thought, or I hope they thought: we have Amazon Prime and we want even more people to use it, so why don't we make fantastic indie movies that you can access if you have Amazon Prime? There is no reason why Amazon as a brand needed to be part of that story for them to have success. Now, not all brands have the reach that Amazon does or the capital to show it in cinemas so it could be eligible for an Oscar, but many brands have channels of their own to put content on. And for those who haven't seen the film it's definitely worth watching. It's all conflict. Devastating conflict.

There are many ways for brands to approach entertainment – if you're OK with creating mediocre entertainment, then avoid conflict and you'll be fine. Most brands are, and the damage with this mindset will probably mostly be in not making something the audience wants to see. It's a waste of money and time. But if you want to have success, and even aim to win in Cannes, then you have to aim to make entertainment as good (or better) than the best entertainment in the world. That's the bar. That's what brands are up against, because that is what the audience will want to see.

The one conflict to actually avoid

When you have a product, service or brand and you want to create world-class entertainment, there is one specific conflict to overcome – that is when your product story is not in line with or natural to the story of the entertainment. This has happened a lot in classic product placement, but audiences these days are trained to spot a transaction a mile away. They know when it's forced in there or when a celebrity is paid to say things they normally wouldn't. It also happens when brands venture into entertainment beyond product placements and when they set out to co-create original content. We saw quite a few brilliant pieces in our jury deliberations this year that did not make it to the top simply because the brand or product felt forced or too much of a stretch to be a truly integrated part of the story. This way of thinking is quite understandable if you consider where advertising is coming from. The notion of branding has been around for millennia; from the burning of an owner's name on to a slave or cattle with a branding iron to marking criminals to the use of maker's marks that stretch all the way back to antiquity; all are signs of ownership, and the desire to claim ownership is still very much around in advertising today.

Sponsorship, for one thing, has taught CMOs that the more real estate the brand takes, for the least amount of money, the better deal you have made. But this is the difference between being a buyer of branded entertainment and becoming an entertainment brand. It's two vastly different ways of behaving, and the difference in what to focus on separates the two. One focuses on telling its brand or product story first and foremost, often at the expense of the entertainment; the other one is focused on creating great entertainment first and making sure that the entertained audience does not leave without somehow knowing that the brand was involved in that joy. The latter is the way to go if you want to win. But there needs to be a behavioural change on both sides of this equation, even on the entertainment side. When a brand approaches Hollywood it is often seen as a much-welcomed ATM, providing additional money that can help with funding a project. Rarely are brands seen as proper co-creators, and the brand story is seen as less important to writers, producers or directors than the creation of their story. This is where brands need to earn the right to be equals in the world of entertainment. Many brands – such as Amazon, Netflix, Hulu, Red Bull, LEGO, Intel, NetScout and Santander Bank – have earned that right, and the list is getting longer every year. In 2018 we will likely see more brands like Facebook, YouTube, Apple, AT&T and many others added to that exclusive list of brands that have been part of making some of the best entertainment in the world. And they'll leave Cannes with their Lions as proof.

The lessons from my jury work and from this chapter are, I hope, pretty clear. The common approach is to avoid conflict when creating entertainment for brands, but I say, do the exact opposite. If I were a CMO I'd seek conflict and would demand it in the same way that I would demand marketing-performance data nowadays. I hope it is also clear that it's not natural for brands to approach conflict, because we have been taught otherwise. And that's OK; we just need to calibrate differently when creating real entertainment. Finally, make sure you avoid one conflict only, and that's the one between the product story and the main story, because you can't trick the audience, you can only lose it.

And I guess that's what's been evident between the lines throughout here: that we are serving an audience first and consumers second in this game, but that they are one and the same.

And about our house, it's still there. Thanks for sticking around to the end.

1. https://en.oxforddictionaries.com/definition/advertise
2. Ries, Al and Jack Trout, *The 22 Immutable Laws of Marketing*, New York: HarperBusiness, 1994
3. http://www.adweek.com/brand-marketing/ werner-herzogs-new-film-future-branded-entertainment-172737/
4. http://www.adweek.com/creativity/see-bbhs-incredible-short-film-home-which-is-finally-online-but-only-for-a-week/
5. *Home* was a coproduction between DokuFest, Black Sheep Studios and Somesuch
6. Snyder, Blake, S*ave The Cat! The Last Book on Screenwriting You'll Ever Need*, Studio City, CA: Michael Wiese Productions, 2005
7. http://creativity-online.com/work/boost-mobile-boost-your-voice/49348

EVERYONE WANTS A DOCUMENTARY (OR DON'T BE AFRAID TO LIVE YOUR TRUTH)

Gabor Harrach, Consultant,
formerly of Red Bull Media House

There is a 'documentary' that no brand ever wants to have produced, although it features all the elements that marketing experts have identified as being desirable for branded entertainment. It is engaging and authentic. The brand is integrated in an organic and credible way. One example of this genre was watched and shared by millions of existing and potential customers, and yet no award was given to the makers of this film. What's even worse is that some executives might actually have lost their jobs (or their Christmas bonuses) over it. The video was shot in April 2017 on a mobile phone (and distributed globally within seconds) by a passenger on board United Airlines Flight 3411, and it shows a fellow passenger being forcibly dragged off the aircraft by airport security at Chicago O'Hare.

This film needs no further introduction because everyone has seen it. It taught a valuable lesson not only to airlines but to all of us: today not only brands and their creative agencies produce films about brands but potentially every customer as well. The same can be said about a viral video shot at a Starbucks location in Philadelphia in April 2018, showing two black patrons being arrested on suspicion of trespassing that sparked wide outrage and made Starbucks close more than 8,000 stores for racial-bias education.

As we move marketing strategies and film production from scripted to authentic, from long development cycles to real-time and from complex distribution deals (to which only the elite of Hollywood has access) to mobile-first, we also encourage every man, woman and child with a mobile-phone camera to become a fearless film-maker. And this is a good thing, because it establishes new benchmarks and encourages us to do a better job not only to service our customers but also to produce content that really matters to people. This was also an important lesson many of us learned in 2017, the year I joined my very accomplished co-jurors (and co-authors of this book) in Cannes at the International Festival of Creativity to award Bronze, Silver and Gold Lions for the best achievements in branded entertainment and maybe a Grand Prix to the best of the best. Following a global trend, my hope was that an unscripted documentary would win the Grand Prix.

Festival-quality content

As traditional advertising loses its credibility and punch, more brands than ever have come to believe that being authentic and real is more important than ever to their customers. Therefore they ask their agencies for unscripted or factual content, leading to the production of many documentaries.

Looking at the sheer volume and quality of the documentary entries, one begins to wonder if the Cannes Lions International Festival of Creativity will one day directly compete with the traditional film festivals, such as Sundance, Tribeca, Berlin, Toronto and Cannes. I would like to argue that winning a Grand Prix, Titanium or Gold Lion for a documentary has already become as important for the careers of its makers as winning a Golden Bear in Berlin or the Grand Jury or audience awards in Sundance.

But does a documentary that serves a brand really need to compete with the work of great auteurs and film-makers that is screened in Berlin, New York, Toronto and Park City? Or does it even have to surpass the work of the great auteurs to make the audience forget that they are watching something that a cereal or liquor brand has produced or paid for? I hope this chapter, and the entire book, will help us find the answer.

Unscripted surge

More than a third of all the 2017 Entertainment Lions were awarded to content based on real stories and real people, and an even bigger percentage submitted factual content to the festival, be it long- or short-form documentaries, TV reality programmes or scripted films inspired by true events. That's already a big win for all those of us who believe that authentic storytelling and branded entertainment is the future of advertising. This trend alone is way more rewarding to me than any award statue.

The surge of unscripted content was also fuelled by the pick of the 2016 Lions Entertainment Grand Prix winner a year earlier, the *New York Times*' VR documentary *The Displaced* that immerses the viewers in the real lives of three child refugees. Despite this landmark success, many agencies and brands found themselves in a crowded space and learned, sometimes the hard way, that coming up with authentic content or a documentary comes at a price and creates big challenges for creatives. Telling a straightforward documentary is a relatively conservative business with established storytelling rules, interview techniques and strict journalistic standards (more about this later) that don't leave much room for over-the-top creativity and, especially, no gimmicks. That makes it difficult to stick out from the crowd but quite easy to embarrass yourself and crash and burn – or, worse, bore your audience.

I once tried to establish a documentary format that would get rid of all talking heads and sit-down interviews to give space for authentic dialogue and make people forget that they were actually watching a produced film. Although the results and the pacing of the films were absolutely beautiful, it was an uphill battle to convince all stakeholders that we could break away from a century-old tradition that a solid documentary is supposed to have interviews.

And the Grand Prix goes to . . . scripted!

Scripted content, in contrast, has the advantage not only of being able to invent characters and storylines freely but also of using film-making techniques. Maybe this was one of the reasons why, despite the surge in documentaries, the 2017 Lions Entertainment Grand Prix went to a fictional entry, science fictional to be precise. *Beyond Money* (*Cuánto. Más allá del dinero*) is an artistically crafted short sci-fi film and a multiplatform consumer campaign created by MRM//McCann Spain for Santander Bank. The jury considered the campaign the perfect combination of a bold, consistent and credible brand message – that experiences are more important than money – with true entertainment value for the audience.

Conventional wisdom is that every great story needs a villain; an important ingredient usually missing in branded entertainment out of fear of coming across as too negative. In *Beyond Money* a brand took the bold step of making itself the villain, or, to be more precise, Santander Bank *villainized* what banks used to stand for. For taking this courageous and precedent-setting step alone, *Beyond Money* needs to be recognized with a major award.

PJ Pereira, our jury president, writes in his chapter of this book that the producers of *Beyond Money* were bringing in the right talent 'that is used to being worth the audience's time' and made the project a 'shining example' of what should be the mantra of our time: 'Think like a marketer, behave like an entertainer, move like a tech start-up,' which is what his chapter is called. While *Beyond Money* was tailor-made to excel in all three categories of this mantra, many brand-made documentaries, even the solid ones, struggle in all of them. They bury the brand message under a convoluted narrative, lack surprising plot points and are unable to adapt to new media platforms to reach their target audience.

No beacon

There was no lack of effort. In *A Love Song Written by a Murderer*, a lovely poem was written by a real-life murderer. The campaign by the Peruvian songwriting superstar Diego Dibos and the agency Circus Grey for the charity Vida Mujer put the spotlight on domestic violence against women in Peru. However, it was later involved in a controversy about the authenticity of the 'real' love letter.

In some submissions the disturbing truth was right on camera. In *The Lick-Hiker's Guide to Inner Strength*, a documentary by Hasan & Partners, Helsinki, the British comedian Ian Wright travels through Europe to lick the dirtiest places he can find, literally, including a public toilet in Russia. It redefined whatever it means to have bad taste, all in the service of the Finnish superfood brand Valio Gefilus. This documentary is one of the most provocative, shocking and polarizing brand films ever. It divided the audience and our jury alike. Its unapologetic boldness and courage were rewarded with a Bronze Lion – but a beacon for where exactly our industry is headed it wasn't.

Perception vs reality of authentic

Most creatives in our industry are not journalists or documentary film-makers (or not used to working with them). As marketers and advertisers we are creators of meticulously planned, storyboarded and polished media products. Optimization is more important than fact-checking. Our perception of the authentic many times outweighs the acceptance of the reality of the authentic. In short, we are control freaks, not neutral bystanders and chroniclers.

People in advertising are used to manufacturing stories (which in documentary film-making is, literally, a crime). Even in the age of fake news and bought social media followers, documentaries remain trustworthy because faking an entire documentary that features a large cast, renowned experts and unique locations is much more complicated than faking a tweet or making up facts. And it would probably take more resources, financial and otherwise, than filming the real thing.

To an advertiser all that matters is usually what's on screen. A great documentary film-maker is also looking for that surprising element that lies underneath.

Capturing the film-makers' equivalent of lightning in a bottle

A few years ago the incredibly talented French cinematographer and documentary film-maker Sébastien Montaz-Rosset captured such a magical moment. Seb's approach is always intimate and unobtrusive. But on this day it was more than that. While filming with his crew in the towering mountains above one of Norway's majestic fjords he randomly encountered the Swiss highliner Bernhard Witz who was practising walking on a tightrope about fifty metres (160 feet) long strung over an abyss more than a kilometre (over half a mile) deep.

For Red Bull's *Ultimate Rush* documentary series, Seb recalls the encounter with Bernhard: 'I didn't know him, and he appeared with two other people. He just warmed up a lot of the time. And I think, why is he doing so many crossings? You know, sometimes you do three, four crossings, and then you do something else. And he was doing it a lot. And then, suddenly, I could see him taking off his Swami, which is not even a [safety] harness but just the belt. And then he's going by the cliff. And he's going on the edge and is sitting on it. And then I go to him and [ask] "Can I film? You're going to cross here?" "Yeah, no problem."'[1]

What follows is what Stephen Schiff, the award-winning writer of *Ultimate Rush*, calls 'capturing the film-makers' equivalent of lightning in a bottle'.[2] Bernhard walks the rope free solo and untethered. Not once, but twice, with 1,000 metres of vertical drop below his feet. It's more than a breathtaking stunt, it's transformative. In front of our eyes the athlete not only reaches new levels of physical achievement and mental focus he actually changes into a different being. To me, this was one of the most intense film-making experiences while working at Red Bull. Bernhard's action was never intended for the energy-drink brand, nor did he perform for Seb's camera. But in my eyes it says everything about the people who live by the principles of the brand. Without saying a single word. It started out unintended, but it couldn't be more authentic. That's what lies beneath a great documentary.

The Displaced

For the 2016 Grand Prix win, leveraging the *New York Times* brand, a journalistic powerhouse and not a bank or a yoghurt manufacturer, was certainly helpful. But it was more. *The Displaced* combined flawless storytelling with a cutting-edge but easy-to-obtain technology and had a distribution strategy to ensure that the readers of the *New York Times* had access not only to the video but also to a free 360-degree video viewer. With *Daily 360* video content to follow every day, who would push the envelope of brand-produced documentaries even further the following year?

Love for the authentic

In spring 2017, when online judging for the Lions Entertainment commenced, I was particularly looking forward to watching the documentaries and factual-content entries. For full disclosure, I used to be a journalist, a documentary film-maker and a producer of factual entertainment before I moved into content marketing for brands. In my first career I interviewed serial killers, school shooters and cult leaders. I testified as an expert witness in capital murder trials and travelled to Guantanamo Bay to discuss 'interview techniques' with CIA representatives (not CAA reps). What the hell happened in advertising for someone like me to end up on the Cannes Lions jury? In short, brands picked up a love of the authentic, and the easiest way to get there, so the theory goes, is to produce a good old-fashioned documentary.

The truth, the whole truth and nothing but the truth

Releasing a documentary comes with a built-in credit of trust. That's a significant advantage over traditional commercials and advertising. Generations of documentary film-makers and journalists who felt obliged to tell the truth have earned the trust of documentary audiences. A well-researched documentary about medical professionals has far more credibility than a toothpaste commercial with a fake dentist. The above-mentioned documentary, *The Lick-Hiker's Guide to Inner Strength*, proves in a crude but credible way how the Finnish superfood boosts the immune system of the film's bacteria-licking human guinea pig. No thirty-second commercial could ever be this convincing.

One of my earlier investigative documentaries was even used as evidence in a death penalty case in Florida. The stakes couldn't be higher. Sloppy work could have contributed to letting a murderer walk free or to an innocent man getting executed in the electric chair. Even if the topic isn't murder but oatmeal, brands not only earn authenticity from producing documentaries they gain credibility and the trust of their audience and customers.

Don't jump (to conclusions)

The responsibility that comes with this trust when producing documentaries for a brand can be as challenging for all participants as producing for a TV news network. I experienced this shortly after taking an executive role overseeing production for a brand studio. One of my field producers called me nervously on a Sunday afternoon from the notorious North Face of the Eiger in the Bernese Alps in Switzerland, where at least sixty-four climbers have died since 1935. One of our athletes was supposed to jump from the Eiger in a wingsuit, but high winds made the jump even more dangerous. The producer wanted me to decide whether the athlete should go ahead and jump as planned or try a safer alternative. Once again, the stakes couldn't be higher. Obviously, safety always comes first. A producer or an executive on the telephone should never make such life-or-death decisions; they should always be entrusted to the athlete on location.

Not *Fearless*

The Lions Entertainment entry I expected and hoped to see the most (but ultimately didn't) was the beautifully produced Netflix documentary series *Fearless*, which features a group of professional bull-riders from Brazil and their quest for titles and acceptance on the PBR circuit, the tour for professional bull-riders in North America and, apparently, 'the fastest-growing sport in America'.[3] It also features J.B. Mauney, the humble and soft-spoken cowboy and bull-riding champion from North Carolina who is maybe the most successful athlete most urbanites from New York and Los Angeles have never heard of.

This documentary series is not only about bull-riding and superhuman achievements but integration and what it really means to be an American hero no matter where you were born.

Fearless is essentially a thrilling yet highly emotional six-hour commercial for the PBR (its chief executive is being credited as a co-producer) and also provides high visibility for Monster Energy (intended or not), one of the main sponsors of pro bull-riders. Even the highbrow *New York Times* had to admit in its review that the documentary series 'plays like an elaborate promo' and that the graphic design and music are 'several levels above those of the cable reality series in this genre'.[4]

Produced on the level of a Super Bowl commercial and attached to a global distribution strategy, all this perfection comes as little surprise. The PBR was recently purchased by WME-IMG, the global sports and entertainment powerhouse. (In 2017 WME-IMG transitioned to Endeavor.) It's exactly the kind of branded entertainment I would like to see more of everywhere – including at the Cannes Lions Festival. But I didn't.

The no-shows

For each great documentary that enters Cannes there might be another one that doesn't. Are some brands afraid to lose credibility when entering a festival that is all about marketing? Has the divide between real documentaries and branded content become so thin and invisible that some producers would rather submit their films to Sundance and Tribeca? Is it considered more effective to have the content speak for itself instead of talking about your own brands and your creatives and yourself? Or is the entry process just too expensive and too complicated for some? I agree with PJ that for each amazing achievement in this field that is not being entered you withhold from an entire generation the benefit of learning from it. This is exactly why we include examples of great branded entertainment in this book even if they didn't enter the Cannes Lions Festival.

No game-changers

As the Lions judging continued over the next few weeks I felt more comfortable screening unscripted entries like *Keepers of the Game*, a two-hour documentary on an all-Native-American, all-female lacrosse team produced by Tribeca Digital Studios for Dick's Sporting Goods, than a short TV spot featuring perfectly cast actors and polished dialogue. *Keepers of the Game* is an inspiring story about empowered female athletes. Some parts – especially the quiet moments of the film – would never work (or have the space to unfold) in a traditional commercial. However, *Keepers* is a relatively traditional documentary with no game-changing elements. The Entertainment jury recognized the work with a Bronze Lion. It was one of half-a-dozen documentaries to win an Entertainment Lion this year. But to make it into this exclusive group it took more than just producing a heart-warming film. Dick's Sporting Goods put its money where its mouth is. The brand not only paid for the film it directly supported high-school athletic teams in underserved communities with $25 million and equipment.

Exclusive ingredient

Dick's Sporting Goods successfully demonstrated what should be in the playbook of all brands and their agencies: to stand out, a brand not only needs to produce entertaining content but also to add an exclusive ingredient to its content that only this particular brand can add, be it its expertise in extreme sports (Red Bull), its unique properties (Marriott) or turning its products into performers (LEGO). However, the word in the agency world is still that nine out of ten clients, when thinking about creating content for their own brand, ask for a documentary showing their happy customers. Obviously this doesn't work any more.

Seismic shift

Back in the 1990s, when I started out in European and US TV, brands were merely advertisers, sponsors and disrupters. A piece of branded entertainment was called an 'infomercial' and was usually relegated to late-night TV, with its true entertainment value coming mostly from its poor, even comical performances and production values. Things, however, started to change in the 2000s, around the time I joined the Red Bull Media House. I served as the head of entertainment and, for more than half a decade, oversaw the production of hundreds of documentaries, TV episodes and pieces of digital content about athletes, adventurers and artists. I witnessed the seismic shift first-hand, when brands such as Red Bull and Marriott turned from being marketers and advertisers to true content producers, programmers and even TV and digital-network operators. It was only the beginning of a trend. Global technology and CPG (consumer packaged goods) brands kept asking me for the right formula to create and distribute authentic content and for help in building content studios. And almost everyone wanted a documentary. An entire industry for branded content was born. What I learned along the way about what really worked for brands and audiences alike is relatively simple and straightforward. It reshaped everything I thought I knew about authentic content.

The new authentic

For starters, I stopped calling brand-produced entertainment 'branded entertainment' because if it's branded in a traditional sense it looks too much like advertising. It is the same if the 'documentary' is actually a two-minute version of a thirty-second spot. It is easily recognizable by having only one plot point and no real story arc and usually being edited to a single song – just like a traditional commercial. We have all heard a thousand times by now that advertising is more about disrupting than entertaining. (Unless it is so disrupting, bold and surprising that it becomes entertaining again. But only a few creatives master the great game of disruptiveness. I count the director Spike Jonze among this small group. In 2017 his eccentric long-form commercial *My Mutant Brain* for Kenzo World, with an amazing off-beat dance performance by the actress Margaret Qualley, won two Gold, two Silver and three Bronze Lions – and, above all, the Titanium Lion.)

Great brand-produced entertainment doesn't need to talk about the brand and constantly display logos. Great content is made from the same stuff – the same DNA – as the brand. And a brand should never hire 'authentic people' or, worse, 'authentic-looking people' to talk about the brand. That's old infomercial thinking. They should feature people who *are* the brand or *live* the brand.

Don't pretend, just be

Red Bull, for example, doesn't use (or 'sponsor') extreme sports or Formula 1 racing to become something else. Red Bull *is* extreme sports and racing. That's the new authentic. The energy-drink brand owns and operates several racing teams, designs its own cars and has sophisticated programmes to develop junior talent for F1 and MotoGP. These initiatives are fully aligned with the in-house content production. We started to produce documentaries about up-and-coming MotoGP riders and F1 drivers such as Daniel Ricciardo and Carlos Sainz Jr several years before they entered Formula 1.

Red Bull land

Do you need more proof? At the 2018 Winter Olympics in Pyeong-chang, Red Bull athletes won thirteen gold, five silver and twelve bronze medals according to social media posts by some of the brand's top executives. If Red Bull was a country and these athletes were competing directly for Red Bull Land, the energy-drink-maker would have been third in the overall medal count – ahead of the USA and Canada. The results are even more impressive when you consider that Red Bull is not even an official sponsor of the Olympics. You do the maths.

Lo and Behold

The authentic approach delivers results. In 2017 the Werner Herzog-directed documentary *Lo and Behold: Reveries of the Connected World* won three Golds and one Silver Lion and about ten other awards for NetScout, a provider of network performance and cyber-security products. No one ever talks about the NetScout brand, but almost everyone in this film *is* part of a connected world, be it Elon Musk, a cosmologist, a Buddhist monk or a woman who is allergic to mobile phones.

A quest for time

There are three aspects of the *Lo and Behold* documentary that really stick out for me. First, together with the BAFTA winner *Home* by Black Sheep Studios for UNDP Kosovo and *A Love Story* by CAA Marketing for Chipotle, it is one of the few Lions Entertainment submissions that I actually watched and enjoyed before I even knew I would be nominated for the Cannes jury. *Home* and *A Love Story* are fictional films not documentaries. However, responding to the refugee crisis by following a family from the UK to Kosovo, *Home* is heavily inspired by real events. Second, *Lo and Behold* was produced by Pereira O'Dell, the agency of our jury president and co-author of this book, PJ Pereira. Therefore, to remain impartial and to follow strict jury protocol, PJ had to leave the jury room while we prepared to deliberate his agency's submission.

But it is what PJ said about his work and similar brand-produced films that really matters to me, because it shows the direction in which our industry is heading: 'It needs to be worth the money to the client, and worth the time to the audience. In most branded content so far, the agencies have been trying to please the brand, and that's all. Now the bar is higher. It also needs to be a good investment of time for the audience.'[5] In other words, as marketers and producers of brand-produced entertainment we are competing for the audience's time, not against other consumer brands but against the might of the established media companies and streaming giants such as Amazon and Netflix.

The message becomes the product

The logical advice is that our content needs to be so well-produced and so much worth the audience's time that we don't need to compete against the streaming giants but are able to leverage them to bring our content to our audiences: the marketing film itself becomes a product that can be monetized. As a jury member I fought hard to not only honour the 'beautiful' or 'awesome and creative' work but also the submissions that had a successful distribution strategy to put the work in front of a mass audience. The children's TV and VOD series *RAD Lands,* another entry by CAA Marketing for Chipotle that has a distribution deal with iTunes, is a great example for this strategy, and it therefore won a Bronze Lion.

The third big question that originated from Werner Herzog's documentary *Lo and Behold* has to do with working with a world-renowned director. Whose DNA is really in this film? Werner Herzog's or NetScout's? Would Werner Herzog have made a similar documentary even without the help of NetScout? Whatever the answer is, there would always be the looming shadow of a big director (especially if he does his own signature voice-over recording, as German-born Herzog does). Personally, I like to work with the best talent available, which can sometimes be an award-winning personality and at other times a fresh talent cast right off the street to meet audiences at their eye level. But the real director, the entity that provides the DNA and footprint, should always be the brand.

How do a brand and authentic content pair up?

Spending hundreds of hours watching content submissions at home and later deliberating in the jury room in Cannes only confirmed what I had learned during my time working with brands. Not just for statistical reasons but to better prepare myself for the challenge, I divided the creation of brand-produced content and documentaries into three main categories as follows:

1. Ideation and execution by a brand
2. Ideation by the talent or a third party, with the brand 'tagging along'
3. Rebranding of an existing story or footage

Each category generates different challenges for a brand trying to be authentic. If, as in (1), the brand has not only generated the idea for a project but also overseen its execution and the production of all audio-visual assets about the project, the outcome can either be the most rewarding or the most disastrous.

A great and still successful example from the history books is *Red Bull Stratos*. When, in October 2012, the Austrian BASE jumper Felix Baumgartner took a leap of faith from the edge of space and delivered a then-record-breaking jump from over 38,969 metres (127,852 feet) above the New Mexico desert, with its precise planning and flawless execution Red Bull made aviation history and broke records in live broadcasting and online streaming. But you don't have to be a rocket scientist to understand how dangerous this live jump in unknown territory could have been if it had not been flawlessly planned and a competent team established, which undertook years of preparation. For that, Felix and my former colleagues at Red Bull deserve all the credit.

There are no shortcuts. Among many rewards, Red Bull won a Sports Emmy for the *Stratos* broadcast. In April 2013 Felix and Alexander Koppel, then the Chief Commercial Officer of Red Bull Media House, took centre stage in Cannes during MIPTV, the annual international market and creative forum for content. They delivered a keynote speech and shared their experiences and some key results. Red Bull did not submit the project to the Cannes Lions Festival, but, in the spirit of being a production house, multiple *Red Bull Stratos* documentaries were produced and internationally distributed.

No gimmicks

I later saw videos from other brands turning dangerous stunts into gimmicks without any real purpose for the athlete or for anyone watching. And, worse, in some cases they needlessly jeopardized the lives of the athletes.

This goes against everything I have ever believed in.

In addition, gimmicks usually don't work for brands any more. Remember, today a brand needs to *be*, not pretend. Luckily 2017 brought forward many great examples of when brands took the initiative and rightfully won Lions.

In the emotional documentary *The Debut*, AB InBev Budweiser, US cable sports channel ESPN and the Africa agency of São Paulo, Brazil, took the initiative to arrange the NBA debut for the Brazilian basketball legend and all-time leading scorer Oscar Schmidt – thirty-three years after Schmidt refused to be drafted to the NBA to make sure that he could play for his Brazilian national team. Our jury awarded the moving documentary a Silver Lion.

In comparison, *Boost Your Voice* by 180LA for Boost Mobile and *Unlimited Stadium* by BBH Singapore for Nike are not classic documentaries but rather innovations and experiences. But both campaigns are grounded in real life. They have a real purpose for anyone who participates. And the initiative and execution are with the brand (or *are* the brand). As detailed elsewhere in this book, during the 2016 US presidential elections Boost stores in underserved communities were transformed into voting stations to give the otherwise unheard people a voice. Nike, with *Unlimited Stadium*, created the world's first LED running track on which athletes can compete against their own digital avatar. For their accomplishments both Boost's and Nike's campaigns received Gold Lions. Boost can rightfully claim that it *does* give people a voice. Nike *is* running, and Budweiser proved by bringing Oscar Schmidt to the NBA that it *is* basketball.

'Now my career is complete. Done!' says a confident Oscar Schmidt at the end of his NBA debut (and the documentary). Many other brands are not quite there. My advice: do it like Oscar; stop talking and start *being*. I urge brands to take the initiative and their own real-life events and actions that make an impact on people, thereby making people care for you to really *become* what weaker campaigns just project themselves to be.

Tagging along

I personally found category 2, ideation by the talent or a third party, the most difficult and risky, with the brand merely 'tagging along' for the purpose of creating content, because execution and outcome are in the hands of others. In addition, sometimes partners do not have the same interests, standards and practices as the brand. This category also includes the most influencer-generated content. And we have all seen how the mindless actions of an influencer can blow up right in the face of a brand – the discriminatory comments by PewDiePie and Logan Paul's suicide images are recent examples. However, the aforementioned documentary, *Keepers of the Game* by Tribeca Digital Studios for Dick's Sporting Goods, shows how a brand can make the right decisions in the choice of its cast, story and partners. The documentary's all-Native-American, all-female lacrosse team would have faced the same challenges with or without Dick's Sporting Goods. The brand was merely a silent partner that added a key ingredient in the donation of sporting goods, which built a successful connection between real people and a brand.

Keep walking

The rebranding of an existing story, category 3, might not only be the least glamorous way to create a documentary it also bears the lowest risk and potential costs for a brand. The results are known before a brand even decides to invest and utilize the story. *Ode to Lesvos* is a documentary series by Anomaly, New York, for Johnnie Walker, supporting the Mercy Corps. Their film crew went back to a small village on the Greek island of Lesvos, where 300,000 refugees had come ashore weeks earlier.

By the time the film crew arrived the refugees were long gone.

The local fishermen tell heart-warming stories of 'fishing for people instead of fish' and of refugee children lining up to kiss them. This is obviously a relatively safe and predictable, albeit highly effective, approach to telling a story, because the outcome was already known. The brand put itself at no risk during the process, and our jury awarded the highly emotional documentary series a Bronze Lion. Is telling the story a noble cause by itself? Does the courage and selflessness of the Greek villagers shine on the whisky brand? *Did* Johnnie Walker help the villagers and refugees to keep walking? You be the judge.

In 2018 Johnnie Walker added a female counterpart, Jane Walker, to its iconic mascot to support women in business, culture and politics and to create a 'symbol to represent the fearless women taking steps on behalf of all', as the official marketing text runs. Although I consider this a step in the right direction in order to connect with today's reality, the brand caught its share of criticism for coming too late to the party once again. The brand strategist Joah Santos writes in a much-discussed LinkedIn post that Jane Walker 'comes off as fake' and that 'it also feels like a brand trying to hijack a cultural moment'. [6]

Picking the right time to enter a cultural conversation seems essential for credibility. Sometimes it's safer for a brand to risk an untested conversation early on, even when the outcome is still unclear (*Boost Your Voice*), than to join an important and rightful conversation too late. (Did anyone just say Pepsi?) Whatever they say, please keep walking, Jane Walker!

'Don't be afraid to live your truth'

One of the 2017 short documentaries that hit the mark in almost every sense and category was *Real Color Stories with Tracey Norman* by Grey Group, New York, for Procter & Gamble's Clairol Nice'n Easy brand, a beautiful redemption story for the model Tracey Norman and for the Clairol brand. Norman was the first African-American transgender model to appear on boxes of Clairol's hair-colouring products in the 1970s. In 1980, while on a photoshoot, her 'true identity' was revealed, ending her modelling career. Thirty-six or so years later Clairol reached out to Norman again and announced that Norman would become the face of its *Nice'n Easy: Color As Real As You Are* campaign. Tracey Norman's core statement – 'Don't be afraid to live your truth' – is not only her personal story but also the story of the Clairol brand. My co-juror Pelle Sjoenell emphasized the importance of this learning in the 'Amping the Tension' chapter of this book: 'Make sure you avoid one conflict only, and that's the one between the product story and the main story because you can't trick the audience, you can only lose it.' The fact that this beautiful and important campaign only won a Silver Lion and not a Gold or even the Grand Prix shows how competitive Lions Entertainment has become.

The street writes the best stories

Telling an authentic story doesn't always involve producing a documentary. Adidas, which is currently incredibly successful with its originals, shoes and athletic apparel, has recently established the Creator Farm in the vibrant Greenpoint neighbourhood of Brooklyn, New York. I visited the Farm in October 2017 and was, quite frankly, very impressed. When I spoke to Marc Dolce, the Farm's Creative Director, he told me it's an 'open-source hub for designers, artists and storytellers'. Marc and his team invite fresh creative talent, sometimes off the street, to join the Farm for three months. The work is not necessarily sports-focused, he says, but 'primarily culture'. In short, Adidas manages to read the street and puts its DNA back into the brand. The resulting story does not have to be a film or a video clip, but it *is* a successful product.

Too much charity?

As in the case of *Ode to Lesvos,* and in contrast to the Adidas Creator Farm approach, many brands and agencies still find the most rewarding and emotionally true stories when working with charitable organizations that bring relief in the face of global crisis and injustice or in the aftermath of disasters. There is nothing more real than a child without parents, a displaced person or an underserved community without access to clean water. However, the quest for the authentic has created problems even within the organization and execution of the Cannes Lions Festival. As Jae Goodman, CEO of Observatory (formerly CAA Marketing) and 2016 Lions Entertainment jury president put it: 'How can a film about oatmeal possibly compete with films about the global refugee crisis?'[7] Some brands and agencies complained that if they were pushing a traditional brand message they would have a lower chance of winning a Lion than the highly emotional charity content. To address this issue the 2017 Entertainment jury used the same tough standards for the brand-led and the goodwill content. We looked deeply at the effectiveness of the content for the commissioning brands and charity organizations. We came back with additional questions for the submitting parties, often requesting proof of effectiveness and even conducted our own research.

New tracks

The organizers of the Cannes Lions International Festival of Creativity heard the concerns as well. From 2018 onwards the festival is beginning the process of separating pure charity work from brand-led work into distinct category tracks. The idea is eventually to have all charity work appear only in the Good track. I applaud this decision.

What is missing?

Suffering is not the only human element that makes a story emotional and enables it to connect with the audience. What about laughter? Humour was clearly under-represented in 2017. The aforementioned *Lick-Hiker's Guide to Inner Strength* was the only funny documentary that won an Entertainment Lion. As a jury we would have liked to see more humorous films, especially in the high art when a brand is able to make fun of itself. Interestingly, the successful 2018 Super Bowl commercials from Tide, Amazon, NFL, Tourism Australia, Doritos, M&M's, Michelob Ultra and Bud Light did exactly that.

Let's entertain!

As marketers we mostly sell products that make people's lives easier and more enjoyable. To be truthful and authentic to this our films should be enjoyable entertainment as well. This is exactly what makes our documentaries different and therefore competitive with the traditional film festivals and the streaming platforms. We don't have to follow the established trails of distinguished auteurs, academies and film critics. We disrupt and surprise. We don't need to hide who pays for our films. We proudly integrate our brands and let their uniqueness contribute to the narrative. We don't whisper all the time; sometimes it's OK to scream. Yet we don't criticize and teach. We take action ourselves and enable others.

We entertain.

1. *Ultimate Rush*, Season 2, Episode 20, 'Unsung Heroes', Red Bull Media House, Wals, Austria, 2013

2. ibid.

3. https://www.nytimes.com/2016/08/19/arts/television/netflix-fearless-review.html

4. https://www.nytimes.com/2016/08/19/arts/television/netflix-fearless-review.html

5. http://www.wodenworks.com/native-content-is-about-more-than-disguising-an-advertisement/

6. https://www.linkedin.com/feed/update/urn:li:activity:6374721615317528576

7. https://www.linkedin.com/pulse/cannes-lions-2017-two-weeks-later-jae-goodman/

FEEDING OUR ANGER

Luciana Olivares, Latina Media

> 'Dr Banner, now might be a good time for you to get angry.'
> 'That's my secret, Cap, I'm always angry.'
> – Captain America and Bruce Banner, *Avengers*

Let me tell you a story. Once upon a time twenty-three beautiful princesses were fighting to win a crown . . . Sorry, that isn't right. On 30 October, in Lima, Peru, twenty-three fierce women fought for gender equality and their rights as human beings. This is what happened at the last Miss Peru Pageant.

We transformed one of the most traditional and viewed shows of the year into a platform to empower women and raise our voices to fight against violence. In Peru, nine teens are raped every day; 89% of the rapists are still without any punishment; 2,379 of the rapes happened in the victims' own homes. Want more statistics? Peru has the third-highest rate of sexual violence committed against women. The awful truth is that terrible numbers such as these are reported every day on TV, in newspapers and on the internet.

However, Peruvians were not paying real attention to this reality. So Latina Media, the network that broadcasts the pageant, and Jessica Newton, the president of Miss Peru, decided to hijack the contest and do the unexpected: during the pageant contestants' hip and bust sizes were replaced by statistics of violence in the country.

Camila Carnicoba, the first contestant to appear on stage, started her speech like this: 'Hi, my name is Camila Carnicoba, and my measurements are 2,200 cases of femicide in my country.' The stage, social media, the whole country and the world went crazy. There were debates about the topic in local and international media. The authorities spoke about it. Even the Peruvian first lady made a pronouncement about what had happened at the pageant, along with other important figures. As of today, the event has reached more than $5.2 million in free press worldwide for a cause that needed to be heard and shouted about. We transformed the princesses into badass warriors, the measurements into statistics that matter, the beauty into an opportunity to see how ugly our reality is, and the anger in our source. Yes, anger, because #MyStatisticsAre did not come from fear or sadness; it was born in the purest state of anger, from being really pissed off.

That experience and the overwhelming responses that we got made me think about our week at the Cannes Festival, about how some of the brilliant ideas we picked used anger as a catalyst to hijack culture and awaken their audience.

Friends don't lie

Fernanda, my ten-year-old daughter, has a new obsession: *Stranger Things*. The time when unicorns were her daily trending topic are gone. Her favourite character is Eleven, the girl with supernatural powers who was kidnapped when she was a baby and confined in a laboratory by a mean guy. One day I asked Fernanda which of Eleven's powers was her favourite, and she said: 'She is a fighter, Mummy, and uses all her anger to move things.' Of course the one who was totally moved was me. My girl understood that anger is a useful emotion, although it has the fewest emojis in WhatsApp. She was so right, and she made me remember how many times I have used my anger to move very heavy things in my professional and personal life. Haven't you done this?

How many times did being really mad about something make you change it? Maybe using the dark side as a source is not bad if you transform it into a powerful tool. Maybe being really green, not like the Grinch who is always complaining but like Hulk, who fights with force and passion, is positive and awakens us from inertia. Maybe anger will make us change from 'Don't worry, be happy' to 'Be worried, be angry', and, of course, we need to be worried if we want to change things.

So, here is my proposal: using our anger to change things as a brand or as human beings is more relevant than ever before. Many of us are pressing the autopilot button and not paying attention, not even to the things that really need attention. Bad news is part of the landscape. We are so familiar with the awful statistics surrounding us that we have become blind – probably because we don't need to see or hear. We need to feel. But if we don't pay attention to issues such as climate change or gender equality, imagine how difficult it will be to get attention for a new soap or a new type of bank account. It doesn't matter if the message is selling a good cause or a car, if it's a not-for-profit organization or a giant retailer, we are not responding to the traditional ways of communicating. So is there any hope? Can we use anger to connect with our audience and society and light our fire?

Go visceral

One piece of advice new writers get from more experienced ones is to write about what bothers you. They are right. Writing about what bothers us makes our art come with emotions. This forces you to go visceral, feel it in your guts, heart, lungs and stomach. That's where intensity comes from.

Of course, all that intensity can be misdirecting. Margaret Atwood, writer of *The Handmaid's Tale*, says that destructive anger makes you destroy everything around you and direct your rage at an object that doesn't deserve it. On the other hand, creative anger occurs when you're able to channel it without panic, to 'create a system, a series of steps to achieve a goal outside of anger'.[1]

Creative anger or, better, hate is the key ingredient behind one of the most awarded and celebrated campaigns in Cannes history: *Grrr*. The work tells the story behind the creation of Honda's first diesel in a unique way. Kenichi Nagahiro, the company's chief engine designer and inventor of the celebrated VTEC engine, hated diesel engines. He hated how noisy, smelly and dirty they were. When asked to design Honda's first diesel he refused – unless he was allowed to start completely from scratch. The result is one of the cleanest diesel engines on the market today, the 2.2 i-CTDi. With this masterpiece Wieden + Kennedy in 2004 proposed to the world of brands the idea of talking about hate as something positive, a passionate force that could actually be turned to good use. But of course the proposal didn't come in a typical way. The agency created one of the most inspiring songs ever made about anger:

> Here's a little song for anyone who's ever hated . . .
> Can hate be good?
> Can hate be great?
> Can hate be good?
> Can hate be great?
> Can hate be something we don't hate?
> Whistling . . .
> We'd like to know
> why it is so
> that certain diesels must be slow
> and thwack and thrum
> and pong and hum
> can clatter clat
> Whistling . . .
> Hate something
> Change something
> Hate something, change something
> Make something better
> Whistling . . .
> Oh isn't it just bliss
> when a diesel goes just like this?
> Whistling . . .
> (Sing it like you hate it!)
> Hate something
> Change something
> Hate something
> Change something
> Make something better.

The lyrics were sung by Garrison Keillor, an American author and voice artist. The ad features creatures associated with environmental protection, innocence and joy . . . butterflies, swans, peacocks, deer, hummingbirds, frogs, chickens, bunnies, seahorses, turtles, goats, penguins, pink flamingos, robins, dolphins, seals and a ladybird. The campaign also came out with an online game featuring a rabbit that visits nine environments, eats carrots and changes shoddy technology into environmentally friendly features.

Why me?

Arun Gandhi, grandson of India's legendary leader Mahatma Gandhi, has a strong relationship with anger. He grew up in South Africa under apartheid, being beaten and bullied. However, he was taught to use anger as the fuel for change. He quotes his grandfather:

> We should not be ashamed of anger. It's a very good and a very powerful thing that motivates us. But what we need to be ashamed of is the way we abuse it. [2]

When anger, irritation and frustration becomes a medium rather than a crutch or something dangerous, beautiful things can happen.

Now imagine your name is Katrina, Andrew or Irma. One day you wake up and read the news about how you or something with your name decided to destroy the planet.

Enraging, right?

That insight helped Barton F. Graf 9000 and the activist group 350 Action find a spot for themselves in culture in a rather hilarious way. In the *Climate Name Change* campaign the idea was to ask the World Meteorological Organization to rename storms and hurricanes after politicians obstructing the climate change agenda. To illustrate how this would work, they put together some fake news stories about these storms: 'Senator Marco Rubio is expected to pound the Eastern seaboard sometime tonight'; 'If you value your life, please seek shelter from Michele Bachman'; 'We've been here two days because of Congressman Paul Ryan. I have friends who are still out there. It's scary, because I have no idea what Paul Ryan could be doing to them right now.'[3]

In the end they couldn't get any storm renamed, but the thought of seeing Hurricane Andrew being called Hurricane Marco Rubio made our days a bit lighter and the climate-change doubters' a little more annoying – which, in the current state of the world, already counts as a partial win. The movement gathered 2.7 million YouTube views, 356,000 unique visitors to the site, 184 million earned media impressions with $0 spent on media, and although no hurricane was renamed it brought a level of attention the organization had never had before.

Give it a little respect

Imagine this terrible disaster: you have no internet! You begin to sweat, you are feeling anxious and miserable, so you decide to call your service provider. A nice robot answers and suggests you remain on hold while you enjoy a piece of classical music. Time passes, and you are still on hold. Your body starts to change and your fangs begin to grow as you transform into a furious wolf. (Just joking.)

The point is that you are really angry – and you are spoiling for revenge. In 2016 in Brazil the first On Hold Music Festival was born. For the country's Consumers' Day, Reclame AQUI, Brazil's top consumer-protection website, turned anger into fun by parking mini concerts in front of the companies that were the worst customer-service offenders. The idea was to give these disrespectful companies a taste of their own medicine: instead of playing good music, they played back the same tracks these companies used in their 'wait until your call gets answered' automated systems. The videos were posted online and got millions of views. They also received a Cannes Silver Lion in Entertainment for Music and two more Lions in PR. Consumers love it; companies, not so much.

Fuck you, sir

Some causes won't allow for light-heartedness, however.

Like the end of democracy, for example.

In 2011 Tunisia faced a terrible truth. In its first free elections only 55% of the people intended to vote, forgetting the main objective of the revolution, which was to fight for democracy. To counter this national apathy Engagement Citoyen NGO, a not-for-profit organization, with the help of its agency Memac Ogilvy, decided to awaken Tunisians' anger.

They put a giant poster of Ben Ali, the president ousted in the 2011 Tunisian Revolution, in La Goulette, one of the most crowded districts of the city of Tunis. With cameras running they started to capture people's reactions. Some were intrigued, some were irritated but most were angry, a feeling that quickly escalated to rage as people realized the real danger of abstention: the return of dictatorship. The poster provoked protests, screams, harsh words and vandalism. Soon the crowd was gathering around the massive poster, throwing ropes around it and uniting to tear it down. But when they did so they discovered another underneath: 'Beware, dictatorship can return. Vote on 23 October' along with the URL for non-partisan and straightforward information about the elections and the candidates.

The message spread immediately (30% share rate online), generating tens of thousands of calls for action, an increase of more than 461% in visits to Engagement Citoyen's website and media coverage everywhere. People spontaneously changed their social media profile picture into the second poster. Within a few hours getting out and voting had become the ultimate act of the revolutionary process. In the evening it was aired on all Tunisian and wider regional channel news. The next day it spread worldwide. They ended up winning two Gold Lions in the Cyber category. More importantly, that year Tunisia's election had an astonishing 88% turn-out.

Oh, fuck the banks, too

Let's face it, banks are not sexy by nature. People see them as a necessary evil – greedy and heartless. I understood this many years ago when I worked as the chief marketing officer of a global bank in Peru. We knew we would not be able to get through to people by talking like a bank; we needed to use something Peruvians really care about, their food. So we used Peruvian gastronomy as an emotional connector between the bank and the audience, changing the typical bankers' way of speaking and hijacking Peruvian culture to conquer people's hearts. Maybe because of that, *Sounds of Conquest*, the amazing concept developed by Caixa in Brazil, made me fall in love. They understood that the best way to be part of the 2016 Olympic Games was not by paying a huge sponsorship fee and putting their logo on big banners; they needed to change the rules and the way bankers communicate.

They hijacked Brazilians' pop culture by using urban music and street art as powerful emotional connectors, creating remarkable content around athletes and local musicians and artists; seven stories of overcoming obstacles, seven songs leading on Spotify, a city covered in urban art, a massive concert, millions of visits and digital shares and, of course, the complete attention of Brazilians on Caixa Economica Federal. They won a Cannes Bronze Lion in Entertainment.

You are so dumb

Branded entertainment is marketing and must accomplish business objectives. At the same time, as my co-author Tomoya Suzuki described in his chapter 'Back to Basics', it needs artistic integrity so that it feels honest enough to grab the attention of a very fickle audience with way too many choices. It's the element that forces you to push the limits of an idea, so it says exactly what it is supposed to say. No compromise.

Where does integrity come from? From things that you, the author, the artist, the creator, the marketer really *feel*. And none of those emotions has proven more useful than anger. Jean-Michel Basquiat, one of the most influential contemporary artists of recent times, used his anger to create his work. When he was asked in 1983 about the influence of anger he replied: 'It's about 80% anger.'[4] Racial injustice and historical abuses of power haunted him and fed his imagination. Basquiat's sustained rage, which began when he was an adolescent, became the engine of his bracingly original art.

There is a kind of rage and indignation that makes one call the target audience of a campaign 'dumb'. In 2013 an Australian campaign got so angry it did just that, but with an incredible twist of creative integrity they did it in the cutest way. Young people in Melbourne, Australia, had exhibited absent-minded and foolish behaviour around trains, and some incidents resulted in injury and death.

That's when McCann Melbourne created a music video with 'funny' cartoon characters dying in ridiculous ways, a contagious song, a karaoke version, a brilliant game, a book – want more? Everything in *Dumb Ways to Die* became a success. The initiative avoided traditional definitions of advertising to create content that is pure entertainment, generating 80 million views on YouTube.

The game became the number-one free app in twenty-one countries, including the USA, the UK, Canada, Australia and Germany, and it reached the top one hundred in 101 countries. In six weeks the campaign gathered an estimated $60 million in earned media and, most importantly, a 21% reduction in railway accidents.

It also became the most awarded campaign in the history of the Cannes Festival, with five Grands Prix and enough Lions to fill a shipping container back to Australia.

Devil inside?

Research in France in 2017 suggested that 65% of French people viewed refugees as a threat. Fear, rejection and anger were among the feelings French citizens harboured about the presence of refugees in their country. Bullshit. Excuse my French, but I assume that was the expression used by the executives and journalists of *Libération*, one of the biggest daily newspapers in France, who were so angry about these findings that they decided to do something to challenge these perceptions. 'The paper is yours for one day,' said the executive director of *Libération* to twenty-one refugees. Twenty-one journalism, design, sports, film-making, photography and science professionals from seven different countries – Afghanistan, Iran, Sudan, Libya, Syria, Russia and Colombia – had total freedom to create, write, design and edit an unforgettable issue that demonstrated the potential for refugees' social integration. Even the President of France took an interview from three of the refugees. The results: a 35% increase in sales and a huge buzz in social media and PR worldwide. However, the most important achievement was helping the French realize that refugees could be part of their society.

This is not a game

It's 2029. We are facing the year of 'mechanical apartheid', meaning the anger and discrimination shown by non-augmented people towards augmented ones. Yes, a futuristic kind of racism. The dark part of human nature is trying to plunge our world into war. However, these days the colour of your skin or your nationality doesn't matter. Humanity is divided – the augmented against the 'naturals'. Don't be scared. This is only the plot of a game, although sometimes science fiction turns out to be pretty close to reality.

Today's cutting-edge prosthetics and augmentation technology allows human bodies to run faster, jump higher, record interactions and see colours previously unseen . . . As you can see, cyborgs are no longer science fiction . . .

That is the point of 'Deus EX: Mankind Divided', a game that decided to tackle a very serious issue and use anger to build its story, generating visceral reactions, sparking and heating an inspiring debate. To launch the game and gain awareness they decided to create *Human by Design*, an integrated campaign discussed in more detail by my co-author Monica Chun in her chapter 'The News It Creates'. For the first time ever important questions were posed about the vision for human augmentation in the future and how far we are we from that reality. The launch of the game was a total success in terms of sales, the summit had a lot of buzz and the US government even received an ethical framework for human augmentation. But more important than any numbers was to see how a game inspired by anger between two groups could become an act of empathy for a whole new community that was given a voice for the first time.

Anger management

In a world of committee decisions (more of this in the chapter 'Advertising Ninjutsu and the Secret Art of Operating in the Shadows' by Jason Xenopoulos), anger may not be a popular idea. You will never win the title of Miss or Mr Congeniality (what a pity!), but you will win a superpower to fight for what you believe. However, the superpower comes with a prescription: two key words – 'identify' and 'reconvert'. 'Identify' because you need to know what shames, irritates, hurts and infuriates you and to understand that those emotions wake up your Batman signal to go and fight for your ideas, cause, gender, community, product, relationships or even life. 'Reconvert' because if you manage your anger you will access a colourful toolbox to use in creating ideas as well as a survival kit to ensure your brand heart is beating as hard as your audience heart. Because you can transform the pure state of anger into the pure state of loyalty, commitment and love.

1. *Anxy* magazine, No. 1: 'The Anger Issue', Spring/Summer 2017
2. http://www.arungandhi.org/2.html
3. http://www.climatenamechange.org
4. https://www.interviewmagazine.com/art/
    jean-michel-basquiat-henry-geldzahler

Part 3
OPPORTUNITIES
AHEAD

WHERE'S THE EXCELLENCE IN SPORTS?

Misha Sher, MediaCom Sport and Entertainment

When I first received an invitation to be part of the Entertainment jury in Cannes, I wasn't quite sure what to expect. I know some of the most inspiring brands in the world are sports brands, particularly in sports clothing. Their ability to tap into people's emotions has enabled them to transcend any single product to sell a lifestyle to which consumers aspire. Most people aren't buying a pair of Nike trainers because they lead an active lifestyle; they buy them because of what those trainers say about you when you put them on. Nike inspires people, as do Adidas and Under Armour, but they are the exception. Most brands involved in sports marketing are still missing the opportunity of connecting with consumers with all the intensity they are open to feel when their senses are connected to one of the most intense experiences we have in the entertainment ecosystem – the experience of sports. Whether brands lack creativity or ambition or both, it certainly feels like a missed opportunity.

I arrived in Cannes with an open mind, curious to see if there was excellence in the space that I had somehow missed. By the end of the week I had been pleasantly surprised by the quality coming from Brazil. Perhaps the beaches there are good for the creative juices because there were some stand-out Brazilian campaigns, which I will touch on briefly. That said, the majority of the work in the field didn't quite live up to my expectations – so therein lies an opportunity.

A 2014 quote from one of the top NBA executives – Vivek Ranadivé, owner of the Sacramento Kings – at the Stanford Graduate Business School's inaugural Sports Innovation Conference perfectly encapsulates why sport has become the Holy Grail for so many brands desperate to connect and engage with their consumers: 'What's the difference between a customer and a fan? Fans will paint their faces purple, fans will evangelize. Every other CEO in every other business is dying to be in our position – they're dying to have fans.'

There is something unique about sport that captures people's emotions. I have been to hundreds of sporting events all over the world, and no matter where I go I experience energy and excitement that simply doesn't exist in any other walk of life. I've seen grown men break down in tears seeing their team win. Sport is the ultimate form of entertainment. Some may argue that that's a stretch, but sport, unlike any other form of entertainment, is an unscripted drama. It's the ultimate triple play – it's live, it's social and it's global. There is always something to talk about.

Sport is littered with stories that people from all walks of life can connect with. It's one of the world's most powerful democratizing forces in its ability to bring together people of vastly different backgrounds.

Over the years thousands of brands have flocked to sport to capitalize on the reach and affinity that Ranadivé is referring to. They wanted to translate sport fandom into the love of their brand. I will never forget the Gatorade commercials with Michael Jordan. They made you feel something, and Gatorade made the brand an integral part of sport. Everyone I went to school with wanted to be like Michael Jordan. They succeeded because even in the early 1990s they inherently understood the power of emotional stories. Every time I saw Gatorade on the shelf I felt a strange affinity with the brand. Unlike many who followed them, they didn't just want to be seen in basketball; they wanted all of us to feel something when we saw their logo. Who could ever forget the famous Nike ad with the Brazilian national football team ahead of the 1998 World Cup? This was before content was a word any of us used and well before anything could go viral. Shot at an airport, it was a beautifully executed piece of branded entertainment that blended music, culture and football without ever mentioning the brand.

But what about others? Instead of thinking of creative execution and emotive storytelling, they focused on pure exposure – as if share of voice miraculously leads to share of hearts and minds. It doesn't. People are inundated with logos and advertising, so unless you can communicate a sense of purpose that connects with them you're leaving a huge amount of unrealized value on the table.

Wake up and smell the coffee

In October 2016 I was invited to 'NBA Crossover', a cultural exhibition in the heart of London designed to celebrate the association's relationship between the league, its players and fashion, music, film and entertainment. I recall walking around all the interactive exhibits and thinking how well the NBA does to combine so many cultural interest points in its core product. Yes, it has superstar athletes whose names are recognized the world over, but there is so much more. In everything from the hip-hop music to the exhibits of iconic sneakers to a mobile barbershop to a 2K lounge, it was clear that the NBA wanted everyone to see it as more than a league and bigger than sport. It is a well-oiled entertainment business, the appeal of which stretches far beyond the confines of the game and taps into people's other core interests in a way that keeps them continuously engaged and tuned in. Sure, the NBA is unique in its attributes, but I couldn't help but think to myself that everyone in our industry will have to take a leaf out of its book. The event was done in partnership with Foot Locker and 2K gaming, which combined to deliver unforgettable branded entertainment for all those who attended.

Sport no longer exists in a vacuum. It's now part of an entertainment industry, where it competes for people's time every day of the week. The implication for brands involved in sports marketing is how they adapt to this new environment. Those who embrace this ever-more-connected world will find new and innovative ways to use sport as a powerful storytelling platform and will reap huge benefits. The game is only part of the equation; social media and digital platforms have extended the experience of following sport far beyond the actual event. The fans have gone from being observers to active participants who crave to know everything around sports and the athletes they follow. There appears to be no end to their appetite, but they are being underserved. Brands involved in sports can tap into this appetite by serving compelling content outside of the actual games and by doing so continuously reinforcing their association. I've felt for a long time that the industry was missing a trick, but in coming to Cannes I was open to the possibility of being surprised. Maybe there was a lot of excellent material that I wasn't seeing. After all, we were tasked with judging around 1,800 pieces of work.

I wanted to see not only how well represented sport was in the category but also how the work stacked up within the broader branded entertainment arena. But after spending more than sixty hours in the room with judges whose experience truly represented the breadth of the entertainment industry my trepidations about excellence in sports marketing were confirmed. While we did see some excellent work from those we've come to expect it from, mostly sportswear companies, sport was a category that was generally under-represented when compared to others.

The question is why?

- Does the industry as a whole still lack creativity and investment in excellence?
- Is there a lack of framework for what excellence can be?
- Is there great work being done that we are not seeing in Cannes? If so, then why?

Our guess? A little bit of everything. But since whining never leads to winning (in sports, marketing or award shows), maybe we'd better look at the few that did win and see what we can learn from them.

We're cool enough

There is a lot of creativity in sports. Look at what Nike did with *Unlimited Stadium*. It developed the world's first full-size LED running track on which runners got to run against and train with their own avatars. Or how about Adidas with its *Original Is Never Finished* campaign? Here is a brand that forever reinvents itself to create its future, using a track made famous by Frank Sinatra, 'My Way', to challenge the idea that nothing can be made original again. The result is a beautiful collaboration with a host of musicians and influencers to remind everyone that doing things 'their way' makes it their own. Then there is *I Will What I Want*, by Under Armour, one of my all-time favourites. There is so much creativity in the way the brand uses a supermodel, Gisele Bündchen, in a boxing ring, overlaid with real-time social commentary to address one of the most pressing issues of the day – empowerment of women. These are all excellent campaigns, and these brands have shown time after time, year after year, that they will make every effort to make their work truly exceptional. But is it a coincidence that these just happen to be hip apparel brands that keep raising the bar against one other? Beyond those, you can find ideas like *The Game Before the Game* by Beats by Dre or Procter & Gamble's *Thank You, Mom*, but you'd have to look hard.

These brands clearly understand the power of stories and have the desire to bring something to the party. It's clear that they don't take their positions for granted and don't expect to build affinity simply because they are in sport. But that ambition is largely missing from many of the others that make up the $60 billion global sponsorship industry. For them it's simple: pay a fee, and the rest will take care of itself. They appear more concerned with share of voice, so the focus is on logos and reach rather than creating anything of value. They believe that their presence and visibility will drive consideration and give them an advantage over their competitors. But share of voice doesn't translate into share of mind, especially when consumers are seeking closer relationships with brands. I love some of the spots around the Super Bowl, March Madness and the FIFA World Cup but often wonder why these same brands aren't going any further and creating great content. Why stop there? Is it because sport is one of the last places where you can still buy an audience's time? And what happens when sport moves to other platforms, as ATP tennis did with Amazon Prime where there aren't any ads? There has never been a better and more critical time for brands to embrace branded entertainment around sports. If ad spots are no longer an option, then how do you get the same audience to engage with your brand? You do so by creating compelling content that brings people closer and makes them feel more connected to the sports they follow.

The content I do see usually lacks any sort of genuine creativity. When working with clients I always remind them that it's not worth doing anything if people won't notice your absence. This, for me, is the question everyone should ask themselves before creating anything. If you're simply replicating something that has already been done, what's the point? What are the chances that anyone will differentiate that it's your brand or develop any affinity if it doesn't stand out? Social posts, ticket competitions, use of talent in advertising, branding at competitions are all good ways of activating, but all of this is expected. We see the same social influencers used in multiple campaigns only because they have reach. It doesn't take much imagination to pay Cristiano Ronaldo for some promotion on his platforms, but does anyone stop and think that when you're the fifth – or, in the case of Ronaldo, twenty-fifth – brand using the same talent, albeit with a different hashtag, that you're hardly standing out?

Where is the bravery to do something different? To be more innovative? To truly leverage the power of storytelling and connect with a broader audience? Because this is what builds long-term equity.

Excellence is not replicating what has already been done. It's creating a totally new and unique experience with a genuine sense of purpose.

If, indeed, there is a lack of understanding of what constitutes excellence in sports marketing, especially as it relates to branded entertainment, this section should address it. While we, as a jury, looked at many different components such as bravery, authenticity and impact, the main focus was always on the story and craft. The story relates to where and how any individual piece of work fits within the current state of the world. It could have been a piece of cultural commentary or something that impacted popular culture. The craft relates to how the story is told. So often we see some great ideas poorly executed or told in a way we've already seen. The best work we judged, be it in sport or other categories, consistently told us stories we hadn't heard in a way we hadn't previously experienced. (*We're the Superhumans* and *The Debut*, two campaigns I will touch on shortly, are perfect examples.) It was always rooted in some insight about the audience the brand wanted to engage. This is as true for Cannes as it is for any entertainment awards and should be true to any brand that wants to stand out. The best work always has these components at heart.

The main question we asked of the work, and one addressed by many of my fellow jurors, was, does it genuinely compete with any form of regular entertainment? At a time when consumers have no shortage of choice, would they choose to watch or engage with the content over or alongside their favourite TV shows? Was it unskippable? For brands investing in branded entertainment around sport it comes down to the ability to engage outside of the white lines. When the game is not on, are you able to serve up the sort of entertainment that can satisfy the appetite of fans? Because, let's face it, outside of games you have to create something special to compete with all the entertainment options that people have at their disposal.

Sure, that's a pretty high bar to set, but why bother to create anything if you're not trying to be excellent? There is no shortage of average work out there. What we wanted to see was something that truly moved us, and the following examples in sport did just that. They were chosen to demonstrate that excellence in branded entertainment in sport can come from anywhere not just the usual suspects we've become accustomed to.

Don't sponsor, contribute!

Whenever I watch major sports events I always find it amusing to see sponsors roll out the clichéd ad reminding me that they are the proud sponsor. There are many proud sponsors, and to most people it doesn't mean anything. Why should I care? What are you doing with this sponsorship that speaks to me, that enhances my experience of that event? I've never seen people get more emotional than when they cheer on their countrymen and -women. There is an enormous sense of pride that tends to attract even the most casual observers who may not be into sport. Now that you have their attention, what are you going to say?

Well, Caixa, one of Brazil and Latin America's biggest banks, knew exactly what it wanted to say and how it wanted to say it to millions of its customers around the 2016 Rio Olympic Games. Caixa is known as 'the people's bank'. Its entire DNA has been built on championing achievements and social inclusion of the most needy members of society. Telling these people that Caixa is the proud sponsor of the Olympic Games would do nothing to strengthen bonds with them. For many, the Olympics became more of a curse than a blessing, as they watched 'state-of-the-art' facilities being built at a cost of billions of dollars while their own circumstances remained modest at best. If there was a disconnect with the people Caixa knew how to address it. As my fellow co-author Luciana Olivares alluded to briefly in her chapter 'Feeding Our Anger', it hijacked Brazilian pop culture by creating a perfect mix of urban music, street art and content to create something that spoke directly to its customers. It wanted to make its customers feel connected to its message – and what better way to do this than through the customers' own stories and their own way of expressing themselves? Caixa wanted to demonstrate that the qualities of great Olympians are the same qualities it sees in many of its everyday customers. The idea was to show that great conquerors go far beyond medals. Many of the athletes came from the ghetto, and the campaign was a celebration of their journeys so that achievement and conquest became something celebrated by everyone.

The result was a beautifully executed integrated campaign that captured the hearts and minds of millions.

Seven original songs were written by seven of Brazil's biggest rap artists and released every two weeks along with a video clip. A special campaign website became a home for the music where people could download the songs, watch their production and access exclusive content about the games and the athletes. The songs were pulled into an album called *Sounds of Conquest*, which was available on Spotify together with a tutorial on how to play them. In the streets each song had a unique graffiti and athlete story, which became a big part of the campaign's visual identity.

Finally, Caixa hosted a live show featuring all the artists. It celebrated diversity, inclusion and the achievements of the Brazilian people.

The campaign is a great example of branded entertainment innovation in sport. While the brand has heritage in sports marketing, the idea and execution behind the *Sounds of Conquest* campaign is a huge step forward in innovation. Caixa understood the true power of storytelling and went far beyond the typical executions we've come to expect from most sponsors, Procter & Gamble being the notable exception. The idea shows a clear understanding of the bank's DNA and the consumers it serves. Yes, many of them are sports fans, but in introducing art, music and popular culture into the creative process Caixa was able to capture and engage in a way that wouldn't have been possible if only sport was part of the equation. From rappers as storytellers to graffiti as visual representation, every detail was an example of excellence in story and craft. Brazilian athletes have competed in the Olympic Games for decades, but never have their struggles and achievements been celebrated and intertwined with the man and woman on the street. Caixa did this beautifully, and I salute it for its bravery. I hope this example serves as an inspiration to any brand that thinks excellence in sports marketing can only come from Nike and Adidas.

Be super

What do Michael Jordan, Pelé, Muhammad Ali, Ayrton Senna, Tom Brady, Wayne Gretzky and Serena Williams have in common? They defined what it means to be great. Some athletes and teams are very good, but some rise above the rest and almost defy logic in what they are able to achieve. I remember the time Michael Jordan took off from the free-throw line and glided through the air for what seemed like an eternity before dunking the ball into the hoop. It was so surreal you had to check your own pulse to make sure you weren't dreaming. If you've followed or read anything about these athletes you can't help but be in awe of their drive to be 'super'. No matter what they achieved, they weren't satisfied. The bar was always being raised. And, as fans, our experience of watching them has often shaped our own expectations of those sports.

I've seen brands that have a similar obsession with being the best, continually rewriting the rules in the art of storytelling. They don't just want consumers to buy their products, they want to influence attitudes and behaviour. Apple and Nike are two that come to mind, and people who buy their products have a strong affinity with what these companies represent. Of course, not everyone can be Nike or Apple, but I have some good news for those who dare to believe that they, too, can be great. And if this example doesn't make everyone feel it's a fair game then I'm not sure anything will.

Can you remember which Rio Olympic sponsor had the most shared ad globally in 2016? I'll save you some time: none of them. That honour goes to Channel 4, an official UK broadcaster of the Paralympic Games. You may be wondering how an organization that doesn't have a fraction of the budgets available to all the top sponsors can create something that becomes such a global phenomenon. The answer can be summed up in ambition and purpose. Rather than focus on promoting broadcasts of the games, Channel 4 decided to engage with consumers about a topic that many chose to ignore: disability. Having heritage in the space from its great work around London 2012, Channel 4 set out to create something that would transform public attitudes about one of the last remaining taboos of our culture. To set out on something so ambitious and brave is one thing; to deliver it in the way it did was quite another.

The three-minute film featuring more than 140 people was a celebration of ability in the truest sense – showing gold-medal-winning Paralympians alongside everyday people performing tasks we take for granted like brushing one's teeth. It featured people flying planes, playing in bands, raising children, tap-dancing, rock-climbing and even driving a wheelchair through a wall. There is even a superhuman band made up entirely of disabled musicians from across the world performing the Sammy Davis Jr track 'Yes I Can'. It was the largest disabled cast ever featured in advertising history, and it exuded confidence and joy on a level we rarely encounter.

It was a truly groundbreaking piece of work, becoming the most shared Olympic or Paralympic ad globally in 2016. Most importantly, the ad helped to shift perception of disability significantly at a time when, according to the case study of the Cannes submission, nearly

70% of UK residents didn't feel comfortable talking to a disabled person.

Consider the level of investment made by brands around the Olympic and Paralympic games and the achievement of Channel 4 becomes even more impressive. Disability is not a new topic, and it's been addressed in many different ways in the past. What Channel 4 did was to take an important societal issue and use sport to elevate it. By creating something that features athletes alongside everyday people, they captured the imagination of millions who aren't even sports fans. The craft of the piece is masterful, bringing us something we are probably aware of in a way we've never experienced before. The result is arguably the most inclusive ad ever created – shattering stigma and stereotypes around disability to better society. That's the art of the possible when you dare to be brave. The truth is that this could have been done by many different brands that activated around the Olympics. Channel 4 don't have a monopoly on great ideas, and it certainly can't compete with the budgets of major sponsors. It set out to create something that's bigger than itself and its business. It put purpose at the heart of the creative, and it's that purpose that millions in the UK and around the world connected with. My challenge to all sports marketers out there is to think of a purpose that goes beyond selling your product. Dare to be super!

Everyone loves a comeback

I mentioned earlier that one of the most captivating aspects of sport is the stories. Sport is filled with stories of setbacks, triumphs, rivalries, surprises, struggles and many experiences we all have in our everyday lives. We love them all, but perhaps none more than the story of a great comeback. Feeling like a victory is impossible and yet having a twinkle of hope that somehow, with some divine intervention, we may, just may, pull a victory from the jaws of defeat. Who could forget the recent NBA Finals where Golden State Warriors, who looked to be cruising to yet another championship against Cleveland Cavaliers, somehow fell short. It made no sense whatsoever. They won the previous year, set a record for regular season wins, were up 3–1 in the series and had home advantage. No team in NBA's illustrious history has ever come back from such a deficit, much less against one of the greatest teams of all time. And yet that's what happened. It almost defies logic, but this sense of surprise, unpredictability and a general feeling of 'what if?' is sport's unique attraction. You may be wondering what any of this has to do with brands or branded entertainment. Well, more than meets the eye.

Sport is not the only place where people love a comeback. Many of the world's most recognized brands have, at one point or another, let themselves or their consumers down. Remember Pepsi's recent ad with Kendall Jenner, which made you wonder who could brainstorm something like that? Or what about Chipotle, which built a brand on being independent and using responsibly sourced ingredients only to sell out to McDonald's? Both have come back, and, in the case of Chipotle, it was a beautiful, self-deprecating piece of branded entertainment that was at the core of rebuilding brand trust.

When we look for similar stories in sport, Heineken's comeback from its sexist ad promoting the UEFA Champions League final in 2014 was simply brilliant. For years the beer industry objectified women and reinforced gender stereotypes to sell beer, especially around football in Brazil. Heineken was no different, and when it decided to team up with Shoestock to offer women 50% discount on shoes online and in stores starting at the same time as the game, it looked like a company tone-deaf to the reality of the changing world in which it existed. The idea that men had to be left alone to watch a game of football in peace is as ridiculous as suggesting that women can't drive. It becomes even more preposterous when you realize that women, according to the case study submitted to Cannes, make up more than a third of the target market, and more than 80% of them feel completely ignored in the advertising. So, well done to Heineken for basically saying: 'You know what? Our bad.' In creating *The Cliché*, the brand didn't just hit a home run in branded entertainment; it showed up an entire industry for the ignorant bunch that it often is and started a cultural conversation that reverberated around the world.

The three-minute social spot focuses on sets of couples out for dinner in São Paulo where the men's menus include a card with an enticing proposition: 'Would you like to be free to watch the UEFA Champions League Final at a Heineken party? Gift your lady a weekend at this spa.' The guys trick their girlfriends into thinking they bought them a retreat, and it's all heading for a predictable ending. Except this time there is another twist. Upon arriving at a party the guys are surprised by a video greeting from their girlfriends who, rather than being at a spa, are at the San Siro in Milan going to the Champions League final. The closing message reads: 'Have you ever considered that she might like football as much as you do?' Luckily for the guys their girlfriends surprise them with tickets to next year's final so that they can all go together.

The spot was a huge success, becoming the most viewed, shared and commented video that the brand has ever created. Given how much Heineken invest in content, that's an impressive feat.

Here was a simple idea that challenged the narrative of an entire industry. It was a clever use of branded entertainment to show brand purpose, something consumers are desperate to see from the brands they love. For the first time, women fans were given the platform that has always been reserved for men, and the results show that it struck a chord. With 22 million views and 200,000 shares, it was clearly something that transcended football and became part of popular culture.

Are you sitting on a great story?

I mentioned at the beginning that people love great stories, especially when they are linked to something to which they are deeply connected. I've had the privilege to work with Pelé, widely regarded as one of the greatest athletes of the twentieth century, and it always amazed me how much people connected to his personal stories. We were once launching a big initiative with Shell where they built football pitches in Rio favelas. This *Make the Future* campaign, which won a Cannes Lion in 2015, was built around the idea that the footsteps of players by day could power floodlights in the evenings to illuminate the pitch, so it was safe. Pelé played an important part and not for the reasons that most think. It wasn't about his profile or his fame but about the story of his name. Pelé's real name is Edson, after Thomas Edison, the inventor of the lightbulb. The year Pelé was born, 1940, was the first year they had electricity in his village. So there we were, seventy-five years on, talking about the progress from the first lightbulb to floodlights powered by players' footsteps. It was a story that few people knew, and now it was part of something much bigger.

Which brings me to perhaps the best example of branded entertainment in sport from 2017's submissions, *The Debut*, courtesy of Budweiser. In bringing Brazilian basketball legend Oscar Schmidt out of retirement to play in the NBA All-Star Game, Bud showed the art of the possible when a great story meets phenomenal execution. The greatest scorer in basketball history and holder of many other records, Schmidt's biggest disappointment was that he never got to play in the NBA, despite being drafted the same year as Michael Jordan. Here is a brand taking a story that was relatively unknown and using every ounce of creativity to make it impossible to ignore. What I loved about this was that it was a perfect demonstration of what's possible when you think beyond the white lines or the time in which the game takes place. In this campaign the game was part of a far bigger and more meaningful experience that touched millions of basketball fans. Bud's delivery of this story, from the initial teaser to engaging content to the game and the subsequent documentary that played on the big screen in cinemas, gave fans something to connect with. They followed because they were moved by the story and felt a sense of pride in supporting one of their own. It was an ambitious idea, but it goes to demonstrate what's possible when you think outside the box. Bud chose the hard way, and if that's what they believe makes their brand a legend then I'd have to agree.

Ambition is contagious

If you've made it this far then I hope you're realizing that greatness can come from anywhere, and what is required is ambition. Excellence is not limited to brands that naturally live in the sports space. Sport is a platform to tell powerful stories that transcend logos. If a Brazilian bank can do it, what is stopping anyone else from pursuing their own excellence in the space?

Well, there are some who don't just pursue excellence but in many ways set completely new standards for others to follow. The problem is when we don't see them in Cannes, and as a result they don't form part of the conversation that sets out the industry's future. Who could forget *Red Bull Stratos*, a project discussed in the earlier chapter 'Everyone Wants a Documentary'? It was one of the best examples of branded entertainment in sport but was never entered into competition at Cannes because the brand might not consider it marketing or advertising.

Red Bull has always been known as a brand that doesn't do ordinary. Everything about its marketing is designed to push the boundaries, to test the limits. *Stratos* was the pinnacle of that approach. Austrian skydiver Felix Baumgartner performed a world-record-breaking freefall from an altitude of 38,969.3 metres (127,852 feet) up in the stratosphere. The event was viewed by millions on live TV and internet broadcast. Reaching 357.64 km/h (843.6 mph), Baumgartner broke the speed of sound, and the data collected was seen as an invaluable contribution to the space industry. When you consider that this was done by a brand, you have to admire the ambition and the risk undertaken by Red Bull.

This was truly an ambitious project, the likes of which we've never seen before. That said, I find it disappointing that Red Bull took such a strong stance against promoting it – as if touching it with the 'dirty hands' of marketing would somehow diminish the importance and appeal of what had been achieved. If the brand genuinely didn't want to capitalize on the marketing opportunity, then how does one explain the narrative 'it's giving him wings' and seeing the brand all over his suit? If this isn't an example of the industry sabotaging itself then I don't know what is. Now each brand is entitled to decide on which forum it chooses to demonstrate its work, and Red Bull did share key findings at MIPTV, but there is a broader question as to whether having a brand at the heart of great content somehow diminishes its appeal. When we're not debating the merits of great work at Cannes then the entire industry suffers, and it shouldn't be that way. Let us be clear about the merits of an awards show like Cannes. It's a moment each year when the industry gets together to discuss the future. It's not an ego play to participate in and aspire to be among the winners.

We didn't get to debate *Stratos* in Cannes, but, given that the purpose of this book is to understand what constitutes excellence, then we would be doing our readers a disservice if we chose not to learn valuable lessons here. Sorry Red Bull!

One of the biggest lessons that sports marketers can learn from Red Bull, and *Stratos* in particular, is the power of consistent and unique messaging. Red Bull has built its entire brand story on being extreme and innovative, with *Stratos* being one of the brand's most ambitious examples. Everything about it had 'Red Bull' written all over the project, and that's invaluable in a cluttered marketing space.

Another lesson to be learned from *Stratos* is the importance of having a purpose. Sure, Red Bull is a business that wants its consumers to buy its energy drink, but its marketing is built entirely on empowering people to test their own limits. It does this because it understands the shift in consumer expectations: brands need to prove their worth. They need to demonstrate a sense of purpose that has the consumer at heart. In the analysis of marketing consultant Simon Sinek, author of *Start With Why: How Great Leaders Inspire Everyone to Take Action*, they nail the 'why' and the result is that their brand transcends their product. There are many energy drinks out there, but none can compete with Red Bull when it comes to a strong brand purpose. I can hear some who are reading this saying, 'Sure, but we can't all be Red Bull', and they would be right. But the challenge is not to be Red Bull. The challenge to all sports marketers is to articulate a sense of purpose with which consumers can connect.

Finally, *Stratos* shows that sports marketing is not limited to paying huge sums of money to established sports properties for the benefits of exposure and association. These are important elements of any marketing, but the key question that all sports marketers should be asking is how those investments will enable them to own and communicate a truly unique brand story that will resonate with consumers. These consumers are inundated with sponsors promoting tickets, money-can't-buy experiences and social campaigns. What are you doing to articulate purpose and empower your consumers? You don't have to replicate *Stratos*, but it's certainly worth exploring the ingredients that made it such a success.

To summarize, excellence in branded entertainment around sport can be achieved by anyone brave enough to try. In a world in which consumers are spoiled for choice, sports marketers should challenge themselves to create something that has a higher purpose at heart than selling a product. The future belongs to those brands that can compete for people's time. This is my opinion, and, rest assured, we didn't always agree in that jury room. My hope is that anyone who reads this book will have learned from our experiences and debates so that the quality of what we see from the whole industry is raised to a new level. Until then, let's just agree not to play it safe.

THE FUTURE OF ENTERTAINMENT: HOLLYWOOD, SPORTS AND GAMING, GAMING, GAMING!

Toan Nguyen, Jung von Matt/SPORTS

What is entertainment?

When I first got my jury invitation for Cannes I thought they were joking. Why? Well, I never actually applied for it. Also, my awards-jury experience in general was close to zero. In fact, I don't even like advertising. I never do TV ads, I never do print ads, and almost every case film for award submission puts me in that Bill Murray mood from *Groundhog Day*. To put it another way: there was probably nobody less suitable to be a Lions judge than me. And yet they brought me in and made me watch more than a hundred hours of material in a couple of weeks before arriving in Cannes and six days straight once we got there.

On the plus side I have one big advantage: I belong to a mysterious and confusing target group – a troublesome crowd seemingly responsible for a host of nightmares, headaches and, most importantly, big shifts in marketing budgets and channels. I am one of those dreaded millennials.

That doesn't necessarily mean that I don't appreciate good artwork or film. In fact, I fought for many films, like *Grow Up* by Mercedes-Benz (Bronze), *Gravity Cat* for PlayStation, *Original Is Never Finished* by Adidas (Bronze) and, most notably, *Single Belief* for whisky brand The Glenlivet (Bronze), which is still stuck in my mind because of its absolute looniness (you basically watch a weird-looking Taiwanese guy doing literally nothing for, like, fifteen minutes). So, yes, we millennials do, in fact, like film – but we just don't like it the advertising way. We like it the Netflix way and the YouTube way, which is the reason why none of those pieces mentioned is shorter than three minutes! Older people tend to think that we're not capable of taking in information in a longer or more demanding form than a tweet or Instagram posting, but they tend also to forget that we were the ones who gave birth to the term 'binge-watching'.

It's fun but also extremely difficult to think about entertainment. I mean not only the word itself but also its meaning – especially within a marketing context. What exactly is entertainment? We may all have an idea what branded entertainment is, but how were we supposed to judge entertainment as a standalone term?

After all, this was Cannes Lions and not the Oscars.

When people think about entertainment they often think about shows. Shows on TV or shows on stage. A quick search on Google Images using the term 'entertainment' will suggest that entertainment is either a theatrical movie or a music concert. Since there was another entertainment jury specifically assigned to music (they even had 'music' in their jury name), I assumed that we had our focus somewhere else. The question was where? I had no idea. Maybe *we* had no idea.

Consequently it's important to understand the basics: which platforms can be considered genuine entertainment platforms; who are the talents of today and tomorrow; and how does technology affect or drive new forms of entertainment? So let's start with a personal observation in full-contact, Generation Y-style, taking no prisoners: I don't watch TV; I watch YouTube channels. I don't know soap-opera actors, but I know Instagram influencers. My thinking is mainly based on different social media filters, hacks and algorithms. But the most disturbing thing you will probably read today is that I enjoy watching other people play video games online.

Yes, I really do.

I might even be sitting on my couch while you read this, watching other people play 'League of Legends', 'Dota 2' or 'Counter-Strike' on my big TV screen at home, which I initially bought for Netflix and Amazon Video. And there is also a good chance that I'm not by myself. Some friends of mine could well be there, too, passing round some snacks, because it's obviously more fun to watch games and matches together. This might sound super-weird to you, but think about it. How many people watch other people play traditional sports? How many people watch other people cook? How many people watch other people get naked and do stuff? Those are all phenomena that have been around for some time, right? So obviously there is something about watching others do stuff that seems to trigger people. And this holds true for gaming, as well, and – hell, yeah, we are talking about millions upon millions of people watching people play video games to win millions upon millions of dollars. Actually, you can win $20 million for winning a single tournament. Wait a moment. What?

OK, let's rewind a bit.

There is Hollywood on the one hand and sports on the other.

As stated above, this was Cannes, not Hollywood. But I'm not an awards guy, I'm not even a creative. I'm a strategist who works in sports- and celebrity-marketing. For the last four years I have been working with sports entities such as the German national soccer team, the German Olympic team, several Bundesliga clubs, a few select athletes and, of course, sports brands like Adidas, Reebok and sports sponsors like Mercedes-Benz. It's mostly been a fun ride, simply because it's more fun to market a soccer team than some Bavarian cheese, the next flavour of deodorant or a banking account (all been there, all done that). My older colleagues – or, as PJ called them, the 'old folks' – have always stated that working with cars is the supreme discipline in advertising. Maybe that used to be true. But right now I'm looking at 29 million hashtags for BMW, 12 million hashtags for Audi, 39 million hashtags for Adidas and 69 million hashtags for Nike on Instagram.

Without doubt traditional sports such as tennis, soccer and American football have been significant drivers of great marketing initiatives. It's superfluous (or tedious) to evaluate the importance of the Super Bowl, especially within the context of the Lions. As a millennial I have a tendency to mix things up: were all those ads created for the Super Bowl, or was the Super Bowl created for those ads? At the end of the day it's simple: sport is really, really powerful. I truly believe that sport as a platform is and will always be king when it comes to its potential to reach consumers. It is by nature a killer application, something with inherent strength and uniqueness through one particular factor: its ingredients are engaging by default. Sport embodies the idea of community-building and loyalty in its fans. Sport is also emotional. It's all about drama – winners and losers. Ultimately sport is about powerful things: humans and personalities.

In an era of constant debate about content marketing and ever-changing Facebook algorithms, it's safe to assume that sport will be the winner. The reasons are many: no other platform can produce content on such a regular basis as sport; no other platform is as naturally tied to anticipated occasions like match days, cups or finals. And yet no other platform is as momentum-driven as sport is when things suddenly go crazy. Sport is indeed a form of entertainment – if not one of the most powerful ones. Also it is culture at its very best.

And this is the very spot where marketing and communication want – and need – to be.

This all seems very straightforward. Yet . . . it's not as if most Lions submissions about sport were of poor quality. From a creative point of view there is clearly a lack of excellence. Most ads, content pieces and activation simply rely on a trivial principle: just sign a cool team, just sign a cool athlete or just be a sponsor of any event and, yeah . . . that's all you need. The problem is that this logic may hold true for Hollywood but it certainly does not for sport. Actors are actors. Athletes are athletes. And you really see what this means when it comes to execution. It's no surprise that we all enjoyed watching that *GQ* video *Ryan Gosling Gets Roasted by His Twin Brother*. It's good writing, sure. And it certainly deserves that Bronze Lion for the sake of bravery by *GQ*/Condé Nast. But it's no Silver, it's most definitely not a Gold, because the entire content piece is just about Ryan Gosling being Ryan Gosling. Likewise, Bill Murray could just play himself and it would be probably a lot of fun. But – and this is important to understand – only a few athletes can pull that off. Only a very few. There is a lack of creativity, there is a lack of acting talent, but there is also another problem.

We've been looking at sports from a general perspective. But this is Cannes. This is a CMO party. From a marketing perspective sport is not always 'sport'. In fact, when we talk about sport and all the aforementioned advantages we are really just talking about a few categories. Let's face it, we always talk about the same sports – especially from a global perspective. Nobody really talks about fencing, tae kwon do, table tennis, volleyball, curling and so on. A rather harsh but truthful way to put this is: all sport is entertainment, but not all sport is entertaining.

So it's no surprise that marketers always opt for the same sports. They all fight for the same assets, teams or athletes and the same share of voice. If you move into sports, you had better be prepared for all-out war! A war for talent. A war for attention. This can be very costly. People close to the scientific and academic field would call this 'a Red Ocean'. There's no need even to clarify that term. It already tells you to avoid it.

When facing that, you basically have two options: you either break through the clutter or you break out of the clutter. The latter means that you focus on something else completely. Instead of trying to get the prom queen's attention you simply go to a different party.

The first option is the obvious one. Breaking through the clutter has been one of the most important, maybe even the dominant, marketing disciplines in recent decades. The reasons have been cited over and over: more products, more brands, more channels and reduced attention span. Consumers are faced not only with many options to buy but also many ways of communicating. Content is everywhere. And I mean literally everywhere. Within this environment the key to success is obviously creativity.

If everyone is campaigning for their car or laundry product, you need to get more creative. This can amount to better insight or better execution, among many other things. *The Bradshaw Stain* by Procter & Gamble's Tide is a good example of breaking through the clutter. It broke through the content by somehow merging with it – just brilliant! There was another nice campaign that didn't make it on to the shortlist, which also showed the power of creativity. Some South American Walmart branch, I think it was in Brazil, became the sponsor of a regional soccer team. But instead of putting its logo on the players' chests (like everyone else), the company chose the back of their shorts, with one fun twist: they swapped the players' names for the names of products and the players' numbers with the product price. Of course, this would never be allowed in Germany, but it was permitted in Brazil, and it shows how you can play around with stuff. Sadly you don't often encounter those kinds of things in today's sports marketing.

Sounds of Conquest for Caixa bank was done really well, because it portrayed athletes in a new and iconic way. Nike raised experience marketing to the next level with *Unlimited Stadium* by combining digital opportunities with actual exercising in a visually phenomenal way. But the work that particularly stood out for me was without any doubt *We're the Superhumans* by Channel 4. It was not only well-crafted and entertaining by nature (owing to the musical show appeal) but also strategically brilliant. At first glance it changed the way non-disabled people look at the Paralympics and disabled people but may also have influenced how disabled people look at themselves. *Superhumans* was for many reasons a game-changer. I know that because I've worked on many Olympic campaigns, also for the Paralympics. Most work is very emotional and touching, meaning a lot of drama and very little comedy. *Superhumans*, on the other hand, developed its own signature, something very joyful, promoting high self-esteem and self-expression. It was different – and it broke through the clutter and traditional patterns. But these are only a few examples – which is, frankly speaking, quite depressing when we're talking about the Lions!

If you look at all the winners you will see how under-represented sports is.

So what does that all mean now? Well, for once it's important to understand that it's important to be different – even in sports marketing. This should be a piece of cake; doing things differently has been in our agency DNAs for, I don't know, maybe for ever. But attentive readers will probably anticipate my next point: doing things differently is not the same as doing different things. Successful ideas find a new twist on the subject that sets them apart. But the question that I want to raise here is why not change the subject entirely?

So, what would you think if I told you that there was something bigger than Hollywood and sports? When we talk about entertainment we ultimately have to talk about gaming.

Yes, gaming.

In fact, gaming might become the biggest thing in the history of entertainment. And I'm talking real money here: $108.8 billion in revenue in 2017. The market has been growing at an average rate of 5%, which represents roughly $5 billion a year. And things are getting even more aggressive. The game 'Call of Duty' had a marketing budget of $200 million; the 'Call of Duty Black Ops II' instalment, in return, generated $1 billion in sales within fifteen days of release. This game is moving more money than many Hollywood blockbusters – and it's not alone. Titles such as 'Grand Theft Auto', 'Final Fantasy' or the famous 'Pokemon' series are all money-printing machines.

Differently put: gaming is a big-boys' game.

And because of the aforementioned advantages it's only getting bigger. So let's go back to the beginning and the strange idea that certain people would watch other people playing video games. Why? Because it's reality, and reality hits hard! We have seen kids watching make-up tutorials on YouTube. We have seen a range of digital-born stars on Instagram who may, sooner or later, change the entire fashion industry. And we're now facing a time when it's sport and entertainment that will be truly redefined.

What if I told you that there is something like competitive gaming out there. There are professional teams, professional leagues and professional players who are playing video games for a living. This happens in stadiums around the world, most of them sold out, while companies such as Twitch (Amazon), Facebook and YouTube stream the games live with regular six-digit to seven-digit concurrent views. How would you feel about this fact: the world championship in 'Dota 2' has a prize pool of more than $20 million! For just one single event. All of this is driven by a strong and growing fan community. Fnatic, a London-based eSports clan, has more than 1.12 million followers on Twitter alone! Faker, a South Korean 'League of Legends' player and something of a Lionel Messi of eSports, counts more than a million fans across different channels such as Facebook, Twitter and – most importantly – Twitch.

So, some of you may be surprised, and some of you may have heard about this, but let me dive deeper into the subject, because there is a lot to tell. And, yes, there are a lot of prejudices when thinking about eSports, so let me address the three most common ones first.

#1 That thing about the nerds

I know the first picture that might come to your mind is probably a teenage boy who's sitting in his parents' basement. You would probably call that kid a 'geek' or a 'nerd' and most likely think he's not someone who's going to date the prom queen. And you could be right.

Sure, the average eSports fan probably doesn't live in the New York's East Village, nor do they drink fancy matcha lattes after attending Vinyasa yoga class. They also don't usually live in artsy lofts with a fixie bike in the hallway or a surfboard on the wall. In fact, it's more likely they're sitting in an engineering or computer-science lecture, learning about macroeconomics, tutoring maths or checking online where they can watch the newest blockbuster. In its original language, of course.

What makes me say that? It's simple. The people who keep up with eSports very likely possess not only above-average English skills but also significant cognitive skills.

If you don't believe me, come and visit an ESL (Electronic Sports League) event and have a look for yourself. The complexity that hits you when commentators analyse strategies, plays and scenarios in double-time English is a pretty good demonstration of the brain capacity of eSports fans who live all over the world. 'Dota 2', for example, one of the most popular games right now, is an amalgam of game theory, as in the movie *A Beautiful Mind* with Russell Crowe, the game prisoner's dilemma and American-football moves coupled with the high speed of basketball. And all that wrapped in bangs, thuds and lots of blinking lights.

So not only are eSports fans not stupid, they are young, too. More than two-thirds of them are under the age of thirty-five. They think globally, they think digitally and, as the numbers prove, they're clever: according to the institute Newzoo eSports fans have an above-average education and income.

So, let's put it like this: eSports fans and players may not be your typical mood-board target group that live in urban lofts, but they aren't the blaring, fireworks-lobbing beer lunatics that can be found in other types of sports. It's most likely that a lot of them will become tomorrow's programmers, aircraft specialists and mobility engineers. Yes, they are the ones who'll go on to have the money.

#2 That thing about the violence

I hear this a lot: eSports and gaming is about bang-bang and violence and forms the perfect boot camp for future serial killers. When most people think about serious eSports they think about 'Counter-Strike', and, again, they are right. 'Counter-Strike' is huge.

The current player base stands at a cool 10 million. Per month, obviously. Sometimes, there are up to 850,000 gamers playing on the servers at the same time. During ESL One Cologne (like a world championship), there were 15 million unique viewers watching the streamed matches online – read that number one more time – and 47.9 million hours of 'Counter-Strike' were watched on Twitch in January 2017 alone.

Even statistically they can't all be maniacs and serial killers.

'Counter-Strike' is among the four most popular eSports titles. That's why prize pools can easily reach into the millions of dollars – on top of an average player base salary of about between $65,000 and $100,000. Think about it. You don't make these amounts of money through senseless aggression but rather technical versatility, reflexes and, most importantly, a high degree of tactical thinking, both individually and as a team. So it's hardly surprising that the whole do-FPS-games-make-you-violent (that is, first-person-shooter) discussion is limited to a few countries. Countries like Germany, where I live, for instance. In other countries huge brands such as Visa, Pepsi, Coca-Cola, Audi and Domino's Pizza have been sponsoring 'Counter-Strike' teams and events for quite a while now, and NBA players and top DJs such as Steve Aoki are even buying their own teams. In comparison, the fact that some countries are still stuck thinking 'Counter-Strike' is for unstable personalities with low impulse control and high levels of aggression is somewhat embarrassing, to be honest.

And even if you dislike guns, there are plenty of other opportunities. 'League of Legends' or 'Dota 2', for instance, are basically cute versions of a Harry-Potter-Meets-Hobbit-World. It's all fantasy with fairy tales, dragons, wizards and werewolves. Speaking of 'Dota 2', this is the game with the $20 million prize pool. I don't know about the income situation of my fellow jury members, but that's quite a sum.

#3 That thing about 'not being a sport'

Some people may argue that eSports is not a normal sport. And they are correct; nothing is really normal in eSports. A global community that is digitally connected, exceptionally clever, gets its entertainment via streams, willingly pays for 'in-game items' (for example, little outfits for your character) and regularly breaks viewership records is anything but a normal sport. Because the fact remains that normal sports – apart from soccer and very few others – are having huge difficulties in many areas. Entire sports are taking place practically without any viewers, and organized sports entities are desperately looking for members. Meanwhile, the eSports kids just have to open up their browser or game client. Long story short: the entry barriers are a lot lower than they are in other sports.

And what about the sweating? Shouldn't sports be sweaty? Another one of those topics . . . Once you've seen how many actions the pros perform every single minute, how precisely they're handling their mouse and keyboard, you can hardly maintain that there isn't a physical component to it. Then there's the mental component as well – and let's not forget that chess is a sport, too.

Professionals practise up to eight hours a day. Before attending big tournaments they move into so-called boot camps, the eSports version of training camps. Some of them have several coaches, and a few teams have even started to work with physiotherapists and nutritionists.

And that's the crucial thing: eSports can help itself to elements of traditional sports, picking up what works best. It can. But it doesn't have to. And that's what makes it so exciting. After all, in some ways eSports is still in its early stages, even though it has already built its own ecosystem. Because of the loose structures in place, it's still possible to shape the scene and participate.

Entertainment is what entertains

We have heard peculiar stories about 'World of Warcraft' and struggling families in South Korea. We have seen the long lines of people buying games and going crazy about new consoles. And there is an entire genre on YouTube called 'Let's Play Videos'. This is simply kids playing games and commenting on them live on Twitch or YouTube. What is happening now is not only an evolution of gaming it's a powerful transition that will bridge different parts of different entertainment industries. It will bridge sports with gaming, with streaming, with talent, with live, with online, with on-the-ground and with a global community.

Yes, eSports is the sport and entertainment phenomenon of the new generation: it's a digital-born sport with digital-born stars. And there is a much stronger feeling of ownership by the fans. They have helped build the eSports scene from the ground up themselves and thus feel strongly about it as 'their' scene. This means they're much more interested in what happens in the scene beyond individual teams or athletes than regular sports fans tend to be.

While we all know those brands and industries that are desperately striving for digital transformation, eSports has managed to build its very own ecosystem. It's all digital by nature – the games, the training sessions, the interaction with fans, the activation, the reach and the views. It is also a rather untapped space for many brands and potential sponsors that still offers the potential for genuine co-creation instead of plain, unimaginative logo placements. We may still lack a definition of entertainment, but we know that it needs to entertain.

So where to go from here?

As PJ, our dear jury president, noted in his foreword, the goal of our gathering and this book is to learn on behalf of an industry that incorporates film, sports, events, VR and maybe gaming. We all quickly understood that this category was different. It had a different nature, a different spin to the work and a different touch on marketing and advertising in general. I think that was the reason they put so many different people from different industries together, and I think that was also the reason why a millennial like me was picked. It's about putting different perspectives together, and it's about developing an idea about what entertainment and branded entertainment is. Sure, it's not well defined yet and not all the work we've seen during our jury sessions was fully statistically representative – I'm sure there is more work out there that would cut it but which was simply not submitted. But if we look at the three best ones, which were *Lo and Behold*, *From the Start* and the Grand Prix-winner *Beyond Money*, we see clearly how far we moved away from traditional advertising. We loved long formats, things that were not distributed across conventional media bookings but rather Netflix, Amazon Prime or even owned media channels. No thirty-second spots, no out-of-home-campaign flights, nothing that works by means of pushing communications with large media budgets. If we think about the three winners, or even all the Gold Lions, we will see that all of them work only and solely on a voluntary basis. And this is important to note: we may not know what entertainment is in terms of marketing rules, but we do know its most important key performance indicator: time, time, time! I'm talking about the time that people are willing to give in order to enjoy an entertaining piece.

Time is probably more precious than ever with all the devices that are available. Our industry – or let me say the industry of my ancestors – was often characterized by the willingness to capture the people's attention by actively distracting them. It was about push communications, about massive media plans and aggressive repetitions, which have now developed into something called 'retargeting'. That being said, it is important to state that my generation is not harm-free at all. We grew up with technology within our daily consumer behaviour, and our self-understanding about privacy and data has brought us to a state in which algorithms and robotics dictate how ads are played out.

In that sense, we are no better. But we are different.

Therefore it's important to acknowledge and embrace the fact we like different things. We like sports. But we like gaming, too. And now those two things are merging. As I have stated above, there are two big strategies: breaking through the clutter or breaking out of the clutter. The solution to both is creativity. And creativity is what lies at the heart of marketing and thereby the festival.

Not everything is bad, my friends. It's a great time to live as a marketer! And here's your shot.

ART, MEET SCIENCE

Marissa Nance, OMD

Science. Yes, while that can be a big and scary word to some, let's all take a step back and remember that it absolutely doesn't have to be. Every one of us depends on some form of science, especially those who consider themselves artists. Behind each creative ingredient, angle, punch or stroke, there is a level of science that is making it possible, even if just intuitively. Which makes these two concepts, art and science, more like partners than enemies. If we view ourselves – we members of the advertising and marketing world – as 'modern artists', by pairing art with science we can create an entirely integrated conversation that delivers everything we need to propel our work towards success. When we sit down to talk about the *art* of branded entertainment, which in our case has a lot to do with attracting the audience to justify the investment, at some point we must touch the science behind that, too. Because it's that science that allows a brilliant idea to be as big as it deserves. Also, let's be clear, by science I'm not referring to the metrics or algorithms behind a campaign, although they have a place; I'm referring to making sure you are being strategic and smart in your approach in addition to being idea- and content-driven.

Since I am driven to view creativity through a strategic lens, I had some challenges while judging the branded entertainment category during the 2017 Cannes Lions. Based on many of the entries we saw, it felt to me as if the industry's focus on branded entertainment exhibited tunnel vision as it locked on to the content or story by itself. We saw very few examples that really balanced this 'art meets science' formula. Which is honestly just silly. There is no shame in creating amazing content, full of creative integrity, that is able to live a full life generating return on the investment (ROI). After that experience my goal was to spend my time with you here, in this book, sharing why this is such an important aspiration for us all to have.

Entertainment. Sales. Engagement. ROI. We recognize these terms and know they are consistently used in reference to the art of branded entertainment, but do any of us really know what they mean? Are we just throwing out the buzzwords we think our partners want to hear? Generally, the eventual funding source of most branded entertainment is a *brand*. With that in mind, in this chapter we're going to explore the basics of what an advertiser should build into and around their branded entertainment strategy and partnerships. We'll also look at the results brands should want to achieve and how they might measure success. Again I take us back to the art-meets-science scenario. I'm hoping to reinforce the idea that if a brand can perfect this balance the returns are limitless.

Content – context – commerce

In 2010 many were still reeling from the effects of the Great Recession. The 'little guys' in particular, who were working to build a life on the back of small businesses, were having a tough time. These companies needed a platform of support, and that's exactly what American Express delivered with *Small Business Saturday*, one of the most awarded campaigns in the history of Cannes. More than an ad campaign, Amex created and funded what I would define as a branded entertainment *movement*, driven by long- and short-form stories (more than traditional commercials) that ran across digital and linear media, content that not only told the stories of these small businesses but was relatable in scope and scale to the audiences they reached, even if those people weren't entrepreneurs themselves. Not only was it delivered at just the right touch points, it was shared by media partners that mattered to the story (including Twitter and Facebook). The context of asking consumers to support small businesses while they were within their personal and 'safe' social-community environment provided an authentic connection to the problem.

The idea worked. As it grew, by 2013 the *Small Business Saturday* platform led to more than $5 billion in sales. It not only generates commerce for the businesses on that one Saturday but has also created opportunities for ongoing revenue throughout the year.

Small Business Saturday is an example of what I believe to be a great branded entertainment programme, and many agree with me.[1] It is brand-funded marketing, rooted in compelling stories that engage the consumer and achieve the brand's desired goals.

Now let's take a deeper look at exactly how to create this kind of successful branded entertainment partnership. We'll detail all of the advantages that advertisers must look to create for themselves as they build out ideas and partnerships to extend brand messages.

First, here's an easy tool to help you remember what branded entertainment programmes should do to be worth your investment:

- It should provide the brand with an incremental level of entertainment, engagement and education through its overall story. Let's call it *content*.
- It should elevate a brand's messaging, functionality and purpose through where that content is placed. Let's call that *context*.
- It should generate a consumer response for the brand through ambassadorship, usage and sales. To preserve the alliteration, we will call it *commerce*.

From now on you'll remember these three Cs to help you stay steady in your journey. *Content. Context. Commerce.* Since we've established that most in the industry have had a head start at understanding the *content*, we'll launch our conversation by examining the industry gaps we find in creating solid *context* and *commerce* for our stories.

Be true to yourself

The most important North Star as you build out a branded entertainment partnership is protecting your brand's identity and its value proposition. Maintaining this at all costs is your goal. So it goes without saying that no branded entertainment strategy will work for a brand that hasn't already done 'the work'.

Before a brand can explore branded entertainment integrations in new (or existing) content, the brand must have a clear sense of self.

What is it? What does it stand for? What is its functionality? Who is it trying to reach? Who is it not trying to reach? Does it have a clear sales or service message? Is there an iconic tagline or image or ambassador that needs to be aligned and protected in the process? These are all important questions to review and understand before entering into a branded entertainment partnership. It was noted in earlier chapters, and I think it's important to remind everyone again here: your branded entertainment work *must* integrate seamlessly into your broader marketing campaign. The brand *positioning* and media *context* are always more powerful when working in lockstep together.

As a part of Procter & Gamble's ongoing *My Black Is Beautiful* campaign, it created the beautiful spot called *The Talk*, which *Adweek* picked as one of the most powerful ads of 2017.[2] In the spot, African-American parents talk to their children about racial bias. They could have stopped there. But they didn't. They expanded into a partnership with the TV show *Black-ish* to extend their African-American-targeted campaign into an entire thirty-minute episode of the show.[3] The ability to link P&G's messaging and tone to a show that consistently delivers similar conversations was more than authentic; it was ideal. There was no concession of art meets science here because the *art* in the show's award-winning writing *was* the science of the brand's overarching consumer outreach. The products were all naturally integrated and, moreover, could be used by any of the talent on-air and no one would think twice. Any of those elements (campaign, show, products) were strong on their own; all of the elements become even stronger together as a seamless conversation.

P&G's initiative is a perfect example of how branded entertainment can enhance a marketing campaign. But a brand isn't just its most recent campaign. Chipotle's award-winning *The Scarecrow* short film is an incredible example of how branded entertainment can do more than enhance a marketing campaign; it can also amplify a company mission. The story of a scarecrow who decides to leave his job at the evil food corporation and start his own organic roadside stand, no matter the cost, actually did more than elevate Chipotle's marketing, it raised awareness around the company's mission statement.[4] Chipotle is a company dedicated to seeking out the very best ingredients it can, raised with respect for animals, farmers and the environment. By creating an entertaining story of uplift rooted in those ideals (with, frankly, very limited branding), Chipotle and its creative partners allowed consumers to connect with the company through engaging entertainment and not just a commercial, all in an authentic and natural way.

If you intend to create branded entertainment as a standalone or one-off tactic, you could be heading down a dangerous (and expensive) path. Confirming you have positioned your product, packaging, advertising, mission and sales initiatives as direct links to your branded entertainment ensures not only success but significant opportunities for cost, time and manpower efficiencies.

Once a brand is sure of itself, finding clarity in the type of channel, partner or content it can align with should be much easier. Reaching women on a male-skewing network makes no sense. Targeting female tweens on an adult male channel won't achieve any goals or elevate any of the existing messaging – or, frankly, work. Placing your curated and protected packaging, mascot, logo or tagline in the context of a completely opposite conversation could harm and even kill all of the equity you have built.

The question to really think about is who you are partnering with. Is it someone who proves to be worthy of your investment? Is it someone worthy of your time and your brand? The most popular person in the room is not always the person you should stand next to. Many partners will insist they know how to work with your brand, but nine times out of ten their promise is being driven by their own goal: revenue. Always work to find a partner with the same integrity and positioning that your brand has in order to secure a drama-free path to success. Never settle.

Set yourself on the right path

One reminder. In terms of context, be open to non-traditional channels that can still authentically convey your story. While partnering with TV, film and/or digital distribution is still the most likely landing place for the content, you might also end up creating an amazing out-of-home experience that surrounds your stories. Simply put, the idea is fairly straightforward: 'Don't fight the natural connection points your content leans into.' Just because you think it would be perfect for the big screen, it may have other ideas and want to end up online. Many of the concepts we saw felt like they could have been so much more, but instead they were implemented to be the 'same old, same old' TV or digital experiences. Take a risk and let your creative ideas live where they want to live.

While judging, one of the most out-of-the-box ideas our group saw was an Xbox activation in the UK. The gaming brand timed the event to take place when the Christmas lights were turned on in UK high streets (a popular annual event) and engaged nearly half-a-million gamers around the world to jump in and be a part of the history of their new game. They knew they had to produce the expected trailer commercial for the launch of their Christmas-themed game 'Dead Rising 4'. But at Christmas TV is cluttered. So instead of simply filming the expected trailer to premiere on TV and online, Xbox built a world into the actual outdoor experience for it to live in. *Zombie Christmas*, the first ever real-world trailer, was built of animated Christmas lights and installed in the Brunswick Centre near Russell Square in central London.

On the day the lights were due to be turned on more than 500,000 gamers interacted to reveal an exclusive new story that only existed outdoors. Everyone in London could visit, and if you weren't in London you could 'feel' like you were there via the interactive cameras on site. The experience became a destination, and millions visited either in person or online. *Zombie Christmas* was one the biggest game launches for Xbox. In the end they beat their anticipated sales goals by more than 30%.[5]

Zombie Christmas is a great use of branded entertainment in the outdoor space while integrating it across social, digital and content spaces. Many of us just don't think of non-digital media as cutting edge or innovative today. That's a shame. Finding a like-minded print brand and audience to share your ideas (written and visual) could be the perfect place to be seen. In the world of podcasts, a brand could launch the next *War of the Worlds* à la Orson Welles and create a timeless activation. Playing in cinemas or on TV doesn't have to be the gold standard for measuring your success; being in the place or places your audience will react to most favourably should be, however.

Letting commerce shine

After confirming your brand alignment and context it is most important to set, maintain and achieve a clear set of goals for results against your campaign. These may be in the form of impressions, awareness or commerce.

While we all know the traditional gold star in ROI is profitability through sales and revenue, it is important to consider that there may be additional milestones for your campaign as it is built and activated. One strong alternative measurement of success for your brands is the value in establishing connections with a brand ambassador who authentically understands, appreciates and approves of your product. Today we call those people 'influencers'. There is a real advantage to be found in their ability to sell your product to those who are going to become repeat buyers. This is especially true for high-end or luxury products. I may not be able to afford a Mercedes, but if I consistently support and value the car publicly those who can afford the car will be listening and will react accordingly through purchase and sales.

Another key measurement is in usage. Many believe usage and sales are the same, but they aren't for any number of brands. There is example after example of brands being used by someone who wasn't its purchaser. Yet once that person uses the product and becomes an ambassador they can continue to evangelize to others, creating interest and *then* eventual sales.

Finally, examine the feasibility of establishing a pre-set tracking measurement for the correlation your branded entertainment will have against your revenue projections. The easiest way to do this is to bring in a retail partner from the beginning. When you're creating goals be sure to have sales consultants from your third-party retailer along with your internal revenue teams for consultation and remarks. Knowing that your investment has to yield two times, three times or more in revenue or commerce gives you a solid benchmark to achieve and work towards. Make sure as you're building towards your retail goals that you have all of your partners in lockstep and they are moving towards them with you. This means making sure you have third-party retail pass-through rights in every deal you negotiate. Then, your shared sales/revenue goals are evident from the start and the definition of true success can be visible to all involved.

But do the numbers add up?

Here we should pause and talk about the overall industry approach to measuring branded entertainment. In short, there is *no* industry standard. Many agencies, brands and channels have their own way of measuring. If the final method of valuation you choose is the ability to determine how close to the goals the campaign was, then your individual equations are fine. If, on the other hand, there are no metrics set and the end measurement is fluid at best, it will be a disservice to the brand, the investment and your audience.

When we talk about commerce I want to stress that this does not mean we ignore the goal of innovative and amazing content. Balance! On one side, you can't assume that by selling with your logo attached to a piece of content it automatically becomes branded entertainment and certainly not good branded entertainment. On the other, waxing poetic without giving any thought to your audience, your ROI and your distribution will likely yield nothing but a wasted investment. If you aren't willing to really go the extra distance you will face ramifications – so much so that I'll remind you that the Cannes Lions juries prior to ours did not even award any Grand Prix recognition in the branded entertainment category for several years running.

Luckily our jury was able not only to award a Grand Prix, we were able to salute a piece of content that truly was a balance of content, context and commerce. *Beyond Money*, as other authors have written before me, was custom content created with Santander Bank. Santander wanted to launch an account targeting millennials but was having a hard time selling to an audience that did not trust it or want to listen. The bank created a seventeen-minute film set in the near future. It was a future in which you could sell and buy experiences stored in your memory. The bank did significant research then leveraged any feelings their audience had surrounding banking and used this film to address them head on. Facing the criticism rather than avoiding it, the bank used the film to create a sense of appreciation and admiration and even trust between themselves and their millennial target audience. Through the film and its positive lessons, in a time in which most banks aren't trusted by anyone – let alone millennials – Santander got its fastest sign-up rate in more than 160 years of history, achieving nearly 35% (!) of its twelve-month business goals in only two short weeks.[6] Extraordinary commerce ROI resulting from just as extraordinary content.

Content vision on point

Next to context I personally believe content is the easiest workstream to follow in a branded entertainment campaign. Why? Here again, if your brand proposition is on point from the start, being able to recognize either new or existing authentic content to immerse it in should be clear. What *does* become an issue at this step in the process is that many advertisers may miss the need to secure some level of supporting quantitative research, insights and statistics to wrap around their content ideation and creation. Again, our goal is always about achieving that art-meets-science result. When you are looking to engage your audience, knowing what and *why* they think a certain way is crucial.

Look what taking the extra step did for Santander. Focus groups, social anthropology, competitive studies will all help you generate content that is suitable, lasting and engaging. Just be prepared to be nimble in your study, since today's consumers are fluid and flexible. Your audience members are changing their minds and desires by the day, minute or second. Also, be balanced. This doesn't mean taking all of the free thought from your idea and making it strictly a numbers game. It just means finding ways for creative innovation to shine strategically and smartly.

Knowing *how* to partner in the creative journey becomes

sometimes just as important as the end content itself. No matter the goal, you must be prepared to act as your brand's first and foremost creative leader. Explore sites that your initial research has told you make sense from a context perspective. Who are the studios and creators that have alignment with your brand's messaging? Just because someone is a leader in branded entertainment with awards and accolades it does not mean they are the perfect fit for you or your story. Sometimes it's smart to look for less known but very synergistic influencers or publishers. There you can find the right message and sometimes for a better price.

You also want to create content that resonates for your brands and your brands alone. Paying for something that any brand could create is worthless and not smart. Doing that with a fellow journeyman, who can represent everything your brand is, shows you're protecting your message and your goals.

During our jury vote, we reviewed a *Lego Batman* campaign that was a partnership between *The Lego Batman Movie* and UK's Channel 4. The film's producers worked with the station to co-create a series of custom content letting Batman 'take over' the airways before the film's release. In character, Batman, voiced by the film's star Will Arnett, handled all of the on-air promotions for the channel during an entire weekend. Whatever was coming next, the little paladin of justice was there to announce it with his irreverent, egotistical, hilarious voice. It was fantastic and *customized* content that literally could only have been made in support of the film. Partnering with Channel 4 was a perfect fit in terms of tone and style. In the end not only was wonderful content co-produced it also led to ticket sales from nearly one out of every six viewers.[7] Amazing!

Schooling our audience

A key factor in telling 'balanced' branded entertainment stories is the entertainment-meets-education value you must find. We know from traditional advertising that it's not enough to engage our entertainment consumers, we also have to educate them on the unique value proposition our specific brand brings them. Show them the functionality or effectiveness or value that they will find by buying our product rather than the competition. This isn't an easy task, and when you're elevating your communication from a traditional ad to branded entertainment it can be even more difficult. Most consumers consider themselves to be savvy and will call you out for marketing to them rather than entertaining them. Knowing your product and the way it can be seamlessly integrated into existing content, stories or talent is a great first step. Taking that thinking further and creating your own unique stories to wrap around the brand is the highest level you can achieve. If you've done all of the work you can and *will* get to that point.

This year one of the jury's favourite ideas was *The Debut*, a partnership between Budweiser and ESPN in Brazil. As mentioned in previous chapters, Bud sponsors the NBA broadcast in that country. They've been a sponsor for years and were looking for ways to elevate that relationship and re-engage consumers beyond running their commercials. When Bud realized that Oscar Schmidt was Brazil's greatest basketball player yet had never played a single NBA game they knew they had an opportunity to tell an important story. This would be a story that would elevate their message while educating an entire generation about an amazing athlete and man. Bud co-produced an exclusive event, documentary and activation around the fateful day that Oscar finally had the chance to play in a game. Everyone in the country wanted to be part of the story, and many appreciated the brand for bringing it to light. Bud consumer engagement was indicative of their consumers' positive reactions.[8] The campaign was *more* than just marketing; in the end it was a movement. It was a touching and moving piece of content; it absolutely aligned with the brand's universe, and it was created by a creative agency and fully executed by the network partner.

See? It is possible.

Be a warrior

We have to reiterate. When you partner with a distributor, channel or talent to bring your story to life be *protective* of your content. It is absolutely OK for you to check background. Explore their social conversations. Understand their messaging and previous work. If anything doesn't line up with your messaging and goals then you can and should walk away. Also, don't be intimidated. Just because someone is a known director, producer or writer doesn't mean you can't stand up for your brand and its needs. Remember, you have a value and the biggest strength you bring is that you recognize the best way possible to bring that branded content message to life. You might look no further than the decades-long relationships many brands have had with James Bond films throughout the years. These participating brands have contributed *millions* of advertising dollars to support the films, providing invaluable support.[9] Positive and mutually beneficial relationships such as those can equal leverage and clout for how your brand is seen and heard. It's important you find vendor partners who understand there is a balance in the relationship that must yield success for all. Today, in 2018, they should be willing to work with you and not against you. The perfect partner does exist for your brand – you just have to be willing to put in the time it takes to find them.

So how does this all come to life?

Here are five ways traditional and non-traditional branded enter-tainment tactics can align with our content, context and commerce approach.

1. 'Retail-tainment'

As mentioned, branded entertainment doesn't have to exist only in traditional channels. With the growing demise of shopping malls, their ownership is constantly looking for ways to reinvigorate foot traffic while creating a source of revenue. Of course, the fact that the USA has an overabundance of space – 2.2 square metres (23 square feet) of shopping space for everyone in the country as of April 2009 – married with the rise in digital spending of all sales means their task isn't easy.[10] This is where branded entertainment steps in.

In Dallas, for example, one mall worked with retail partner LEGO to add a $12 million 3,700-square-metre (40,000-square-foot) LEGO Discovery Center and a 93-square-metre (10,000-square-foot) miniature golf course made with LEGO. This allows for LEGO to create an immersive entertainment experience for consumers while promoting its products and sales. In Shanghai, visitors can visit a new six-storey 3,440-square-metre (37,000-square-foot) House of Barbie. While there, consumers can do much more than just shop. They can model Barbie-style clothes, learn to sing and dance to the 'Barbie Girl' song and dine in the café. A highlight is a visit to the Pink Room, complete with a bar, karaoke, DJ and pink martinis. There is a day spa, a hair salon and shopping for more than 1,600 Barbie products.[11]

Retail-tainment isn't new. Apple stores have been entertaining consumers using their brand messaging and tonality since the advent of their unique store model. With their Genius Bar and hourly tutorials, the staff regularly promotes the Apple brand for purchase while engaging the consumers in real time. They know they have piqued customer interest at a highly effective purchase-decision-making point.

2. Immersion marketing

I call taking your branded entertainment concept to multiple touch points that will engage and move consumers to purchase '360' or 'immersion marketing'. Creating a consistent surrounding drumbeat using the talent, messaging, content, imagery and ideas behind your branded entertainment is not only effective but can also be cost-efficient in terms of reach and scale.

In the USA one popular consumer packaged goods company (CPG) wanted to engage Hispanic women hoping to increase sales of its product within that market. The company knew this was an audience that was discerning and very clear in its likes and dislikes. Speaking to the audience in an inauthentic way would only damage their relationship and could potentially decrease rather than increase sales. With its agency and the leading US Spanish-language broadcaster, the company created a custom 360 platform specifically to reach its target audience. The content was filled with tips and ideas to help make life easier for viewers. Some of these tips included placement of the company product usage and messaging as the 'hero'. The platform lived on TV, audio, streaming, online and through top influencer talent. Most importantly, the programme was able to live within a retail partner's ecosystem. Together with that retail partner the CPG was able to predetermine the metrics of sales success they wanted to achieve. During the span of the programme they were able to create custom activations with that retailer which helped their sales increase by more than 40% year on year.

When you have a clear vision of where your target is, how they want to be approached and what they want to hear, you are prepared to create entertainment that can effortlessly surround them at all valid touch points with your brand's message and functionality.

3. Native content

Unless you're hiding under a rock as a marketer or content creator you'll have heard the buzzy phrase 'native content'. Many people and companies in our industry like to equate native content with branded entertainment. That should not be the case. Much like retail-tainment or immersion, native content is a form/channel of branded entertainment but by no means sums up the category as a whole. When an advertiser is making an ad buy and can extend beyond a traditional ad to more of a customized partnership with the media vendor, who will then also distribute the content, they are following the native content trend. Simply put, think of branded entertainment as an overarching strategy, while native content is a tactic, specifically deciding to work with one synergistic partner in both your editorial and distribution.[12]

In 2017 Samsung partnered with popular animal blog 'The Dodo' to highlight the Galaxy S8. After realizing that a high majority of its users were animal owners and lovers, Samsung knew this could be a solid aperture to reach them. They went to 'The Dodo' and asked for 'native' content to be created and then distributed on the site that integrated their products and leveraged this insight. 'The Dodo' produced a short film about a photographer who snaps adorable shots of rescue dogs wearing floral headgear. The film racked up an incredible 12 million views on Facebook alone, and the Samsung brand integration was perfect. Subtle at first, with the photographer snapping a few photos on a Samsung device, it was then woven in again via an interactive gallery using Samsung's Gear VR device, before you finally realized that the entire video was created on a Samsung Galaxy S8. Samsung is our hero.[13]

Be sure to fully understand the difference between your broad branded entertainment strategy and the integrated tactics you can then use to support it. Native, immersion or more traditional media can all provide the desired results within the right budgets and channels.

4. Branded webisodes

Marriott International's Moxy Hotels partnered with YouTube to create the *Do Not Disturb* series in which YouTube celebrities created custom content that aligned with Marriott guests' interests. Marriott made sure to secure deep consumer insights and research before initiating its content, so it felt confident its stories would be appealing and engaging. Here the brand specifically aimed to reach millennials. Because of the young target audience it made sense to use social media statistics as milestones.

After measurement, Marriott saw social media mentions

increase by 167% from the previous quarter. Additionally, as a result of the series, the average time spent on the Marriott YouTube channel increased from forty-three seconds in the previous quarter to two minutes fifty-four seconds during the campaign – a 270% increase.[14]

5. Never been done before

Sometimes you have to take a gamble and go for a big branded entertainment partnership to really make your brand and its message stand out. This means you're going to have solid insights, a great team and as much preparation as you can possibly secure. But if it works it could work big, just like it did for Tide's Super Bowl *The Bradshaw Stain*. The piece was a winner at the 2017 Cannes Lions Festival in multiple categories. In partnership with one of the world's biggest entertainment platforms, the Super Bowl, Tide was able to create a never-been-done-before approach to content by integrating into the live game's half-time show, then taking that conversation seamlessly into their already produced ad content storylines during the commercial break before finally come back to the live show for the audience pay-off.

The story was simple. Broadcaster Terry Bradshaw was seen on live TV with a stain on his white shirt. How would he clean it before the end of the game? The story then went to the already produced ads where we see Terry's journey to clean the shirt. Then when the show came back live he was wearing a cleaned shirt again, thanks to Tide. The consumers were able to follow the journey to see how Terry Bradshaw would solve his stain problem, understanding eventually that Tide was the true hero of the game. Tide was able to clean the stain *and* entertain everyone in a new and innovative way. The brand saw 4.8 billion media impressions, over a hundred tweets per minute, 600 'free' media placements/mentions and, *most tellingly*, they saw a 22% *increase* in their sales numbers.[15] One important thing to note: when you are trying something that has never been done before you may have to take a giant leap of . . . faith.

Yes, there were without a doubt pages of reasons why the agency and the client should *not* have attempted to bring this programme to life. It was complicated. It hinged on talent. It could have been overshadowed by the game . . . It was live! With big risk comes big reward, and there is something to be said for having the faith that your insights, research and preparation will bring success. And even if it doesn't, you tried something that had never been done before. You *tried*!

So is this really going to work?

The million-dollar question seems clear. Is branded entertainment the future? If we've succeeded in achieving our content, context and commerce, does that mean these partnerships and platforms are the primary tactics brands should use to achieve ROI? I think it has to be a large part of our marketing future, but, unfortunately, with the fast-clip growth of the marketing industry and technology, no one can truly answer that question for sure. What we can do is look at the surrounding environment and influences to track trends and possibility. Specifically, be aware of what is happening today and what will happen in the near future as you evaluate branded entertainment tactics within your brand's marketing plan.

Even if you don't agree with branded entertainment, this may be our only path forward. While that sounds a little ominous, it may not be far from the truth. Today consumers have so many choices. They can view their content in so many ways. A common denominator is that they can do all of this *without* having to watch a single traditional ad. Streaming and on-demand enables viewers to pay for the right to avoid ads. With that there may be no other option but to find positive and authentic ways to partner directly with the content and integrate brand messaging. If done well, all of the parties involved can find success and benefits. If done poorly, everyone is looking at a negative response – *especially* the brands involved.

So if you are an advertiser creating branded entertainment partnerships in this chapter I hope we've established the journey you must take. You must be true to your brand's positioning and context. You must know your audience and create authentic content for them. You must establish measurable commercial goals from the start and a clear strategy on how to meet them. If you are able truly and honestly to say you've done these things then you will have a chance of creating incredible content and finding the success you deserve.

Good luck!

1. http://adage.com/lp/top15/#smallsaturday
2. http://www.adweek.com/brand-marketing/parents-have-the-talk-in-powerful-my-black-is-beautiful-campaign-from-pg/
3. http://variety.com/2018/tv/news/procter-gamble-blackish-tv-advertising-abc-1202664501/
4. https://www.chipotle.com/company
5. http://jacobjim.com/zombie.html
6. https://www.youtube.com/watch?v=sxwciMHwfto
7. https://www.campaignlive.co.uk/article/lego-batman-wins-day-warner-bros-channel-4/1448011
8. http://www.digitaltrainingacademy.com/casestudies/2018/01/budweiser_revives_a_brazilian_basketball_legend_to_share_its_core_values.php
9. https://www.theguardian.com/media-network/2015/oct/22/spectre-james-bond-007-brands-marketing-sony-heineken-belvedere
10. https://www.whitehutchinson.com/leisure/articles/retail-tainment.shtml
11. ibid.
12. https://en.wikipedia.org/wiki/Native_advertising
13. http://adage.com/article/agency-viewpoint/10-branded-content-partnerships-2017/311725/
14. https://contently.com/strategist/2016/02/23/study-branded-web-series/
15. https://www.cnbc.com/2017/06/27/the-best-advertising-campaigns-that-won-awards-at-cannes-lions-in-2017.html

Part 4
THE BUSINESS

THE HOLLYWOOD WAY

Jules Daly, RSA Films

Forget budgets. Forget the superstar director or in-demand actor – even platforms and length. Forget them all.

If there is one thing I have learned from working with Ridley and Tony Scott for twenty-eight years it's that every story starts with an idea. Find an explosive one; everything else takes care of itself. That's how they made *Blade Runner, The Martian, The Good Wife, The Andromeda Strain* and so many other unforgettable stories.

To this day I see Ridley's face light up when that spark ignites. He picks up a pen and a piece of paper and starts to draw. A mountain, a face, an ocean, a building, a piece of wardrobe. One second, and the idea comes to life. Pure, singular, beautiful.

Of course, eventually that purity is challenged by reality. Constraints, surprises, inconsistencies . . . But the quest for the right idea (and the right way to express it) requires a resilient spirit. The challenges always push creators further. And when they find the solutions it feels electric.

It was that unstoppable search for the perfect expression of a pure idea that made the Scott brothers two of the greatest storytellers across many generations and platforms. Under them my training has been like church. I've watched the duo work under their divine inspiration, transforming ideas big and small into revolutionary projects that change everything around them. Whether it is a feature film, a TV series, a commercial, branded entertainment or even now the six-second bumper ad, their enthusiasm, and that of those they trained, has always been the same.

Looking at the work we judged this year I could recognize signs of the same passion, and that is an inspiration. So I thought I would share some of the things I've learned from those two and the crowd of brilliant film-makers with whom I have worked in the past three decades; lessons that may help this new wave of talent mixing brands and entertainment into the best versions of themselves. Maybe one of you will come up with the next *Thelma & Louise, Alien* or the '1984' TV ad for Apple.

No matter what, keep pushing

Ridley and Tony are two of only a few leading directors who have produced content for different media – movies, TV and advertising – that have been published on such a variety of different platforms: the big screen, the small screen, digital and VR. I have been blessed to have learned from the best.

Neither ever stopped the process of creating and nurturing an idea. If inspiration called, they always answered. And since, at least for them, it was always calling, working with them was a constant happy search for answers from anywhere, on all levels. It's a way of life. A very curious, obsessive and unstoppable one. Ridley is still a creative mind after cameras start rolling. Tony would cut and paste a script, commercial or film up until the final second of the last day of shooting. He was always striving to make it bolder or stronger, always pushing to find a deeper meaning.

That shows in the work. If you watch any of the movies or commercials made by the Scott family you will be surprised – by the unexpected, the bold and the original. They have driven producers crazy, but their persistent vison always turned a great piece of work into a brilliant one.

> There's a little thing on your shoulder called intuition, and it whispers in your ear. Everyone has that, there is a voice telling you to do something. Most people ignore it – but you must listen to it. I do it every day, all day. – Ridley Scott

Explorers, go explore

In 2001 BMW and Fallon approached RSA Films to launch a dark action/comedy series of the ilk that only Tony Scott could create. The three-part series starred Don Cheadle, F. Murray Abraham, James

Brown, Gary Oldman, Clive Owen, Danny Trejo, Ray Liotta and Dennis Haysbert among others. It included three 'subplot movies' that furthered the plot and incorporated an alternate-reality game for avid fans.

Hostage, directed by John Woo, was the first episode. The FBI enlists 'the Driver' in an attempt to remedy a hostage situation gone awry. As more information about the kidnapper and the victim are revealed, the situation becomes ever more complex.

In Episode 2, *Ticker*, directed by Joe Carnahan, dangerous stakes come into play as the Driver and his wounded passenger are fired at from a helicopter overhead. The helicopter shoots at a briefcase as it begins to count down. What's in the briefcase and who is this mysterious passenger? All is revealed in this episode, which features a BMW Z4 3.0i.

James Brown plays himself in the third episode, *Beat the Devil*, directed by Tony Scott himself. According to the film, the soul legend made a deal at the dawn of his fame to trade his soul for his career. Considering his status now, he hires the Driver to renegotiate said deal, offering a new wager instead that takes the Driver to the Las Vegas strip for some action and adventure.

Looking back, it sounds like an idea that, of course, should have been made. But step out of your time machine and take a good look around. Back then there wasn't such a thing as branded entertainment as a discipline. Long formats were sixty-second spots like Ridley's '1984', made for Apple and Chiat\Day for Steve Jobs. Speeds in those days were such that you'd have to download overnight, yet, against all the logic of that time, it happened – and changed advertising for ever.

These films are still seen as a benchmark of branded entertainment – brave and with the scale to cross platforms. Many car companies (Audi, Jaguar, Mercedes, Ford – see below for examples) have since used fictional content with celebrated actors as a way to try to build their brand and create an emotional link with their audiences. It all started there, with David Lubars's (then at Fallon Worldwide now Global Chief Creative at BBDO) and Tony's drive to explore.

Fast forward to 2018. We've moved on so much.

We are surrounded by a wealth of platforms desperate for ideas to keep their audiences entertained and thrilled. There is financing available to us from all walks of life, from brands to streaming services to private financing.

A great democracy has been born. Every age and demographic in most corners of the world with Wi-Fi and access to smartphones can create their own stories, film them and send them out into the universe. You no longer need millions of dollars and a cast and crew of hundreds to tell a story that reaches and touches people all over the globe. There is a plethora of platforms on which you can publish your content – YouTube, Facebook, Instagram, Snapchat – and the content is valuable in a very different way to traditional content. It does not compete with cinema blockbusters but sits alongside them.

Our diverse needs, after all, are met across multiple platforms. We curate our own content consumption – from *Game of Thrones* to the latest *Star Wars* film to content from social media influencers, our friends and families. We look for different things at different times. We may want to binge-watch on Netflix, practise yoga with YouTube, go to a cinema to experience a movie in all its dimensions or virtually attend our friend's wedding via Instagram stories. The content might not win an Oscar . . . but it might win a digital Emmy or a Webby or a Lion . . . there are multiple parameters for judgement and accolade. And don't be fooled: the greatest names in entertainment are all watching closely, looking for opportunities to explore this new world themselves.

At the heart of this new world is branded entertainment. It is on the point of finally becoming what we have all been searching and hoping for. The democracy of platforms has allowed branded entertainment to become mainstream because the risk of creating an expensive one-off project has been eliminated.

Spreading the word

We at RSA are lucky enough to see many powerful branded-content projects. More and more brands and agencies are spending time pitching, designing and creating what I believe is our future. But there has never been an instance in the infancy of one of these projects where our partners haven't asked us if we had any ideas for distribution. Of course, posting on a brand's website is the first rite of passage – and largely a good start. But how do we get these ideas past just our industry? How do we reach a larger audience? This to me is the golden but elusive ticket.

BMW Films first launched online before premiering on DirecTV. The films were so successful that DirecTV rethought its advertising strategy to incorporate other companies' ads on their vacant channels. That was in 2001.

Distribution. Seventeen years later our nemesis remains.

I applaud the courageous agencies that are coming up with ideas and partnerships for longer content. I applaud those who push their clients to try to release their stories in new spaces. But how do we curate and support content for new platforms? So many beautifully crafted films of all lengths are not seen by the size of audience they deserve. Take *Lifeline* from Qualcomm. This Cannes Entertainment Lions entry is a thirty-minute psychological thriller in which the phone becomes one of the protagonists. It won a Bronze Lion. And where could you find it? Either on the brand's own website or lost on YouTube. All that investment in a genre piece of entertainment that did not get the audience it could have done. If we fix this issue the market will explode with potential and positivity. Even those less adventurous brands, the more cautious spenders, will then open up and start the next stage of this journey.

Media agencies know what to do with a thirty-second spot, but they haven't cracked the magic formula of where and how to distribute branded entertainment. They have some thoughts and tactics, which our co-author Marissa Nance explores in her chapter 'Art, Meet Science'. But we need more than partnering with current channels if we want to give great ideas the visibility they deserve. Of course, YouTube has been a game-changer; Facebook with its Watch tab may also stand up to compete with it. But neither platform really helps us communicate and properly support our product. Once we've made strong, creative content with the brand at its heart, what do we do with it? Where do we put it to ensure it wins the audience it deserves? I'm afraid I don't yet have the answers, but am watching how the landscape changes over the coming years as the most courageous brands and film-makers continue to innovate and experiment.

Best practices

The beauty of travelling to uncharted universes is that you can invent the rules. Trying doesn't hurt that much. It didn't hurt when David Lubars and Fallon came to us with *BMW Films*, and it doesn't hurt now with so few 'best practices' established yet.

So be brave! Invent a format. Shoot big. Make a full season of a TV series. Create a mega-concert, a feature film with the brand at its heart. Work with the best planners to find new ways of getting your content out there.

In 2017 we saw *Lo and Behold*, which was funded by NetScout and distributed to cinemas around the world. Not only that, it was directed by none other than Werner Herzog. They dreamed, dared . . . it happened.

Another of our Gold winners, Lacta's *From the Start*, started as a web series that went on Greece's main TV channel, the same journey made by the BMW films. And I mean that as a compliment. We are not here to take pride in the distribution but in the ideas that inspire everything and everyone. How we reach the audiences is something we should all be sharing more and discussing more. So much so we even created a chapter just for this: read Samantha Glynne's contribution 'Ideas That Scale' if you want to know more.

Collaborate

In 2018 Alejandro G. Iñárritu won another Oscar at the Academy's Governors Awards. The recognition came for his VR installation 'Carne y Arena', currently being exhibited at the Los Angeles County Museum of Art. The *Hollywood Reporter* said that 'Carne y Arena' is the first film production to truly capture the need for a 360-degree canvas. What no one is saying (yet) is that it happened as a partnership between Legendary, Emerson Collective, Hyundai and Prada.

Movie-making is a visionary art, yet it thrives on collaboration. In the past that happened between directors, actors, directors of photography . . . now brands are being invited to join the creative process, too.

Master film-makers such as Stefano Sollima (*Gomorrah*, *Sicario: Day of the Soldado* – a.k.a. *Sicario: Soldado 2*) have led the way. This year he directed *Campari Red Diaries 2018: The Legend of Red Hand*, a thriller that tells the journey of a woman, played by Zoe Saldana, in pursuit of the perfect cocktail. As yet this is destined for distribution on YouTube, but let's see if it goes beyond this platform.

Jake Scott has been another evangelist for the art form. He created *The Gentleman's Wager* with Anomaly for Johnny Walker Blue Label. It starred Jude Law and Giancarlo Giannini and is a playful take on a wager that the two friends set for a priceless boat. It debuted at the Venice Film Festival – a fitting premiere for a great piece of branded entertainment. 'The story form insists on living,' says Jake. 'It is fundamental to human communication and how [his] story is recorded. The advent of branded entertainment proves that audiences exist to be entertained and delighted, not tricked into buying something because we all love a good story.'

Jake also worked with Ford on the short film *Le Fantôme* (*The Ghost*). This eight-minute film centres on an enigmatic stranger and a couple who no longer exist. It stars Mads Mikkelsen as a hitman in pursuit of a couple starting a new life under witness protection. As he watches the pair closely and is about to attack, he gets distracted after catching a glimpse of their new Ford vehicle from afar.

The talent

Brilliance may come from both behind the camera and on-screen. Damien Lewis starred in Jaguar's *Desire* film with the Brooklyn Brothers, directed by Adam Smith. Judd Ehrlich (*We Could Be King*) directed the hard-hitting documentary *Keepers of the Game* for Dick's Sporting Goods, which garnered a Bronze Entertainment Lion in 2017.

Sometimes it comes from somewhere else. On 24 July 2010

thousands of people around the world uploaded videos of their lives to YouTube to take part in *Life in a Day*, a historic cinematic experiment to create a documentary film about a single day on earth.

Directed by Kevin Macdonald and executive-produced by Ridley Scott, *Life in a Day* wowed audiences around the world. And then it became scalable. It expanded to include *Britain in a Day*, *Israel in a Day*, *Germany in a Day*, *India in a Day* and the award-winning *Christmas in a Day*.

At Cannes Lions we saw a brand take this big idea and own it in the guise of *Spain in a Day*. This documentary feature was directed by Isabel Coixet and was a wonderful tribute to Spanish people experiencing life, love, grief, joy, hardship, cooking and eating. The company behind this film was Campofrio, a Spanish food group with many well-loved brands. The idea was not a new one, but the partnership with the brand was both synergistic and explosive.

Get in early

There is a saying in screenwriting that goes like this: 'Enter late, leave early.' When it comes to the future, though, that doesn't apply. Once a big trend takes shape, you want to be experienced in it already, because once it becomes hot no one will want to wait for you to learn. Right now this future is called VR and AR.

The Spielberg-backed VR start-up Dreamscape Immersive recently grabbed $30 million led by AMC and Nickelodeon to bring headsets into cinemas. Although AMC has an existing relationship with IMAX, Dreamscape is constructing a slightly different immersive platform: a location-based, room-scale experience. One of Dreamscape's strongest bets is that VR will save shopping malls. Currently there is a pop-up cinema on the first floor of the Westfield Century City shopping centre in Los Angeles called Alien Zoo: a twelve-minute multi-sensory experience that involves gearing up with sensory-equipped gloves, shoe covers, a backpack and a headset. This media provides enormous potential for brands who want to create truly immersive storytelling.

VR is a bridge, albeit one under construction, for humanity's transition from personal devices to personal universes. Everything we know is bound to change – today's computers and phones may be equipped with technology ranging from computer vision to blockchain, but all digital interfaces that we know today will have to be rebuilt from the ground up. At this moment there are more than 450 companies developing infrastructure, tools, platforms and applications for the entire virtual/augmented/mixed-reality industry. VR is expected to cause disruption on a vast scale, completely revolutionizing enterprise applications, education, social media and the $2 trillion entertainment market, all the while opening a door to a new way of being alive.

VR, too, supports our entertainment and is a game-changer in the world of marketing. I don't believe it's time to see an entire movie in VR, but its turn is coming.

Right now its strength is the experience – an additional, location-based event that can extend a product's story across so many beautiful ways and avenues. As mentioned, we did a sophisticated VR piece for *The Martian*. It has been celebrated as one of the most pioneering pieces of VR to date. We opened at Sundance in 2016 to rave reviews and six-hour-long queues in the snow. We followed it up with a prequel to a bigger piece for *Alien: Covenant* called 'In Utero', a 360-degree virtual reality journey into a living nightmare that offers a terrifyingly close and personal encounter as an alien neomorph at the time of its birth. 'In Utero' enables fans to experience the very first memories of the neomorph in an immersive environment. The 360-degree video had its debut on the Oculus app through the Rift, and Samsung Gear VR headsets then became available via Google Daydream View, HTC Vive and PlayStation VR.

In 2017's Cannes Entertainment Lions it was a pity that the VR projects did not receive the support they needed in the judging room (not enough equipment, entry guidelines that did not necessarily suit VR projects). Unfortunate. But I suspect that in the next few years VR is going to be a very important element in the branded entertainment space.

Love is hard to find

Ten years ago I told Ridley that audiences would watch *Gladiator* on their mobile phones. He looked at me as if I was crazy.

Now I am saying it again: dive into the new platforms.

So how do we move forward into this universe? First of all, make us film-makers part of the solution. Call upon us to be your partners and grow that idea. Every good idea is only one step away from landing on the right desk. If one production company or partner doesn't love it, call the next. Then, once we're on board, push us to be better, find people that are like-minded to be adventurous and courageous.

Do not settle for the norm.

The exciting thing about our time in advertising and entertainment is the variety of platforms. We have so many new options and innovative technologies – streaming, live events, VR, social platforms. But it also seems a bit chaotic, and that is where production companies need help to talk to the right audiences via the right media. This means that everyone is looking for partners to make good ideas happen. But it also means that things need to be really thought through. Working with planners and strategists has never been more important. The layers of support around a brand or idea are more vital than ever to the process.

The economics

Another lesson you learn in Hollywood is that money does the talking. Until you have the funding you have nothing. So if we want to take a film-maker approach to branded entertainment we need to ask ourselves: where is the money?

When you come home at night do you watch TV with commercials or do you watch Netflix? How our lives have shifted from watching network TV to streaming. Money is shifting and being spent in different places. The way forward is to be a part of solving that spend and creating this new world together so that it becomes commonplace. But we will not get there unless we break barriers and rules and encourage our partners to be the courageous ones.

At RSA we've been doing our homework. For years our company has had a few different divisions that work side by side. Now we work in sync. The film and TV worlds are supported by our new team at 3AM – not the time, the company. 3AM is a creative accelerator, working with film, TV and video-game creators to generate marketing and narrative opportunities from development through launch and beyond. Created specifically to meet the marketing needs of film-makers in a rapidly evolving industry, the operation was built to generate attention-earning content and strategic alliances between brands and movies through a unique approach that cultivates story, marketing and distribution from the very start of every project.

In 2018 the company has evolved to partner with television producers, gaming publishers and entertainment brands. We create alternative content and its distribution for the product we make – from a TED talk with Guy Pearce for *Prometheus* to a beautiful film called *Meet Walter* with Michael Fassbender for AMD to promote *Alien: Covenant*; from our VR project for *The Martian* to short films released on actors' Twitter pages for *Blade Runner 2049*.

And the talent is on board. They are more and more apt to embrace this way of marketing the film – this superpowered form of influencer-marketing – especially if they believe in it. They work a little longer one day or come in early on Saturday morning.

In fact, producing short content is a way to keep superstar talent invigorated, both in front of and behind the camera. Actors are trying their hands at directing and loving the challenge. As content creation becomes democratized, creators are embracing the problems that need solving in terms of telling a story. Directors are using a different muscle that some never realized they had after being behind the camera for so long. Matthew McConaughey, Ewan McGregor, Kristen Stewart and soon Bradley Cooper are all actors who are enjoying the new realm of directing spots or branded content.

But in the meantime my warrior cry is that brands and agencies should take the risk. Reach out to any film-maker, director, producer or writer that you want to work with. The magic about right now is that the current culture of curiosity makes anything possible. Everyone is open to a grand idea in big or small formats. Elevated talent on- and off-screen aren't opposed to partnering with brands or agencies as long as the idea is stand-out. Talent agencies are open and supportive to sharing great work with their clientele. But, as ever, nail the idea. Make that magic. Yes, big budgets can sometimes push it faster and open doors more quickly, but brilliance will always make it to the right hands.

Start, now

Brands are in a unique position to be ambassadors to this content. Technology and distribution are continuously changing the opportunities for you. So what can we do to further the cause? Start a film school. Give kids at high schools and colleges the chance to tell your brand's story with grants or small festivals. Help us challenge ourselves. If you work with a brand and you want to make a film, call a producer, call a director. Come up with your idea. Be flexible as to the process, because that's how great ideas get produced – in a messy, unstable and unpredictable way.

You either give up your step-by-step approval process or you have nothing to do in here. (PJ Pereira's look into some of the Grands Prix in the category in the final chapter of this book goes deeper into this.) But more important than anything is that you must start doing something.

Much of the pressure lands on us film-makers and the future film-makers. As Ridley said at BAFTA 2018: 'Go out and make a movie this weekend or stop moaning.' One of his favourite phrases is 'Just do it.' It's a rallying cry and a challenge to just get out and start shooting something. There are fewer excuses now than ever. Make a film on your phone. Tell your story and let the audience see your ideas come to life. Post it on Facebook or Instagram – and learn. If it's good, there is a chance that it will be seen and shared and – 'bam' – you are legitimate. This content might not win an Oscar or a Cannes Lion, but it might start you on the path to winning. Agents, managers, studio execs, presidents of production companies, we look at everything we can get our hands on. We scour these platforms for magic. So, film-makers . . . the world is your oyster.

Lead the way and others will follow. With luck the plight becomes the flight, and the landscape shifts. For those forward-thinking brands, we thank you for leading the way.

WHAT'S IN IT FOR THE STARS?

Carol Goll, ICM Partners

For years celebrity brand endorsements were the little dark secret in which only a few artists would participate. The criteria were usually that, first, it had to be a brand/company that wasn't completely embarrassing, second, it had to be shot and marketed in a country outside of the USA, preferably where the language of the campaign was not English, and, most importantly, third, it had to pay a lot. There were exceptions, of course – beauty, luxury and high-end fashion campaigns were acceptable for artists in the early years – but for the most part celebrities were looked down upon for endorsing a brand.

A few years ago I had an iconic actor client pass on an opportunity for a Chrysler Super Bowl spot. He was not ready to be seen in a commercial in the USA and interpreted the creative treatment and copy in a way that did not feel authentic to him. Having knowledge of the spot I was interested to see who they would eventually cast, and in this case it was Clint Eastwood. The spot won many awards and received fantastic reviews. Eastwood was not one to partake in many commercial spots, but he must have interpreted the creative treatment to be more of a fit for him. It was a moment of understanding and learning for me, finding that first and foremost it is the story or content that drives the decision for many celebrities in determining whether to be associated with a brand campaign. Today brand partnerships are not only a lucrative element in an artist's career but also a crucial aspect of awareness in the entertainment industry and consumer marketplace.

Working with a brand began to be acceptable with the advent of the internet and social media. The new digital landscape caused a seismic paradigm shift in how we consume media, including film, television, art and music. The new frontier gave us unprecedented viewer insight data, and both brands and celebrities were able to capitalize on this by tailoring their marketing and image according to consumer preferences. Films, long derided for their clumsy product placement, began pursuing organic brand relations that were relevant to the narrative. Musicians, especially those in the urban genres, began rapping and singing about their favourite products. Brands became an essential and embraced tool in the creative community, and the stakeholders in those brands took notice.

Celebrities involved with advertising and brands are no longer looked on as 'spokespeople' for a company. There are a few brands that still use celebrities in that way, but branded entertainment has shifted the paradigm. Brands tend to think of branded entertainment as a balance between the results they need to achieve and the needs of the audience. Celebrities are 'headliners' today, as they bring their own audience with them, so this is a big reason why companies enlist well-known names in campaigns.

Nevertheless this concept is nothing new to Hollywood – going back to the days of Clark Gable and Marilyn Monroe. Big names sell cinema tickets. Attaching Meryl Streep or Leonardo DiCaprio to a film often guarantees that is it worth watching or taking the risk in purchasing a ticket. If brands really want to get closer to the entertainment business they need also to engage the passion and interest of a third group: the talent. You need to think about how to make an idea interesting to artists to persuade them to participate if you really want to make something memorable and shine.

Digital and social media have made it possible for celebrities to build their own personal brands and ultimately their own media platforms. Information about a star is readily available just by looking at an app on a phone. We know what the celebrity likes, doesn't like, eats, wears and consumes, thus establishing a link of authenticity. Brands love organic associations with their products, and celebrities know it. As Jay-Z so eloquently put it, 'I'm not a businessman, I'm a business, man'.[2]

Being a headliner doesn't always mean being in front of the camera. Celebrities are often drawn to a commercial branded entertainment project as a co-creator. Big Hollywood names want to ensure the entertainment is high quality and a strong reflection of who they are as artists. No one wants to appear in a bomb of a film or receive terrible reviews on an album. Consumers know when a star is selling out because it does not feel authentic to that celebrity's own personal brand, ethos or artistic sensibility. Whether it is improvising lines in a script, writing or directing a project, having input – big or small – and approval to do this is an important element for talent who sign on with a brand.

As an agent I've been in negotiations with companies on behalf of celebrity clients when companies are concerned that giving celebrities creative input and approvals means they will lose control or the talent will become so demanding that it will be too challenging to work with them. I always relay to the brand that this will only boost the project's appeal. And often it is the level of comfort necessary for a celebrity to come on board with a project in the first place.

As you can see, it is not just about the money when celebrities partner with brands. First and foremost it is about the creative treatment. Artists are unlikely to bruise their image or reputation on a branded entertainment project that is not good or on which they do not have input. Depending on what they gravitate towards creatively, artists may look for a variety of elements in deciding whether they will work with a brand. They may be tempted by the chance to access new artistic avenues such as singing in another genre, playing characters they love or reprising a signature role from a past project, or they may be seeking to escape typecasting. Artists like to stretch themselves, and I always encourage brands to let them do it. They are experts in their craft, folks. The meat, the real meat is here. Good branded entertainment needs to be as compelling as an award-winning film, TV show or song.

It's not only celebrities who are embracing brands. More often than not, advertising agencies are looking to creators of traditional entertainment to develop and produce branded entertainment. Writers, directors and composers are often brought in to help create relevant consumer marketing. This top-down approach to producing great content lends an authenticity to product marketing and has removed the taboo around celebrity brand endorsement.

Although 2017 was my first time participating in the Cannes Lions jury process, I had previously secured roles for two ICM Partners' clients in the Intel and Toshiba short films in 2013 and 2014 that won at Cannes Lions. In 2012 Intel and Toshiba presented a social film experience called *The Beauty Inside*. The film, directed by Drake Doremus, who directed the Sundance Grand Jury Prize-winning *Like Crazy*, and produced by Pereira O'Dell, starred Topher Grace, best known for his role in *That '70s Show*.

The project featured an innovative format of six filmed episodes interspersed with interactive storytelling that all took place on the main character's Facebook timeline. The film was innovative in that the viewer was able to interact via social media and play the lead role throughout the story. *The Beauty Inside* garnered 70 million views and won several awards, including a Cyber Grand Prix at the Cannes Lions Festival. The things that drew viewers to this project – a compelling script, good story and a strong director – also drew Topher to star in it. It was an innovative vision that had the backing of two massive brands, and that freedom to innovate within the traditional medium of film was another plus for this incredible actor. It did not feel commercial in the traditional sense of the word, where brands exploited an artist's name and likeness to help sell product through association. This demonstrated how innovative storytelling drives strong audience engagement through superior branded content. Intel and Toshiba are examples of brands that went to the Hollywood community to create content that was not only a marketing tool for their company but an engaging and award-worthy entertainment. These were all attractive elements tending to encourage the actor's participation.

Track record

When Intel and Toshiba were casting their 2014 short film *The Power Inside*, I already had a good indication of how successful these projects could be and how artist-friendly they were from a brand standpoint. Once again working with Pereira O'Dell, they cast Harvey Keitel, perhaps best known for his work in *Pulp Fiction*, as the lead and went on to win several awards, including the Cannes Lions Cyber Bronze.

By casting a legendary and recognizable dramatic actor such as Keitel in the film, Toshiba and Intel brought the film to life in a credible, compelling and engaging way. Once again, this was a piece of content, paid for and envisioned by two massive tech brands, yet it was not a traditional commercial project. As one of the most revered and coolest actors in Hollywood, Harvey needed this to feel as authentic to himself as starring in a Hollywood passion project might. He brought the character to life as no one else could through his unique 'brand of cool'. The content was compelling and filmed with a cinematic quality, so the audience was engaged. It was authentic to Harvey because it didn't feel like an 'ad' but rather a short film with a great story and compelling role.

Expanding the audience

There was more to Harvey on Intel and Toshiba's *The Power Inside* than just a good script. It was a connection to a new audience, since it was marketed to a millennial crowd through the internet. It tapped an entirely new fan base for him. While millions of moviegoers remember him from *Reservoir Dogs*, *Pulp Fiction* and *Bad Lieutenant*, the target audience may never have seen any of his films. The marketing behind the short film was also unique for a commercial project, as it was in the same vein as marketing a film, complete with movie posters that were displayed in large metropolitan areas.

When I see brands choose celebrities to work with who may not currently resonate with their audiences, I cheer them on. By thinking outside of the box companies often find much bigger names who are much more enthusiastic about participating in a project because the parties are aligned in their quest. This simple concept may elevate the attention a campaign receives just by a smart casting decision.

Headliners are media

For close to a decade I've run the Global Branded Department at ICM Partners, one of the world's top talent and literary agencies. The Global Branded Entertainment division represents actors, comedians, directors, musicians, TV personalities, broadcasters and sports stars in the commercial space. But my career as a commercial agent representing talent is rather unusual, as instead of starting in the mailroom at a top Hollywood talent agency like most of my colleagues I launched my career in the automotive industry. For more than thirteen years I was an executive at Mercedes-Benz USA, where I ran the department responsible for entertainment and lifestyle-marketing initiatives. Because of my background I often wear a couple of different hats and view branded entertainment from dual perspectives – that of the artist and that of the brand.

I see the use of celebrities in campaigns, endorsements and branded entertainment differently when I am representing a brand from when I am representing the talent. In many cases artists view brand partnerships as an opportunity to build their own personal brand. Many use work with brands in order to diversify their cultural impact (and revenue streams) by creating new business through endorsements and branded entertainment. Artists who can make the brand associations authentic to their core values can even become brands themselves. The projects celebrities choose to be involved in need to be organic to who they are as people, the message needs to be authentic and it needs simply to make sense to the consumer. If consumers are confused as to why someone is featured in a campaign, it tends to be the wrong fit. If consumers don't 'buy' into the association then they don't buy the product or the idea that the marketer is trying to sell. It's that simple.

When brands hire a celebrity for a campaign, they want the association or the 'rub' on their product to make it stand out and grab the consumer's attention. Big social media followings among artists are very important, as brands want their campaigns to be seen and engaged with by the artist's most loyal fans. Brands can measure their return on investment by looking at an artist's social media engagement analytics and other factors to determine if their fans will ultimately purchase a product. Many brands are finding this type of media buy more effective than traditional media, such as an artist featured with a product on a billboard, as measurement is directly linked to the artist through their social media channels. The playing field keeps changing, and artists are aware of how critical it is to have an engaged fanbase.

There has not been a celebrity campaign I have worked on during the last couple of years in which consumer and audience engagement with social media wasn't an integral part of the campaign. In most brand castings, social media following is not only a strong indicator of which artist is right for a campaign, it is often the deciding factor. This practice is not unique to the brand world: film studios, TV production companies and record labels also drive consumer engagement through social media now more than ever.

Driving pop culture

In the 2017 Cannes Lions Branded Entertainment category there were only a few select campaigns that used celebrity talent. Some were in front of the camera and some were behind. One of the most notable campaigns was Adidas's *Original Is Never Finished* digital video. This ninety-second film won a Bronze Lion in the Branded Entertainment Category and a Grand Prix in the Branded Entertainment for Music category. I vividly remember watching this spot when it debuted during the 2017 Grammys, and I was mesmerized, so when it appeared on the Cannes Lions ballot for award consideration I was not surprised.

Adidas had always been a runner-up to Nike in both sales of trainers and cultural perception. While Adidas sat on the sidelines, Nike told the consumer to 'Just do it' and in doing so created a cultural cachet that is matched by only a few brands throughout the world. It cornered the market in traditional advertising for its segment, outfitting and collaborating on custom product with the highest-performing sports stars in the world. To gain ground on its rival, Adidas needed to redefine itself and did so by shifting its focus from sports terrain to the streets. It made its product about lifestyle and used branded entertainment to cement the emotional connections between product, celebrity and art. It moved into a new segment through high-fashion partnerships with notable cultural luminaries such as Kanye West, and in doing so elevated its brand equity in the mind of the consumer.

For this latest piece of branded entertainment Adidas focused on the idea of creation and originality. *Original Is Never Finished* explores the idea that driving culture forward can redefine what is truly original. Produced by RSA and created by Johannes Leonardo, the film featured a mix of modern-day creators, such as hip-hop artists Snoop Dogg and Stormzy, basketball legend Kareem Abdul-Jabbar and artist Petra Collins. They set the film to a version of 'My Way', the classic song associated with Frank Sinatra, which was remixed (including some of Sinatra's recording) into a more contemporary and epic anthem. A very clever choice. Here was a track that has been covered so many times and in so many different ways, but they were able to make it feel fresh and original again. The spot featured Adidas's EQT line but didn't flaunt it, so it didn't feel like a commercial in the traditional sense. The EQT line drew stylistic cues from the heritage of the brand, specifically an Adidas collection from the 1990s. Like the song, they modernized the product for today's consumer and made it original again.

The imagery of the spot further enforced this concept. In it Petra Collins reimagines Sandro Botticelli's *The Birth of Venus*, while Snoop Dogg recreates his *Doggystyle* album cover with a surreal chase scene. The spot featured a multi-generational cast, including other contemporary pop culture influencers such as Dev Hynes, Mabel and Lucas Puig. Adidas tapped into the cultural ubiquity of icons such as Snoop Dogg and Frank Sinatra – pop-culture revolutionaries who remain relevant today – to make their point that history not only repeats itself but is always reinventing itself. The video and the talent themselves suggest that consumers have choices, and crossing boundaries and reimagining oneself allows for a new perspective and fresh thinking. From there, they pass the torch to a new generation of creators and inspire them to redefine the originality in their own terms.

In the Adidas press release Alegra O'Hare, Vice-President of Global Communications Adidas Originals and Core, declares: 'Everything we do for Adidas Originals is a work in progress, as true creativity is never finished . . . We are constantly challenging ourselves and breaking down the boundaries that limit imagination;

we hope to inspire all creators to do the same. We first raised this idea in 2015 through our superstar work, questioning the very meaning of the word. We then continued with the notion of the current dystopian future, by motivating consumers to take [sic] future into their own hands and create it. Now with Original, probably the most important and centric concept to our brand's ethos, we elevate the trefoil's storytelling, as we look into what it really means to be original, questioning its very essence.'[1]

As Adidas reinvents itself, branded entertainment using celebrity partnerships continues to push the boundaries with well-known personalities beyond the endorsement and commercial exploitations of days past. It is an exciting, ever-evolving time for branded content, and the use of celebrity is much more than skin deep. There needs to be authenticity and an organic quality between the personality and product.

Kenzo's *My Mutant Brain*

When luxury fashion houses started to create short films to highlight their fragrances, cosmetics, clothing and accessories, the ingredients got copied over and over. Too serious, pretentious and trying too hard to be filmic and entertaining, they lost their effectiveness – if they ever had any. Consumers began to wonder whether the brand was trying too hard. Celebrity spokesperson: check. Well-known film director: check. Cutting-edge cinematographer: check. Social media and digital engagement: check. It's been done by Louis Vuitton, Armani, Dolce & Gabbana, Burberry, Calvin Klein and others. They are all very good, but as this concept was repeated over and over its value in the branded content space plummeted.

So what made Kenzo's film *My Mutant Brain*, for their new fragrance Kenzo World, a branded entertainment surprise and Cannes Lions winner? It had the same ingredients. Star Director: Spike Jonze. Celebrity actress: Margaret Qualley, star of *The Leftovers* and daughter of Andie MacDowell. Choreographer: Ryan Heffington, responsible for the frenetic music video for 'Chandelier' by Sia. It's over the top, far-fetched and frankly out of character for a branded perfume ad. The film is four minutes of dancing by a character played by Qualley, who leaves the ballroom hosting a stale gala to career around the halls, dancing and contorting as she goes. The brand presence only shows itself at the end when a giant floral eyeball, a visual used by the brand in its packaging, appears and Qualley dives through.

Kenzo took a much-used timeworn formula for perfume campaigns, featuring a pretty girl and a bottle, and turned it on its head, making it a parody of the self-important arthouse pieces created by other brands. Celebrities enjoy creating art and commentary, and this project accomplished both objectives by securing participation from artists who wanted to do something unexpected and radical in the beauty category.

Tide's *The Stain*

In 2017 there were very few celebrity-fronted campaigns to make it to Cannes Lions' final prizes. However, there was one campaign that really stood out for me, and it would be remiss of me if I did not mention it in the context of celebrity in branded entertainment: the Tide Super Bowl LI campaign that featured Terry Bradshaw, entitled *The Stain*. The content was an incredibly clever use of a celebrity being integrated into the game that stood out from a typical commercial spot.

With more than 110 million viewers and the price of a Super Bowl commercial reaching $4.5 million for a sixty-second spot in 2017, advertisers have had to up their own game year after year in creativity, originality and keeping the viewers' attention. The Super Bowl is more than the biggest American-football game for NFL fans; it also features some of the most creative and memorable commercials and branded content.

The allure of a Super Bowl campaign is strong for artist consideration. I have many celebrity clients that have shied away from commercials unless it is a Super Bowl spot, because the content is often special and unique. So many of these spots have captured the zeitgeist of pop culture while elevating the awareness for the brand and introducing talent to new audiences. And, simply put, the creative treatment can be really good. There is a bit of cachet for an artist to be featured in a smart Super Bowl spot, especially if it is unexpected, authentic and compelling. In many cases an artist's decision to accept an offer to participate in a commercial campaign is based on the story and the script and is less about the brand or product.

Tide featured four-time Super Bowl champion and current Fox NFL analyst Terry Bradshaw, because he is a fan favourite who is also known for his good humour and friendly demeanour. As a likeable sports personality Terry was an authentic choice of talent for Tide, and the media execution made this spot organic in his role as an on-air analyst.

The campaign description was simple. Laundry stains are a part of life – no matter who you are and where you might be. Many of us have experienced those unfortunate and embarrassing human moments where we have noticed a stain on our clothes before a big presentation, meeting or date. With this in mind, Tide's strategy was to create a stunt whereby it would subvert the viewers' expectations by having it look like they were not watching a commercial. It accomplished this by making it seem as though Terry was live on-air when he discovers a barbeque stain on his shirt. There was no branding, so viewers could speculate if the stain would still be there after half-time, building suspense and anticipation.

To pull this off, both the live set-up and the commercial had to look like real life in real time, with Terry's relatable nice-guy personality. About ten minutes later Tide ran a commercial in which you see Terry freaking out and taking a panicky car ride in an effort to eliminate the stain. Viewers finally got it, received a big pay-off, and the reaction was positive. It was a clever, memorable ad that turned a viewer 'wince' to Terry's wink.

We debated on the Cannes jury whether this was true branded entertainment or just a clever branded commercial stunt. Today branded entertainment encompasses the new world of advertising and branded content in so many different forms that the phrase ultimately just means content that is simply entertaining. Whether you like the bit or not, it was a compelling standpoint and smart use of a celebrity. Tide could not have made this stunt work without Terry Bradshaw, and he was the most appropriate celebrity to bring this to life. For Terry it showed a different side to his personal brand. And for those millennial viewers who did not grow up with Terry Bradshaw from his iconic days as star quarterback for the Pittsburgh Steelers, they formed a connection with his comedic personality.

This was a clever use of celebrity and media execution on a huge stage that was daring and took the moment into the social media sphere where the conversation drove engagement and buzz. While it wasn't noted, it feels that this was not a 'casting' situation but a creative idea being developed with particular talent in mind. In my line of work I see more and more of this with celebrities, given the growth of digital and social media. Building stories around the personality or character of an artist's own personal brand often yields the most authentic connection between audience and brand.

When the stars align

Hollywood has never been closer to brands than it is today. It starts with a strong narrative and good storytelling. There are longer formats, shorter content moments and teasers, new distribution funnels and more opportunities for consumers to engage with the product. Brands are becoming much more sophisticated in casting talent for commercial and brand projects because an artist's personality and ethos are often critical in making an emotional connection to a product or service. Branded entertainment is the emotional connection between the product message and consumer. And celebrities often help amplify that message, being who they are while bringing their loyal fans into the mix.

Coming back from Cannes Lions last year after serving on the jury I was even more excited about the branded entertainment landscape than ever before. Content, storytelling and advertising is getting even more compelling because of new media distribution channels, social media engagement and Hollywood's involvement as a creator and innovator. Celebrities featured in commercial or branded campaigns are no longer taboo – in fact, they are often important elements in helping stars themselves distinguish their own personal brand within the zeitgeist of pop culture.

When I first came to ICM Partners as a talent agent I got to understand fully the pride and excitement agents feel when they are honoured and thanked at awards shows by clients, whether for being supportive or for helping to secure a great role. I feel the same when a client of mine is recognized for an outstanding role or collaboration in a branded piece of content. Great entertainment is great entertainment, whether it is brand sponsored or studio supported. Is this convergence of brands, storytelling and entertainment the future, or is it just reinvention of the past? Remember when a laundry soap brand supported daytime content called soap operas? Original is never finished . . .

1. http://news.adidas.com/us/Latest-News/adidas-originals-launches-original-campaign-and-film---original-is-never-finished-/s/8b2cd3d4-fd68-4bab-8ae3-90dc35f0095b

2. Kanye West featuring Jay-Z, 'Diamonds from Sierra Leone (Remix)', © 2005 Andre Benjamin, John Barry, Devon Harris, David Sheats, Don Black, Antwan Patton, Kanye Omari West

IDEAS THAT SCALE: HOW TO CREATE A GLOBAL TV FORMAT

Samantha Glynne, FremantleMedia

Imagine a single advertising campaign so powerful that it lasted for over a decade, worked in more than fifty countries, was successful across TV, digital and social media and won multiple awards.

And now imagine that the brand did not need to pay for the campaign because broadcasters around the world funded every cent of it. And the more the campaign travelled, the more money it recouped, making it a highly profitable business.

Do I sound like a raving lunatic? This is the business of international television production, where scalability of content is key. The strongest TV formats are created with the potential to travel across seasons, territories and platforms. Each format becomes a brand in its own right. It may evolve and adapt to the nuances of the local market, but it has the same identifiable structure and values at its core.

These TV formats are conceived with great care, designed to have a long lifespan and international appeal. They are nurtured to keep them evergreen. They attract huge highly engaged audiences who actively choose to spend time with them. They maximize an initial investment to become profit centres. This is because their lifeblood is their intellectual property, or IP.

Wouldn't it make creative and economic sense to see global brands such as McDonald's or Nike create their own branded entertainment in the form of long-running international hits? To evolve 'I'm Lovin' It' into a family entertainment format, to turn 'Just Do It' into a global competitive-reality show? After all, Red Bull took 'It Gives You Wings' to create the world's biggest branded content powerhouse. They embraced and grew their IP.

Love your IP

According to the WIPO (World Intellectual Property Organization): 'Intellectual property (IP) refers to creations of the mind, such as inventions; literary and artistic works; designs; and symbols, names and images used in commerce. IP is protected in law by, for example, patents, copyrights and trademarks, which enable people to earn recognition or financial benefit from what they invent or create. By striking the right balance between the interests of innovators and the wider public interest, the IP system aims to foster an environment in which creativity and innovation can flourish.'

I believe that branded entertainment has the potential to own IP and become a self-financing way to reach the hearts and minds of audiences who choose to spend time with content, regardless of whether or not it has been funded by a brand. The collaboration between TV production companies and the advertising industry can lead to a new branded entertainment model. With the growth of OTT platforms, the terms 'TV', 'digital' and 'branded' are now beginning to merge, and the only true requisite is that people want to be entertained.

IP is the core business principle of the world's biggest production companies. Billions of people around the world will have seen local versions of the world's most popular shows. In the non-scripted business, Sony Pictures' *Who Wants to Be a Millionaire?* has travelled to more than 115 territories. Endemol Shine has *Deal Or No Deal* in eighty-eight countries, *The Money Drop* in fifty-eight countries and *Big Brother* in fifty-five. Talpa's *The Voice* is shown in fifty-nine countries. All of these shows continue to grow and travel to new territories.

Having worked on both sides of the business – in TV and advertising – I am aware of the different values that both entities revere. In advertising, annual campaigns mean that the pressure is on to refresh and renew. Sometimes the greatest creative ideas are adapted, convoluted and even obliterated to make way for the next big shiny thing – and the only thing left is a copy line, which has its own sell-by date. Original and groundbreaking work is awarded, but little credence is given to the lasting power of a returnable message;

plus, the constrictions of a thirty-second spot don't usually allow the flexibility for local nuance and language.

But I still raise the challenge to agencies and brands to join hands with IP creators and nurture a new long-term way of doing business.

TV is big business

I work for FremantleMedia. We're one of the world's biggest production companies. We've got offices in thirty-one countries, and we produce and distribute 20,000 hours of content every year. We pride ourselves on creating irresistible entertainment and have many famous TV formats that travel the world – *The X-Factor* (a Fremantle/Syco show in fifty-five countries) and *Idols* (a Fremantle/Core show in over fifty territories), *Family Feud* (seventy-one territories) and *The Price Is Right* (forty-two territories), to name a handful.

The jewel in our IP crown is *Got Talent*, which was created by Simon Cowell and we co-own with Syco Entertainment. It has been produced locally in seventy countries and sold as a tape (the anachronistic term for a finished programme) to over 200 territories. Over eleven years it has attracted more than 43 billion views on YouTube and is consistently the number-one show for broadcasters in wildly diverse territories, from the USA to Spain, from Norway to Mongolia. It is the *Guinness World Records*-holder for 'the most successful reality entertainment format in the world'.

As you can imagine, it's not easy to create a global mega-brand that crosses borders and cultures and languages. It takes time – and a lot of creative and strategic work – and it involves collaborating with our partner Syco and the best development producers from all over the world to make sure that the show is relevant to different cultures and countries.

Got Talent is a great case study for travelling IP and there are many lessons that the advertising world could learn to apply to branded entertainment.

In 2016 FremantleMedia was invited by Cannes Lions to present a panel on the Inspiration Stage about creating global IP via *Got Talent*. FremantleMedia's Director of Global Entertainment, Rob Clark, explained the journey of *Got Talent* from concept to mega-brand. He stressed the importance of the four pillars of a successful format: 'First, it should be scalable and work on a huge budget, such as in the USA, but also as a small budget for emerging markets. It should be returnable – *The Price Is Right* has been on air continuously since 1956. It should be transferable, with no cultural barriers. And, finally, it should be promotable; you should switch on a TV anywhere in the world and recognize the look and feel of a strong TV format.'

The obvious starting point is being able to identify a successful piece of IP. The TV pilot in the UK didn't even go to commission. Despite this, we remained confident in the concept, largely because our network of producers around the world loved it and were adamant that it would work. It was this surge of internal confidence that kept us going.

We took the show to NBC who commissioned a pilot. The original host in the USA was Regis Philbin, then a famous daytime-TV celebrity, and the show started to look more like a global format . . . but it still wasn't quite there. We continued to share the concept with our creative network around the world – it was commissioned in France, Portugal, Russia, Australia, Belgium and Greece, evolving as it went.

The real shaping of the format came with the first series of *Britain's Got Talent* in 2007. The head creatives at Syco and Fremantle always believed this show had themes that worked on a global level – variety, humour, family, dreams coming true, competition, talent. With the UK series we began to get to grips with what worked in the production –the presenters remaining backstage, for example – and we understood better which elements of the show could be localized for audiences.

Go global, feel local

An important element also became clear: the show reflects the cultural make-up of a nation, and, although it is global, it must appear regional. Here's a quick test to see if a piece of content can become a global mega-brand: is it transferable (easy to adapt); is it returnable (recover the investment); and is it scalable (reaching as many territories as possible)? This is a really simple way to look at the potential of branded entertainment at the very start.

The *Got Talent* format became what it is today when, in Series 3, a woman called Susan Boyle walked on to the stage. Her performance of 'I Dreamed a Dream' from *Les Misérables* has become one of the most popular TV clips of all time on YouTube. To date it has had an estimated 630 million views. If you've never seen it you should seek it out – it sends shivers down my spine every time I watch it.

Those few minutes of content with Ms Boyle encapsulated everything about the show that has made it a success: dreams coming true, outstanding talent, entertainment for the whole family . . . and it also captured expectation, surprise, redemption; a moving voice, a humbled Simon Cowell, a win for the loser. And it catapulted the format on to the global stage.

On a practical level, as more and more broadcasters started to commission the format, we needed to protect it and become strong brand guardians, in the same way that consumer brands look after their own equity.

We developed brand bibles and deployed flying producers around the world to make sure that the format was being produced properly. From the number of judges to the positioning of the presenter, we worked alongside Syco to oversee integrations with advertisers, insisting that our central marketing and creative teams managed approvals on all logos, idents, products and merchandise. Once we were confident about the core elements that needed to remain, we could allow our local teams to make the show relevant on a regional basis.

So we identified a hit, looked after the format globally; the next issue was how to keep it fresh. We had to be nimble enough to keep the brand innovative but clever enough to know what worked. Simon Cowell has always been a key driving influence in how the show reinvents itself, and one of the most successful changes we made to the show was the introduction of the Golden Buzzer, which allowed judges to catapult their favourite acts into the finals. It wasn't rocket science, but it added a different dimension and created a bigger moment in the studio with the audience yelling, 'Push the button! Push the button!'

Got Talent also provides an amazing partnership platform for advertisers who want to reach a highly engaged audience. The show attracts brands from every sector – from food and beverages to cars, from tech to finance. It's a big part of Fremantle's and Syco's businesses. Every year we do more than 150 brand integrations on *Got Talent* all over the world – from the branded cup on the judges' desks to Facebook Live streams to licensing and events.

In 2017's Entertainment Lions there were impressive case studies from lots of different genres – but very few from what could be called factual entertainment, which is where *Got Talent* sits. One that I loved was *The Lick-Hiker's Guide to Inner Strength* from Finnish dairy brand Valio Gefilus, which won a Bronze Lion for online non-fiction of fifteen minutes or longer. Ian Wright from the TV series *Lonely Planet* created a comedy documentary in which he travelled around Europe licking the filthiest places. This is not yet a format because it's only a 'germ' of a big idea – but it could grow to become a larger-scale travel series with a competitive element or a segment in global show. It reminded me of an element in Fremantle's game-show *Total Blackout* (which travelled to nineteen countries) called 'Lick It'. Contestants would have to lick everything from chicory prawns to a man's belly in total darkness and guess what it was they'd tasted. Similar idea, totally different application and context (it sat alongside 'Smell It', 'Touch It' and so on).

Scripted at scale

So that's a snapshot on factual entertainment brands. The much trickier genre to achieve at scale is scripted. It's entirely possible to deliver drama and comedy season after season (*The Simpsons, Law and Order, Dallas*), but this does not usually involve producing multiple versions of the show in the USA and Asian or European countries. Instead, it comes from the number of tape sales (the same version, redubbed or subtitled in local languages) to different territories. *NCIS* has been running since 2003 and is now seen in over 200 markets, having been dubbed and subtitled into fifty-nine different languages. *CSI* had almost 800 episodes across fifteen seasons, and the tape was also sold to more than 200 territories. From the UK *Midsomer Murders* has aired in over 200 territories and *Downton Abbey* in sixty.

I'm always on the hunt for scalable branded entertainment case studies, and there aren't enough of them out there. One of the outstanding ones in recent years is the work that Pereira O'Dell created for Intel. The series includes *The Inside Experience* (2011), *The Power Inside* (2013) and *What Lives Inside* (2015). These films are beautifully crafted pieces of entertainment that focus on different Intel projects, often with audience interactivity at their core. They play off one central idea and scale that into different executions.

All of them won awards, but *The Beauty Inside* (2012) was the most lauded. This web series centres around Alex, who wakes up every day in a different body. The plot has been dealt with in numerous other chapters in this book, and PJ Pereira's story about how it came to be is insightful. This series taps into ancient myths and stories from around the world that deal with metamorphosis and shape-shifting, and it appeals to the fundamental human desire to find and keep true love. The creators took this already potent IP and made it universal for modern times. They used social media to turn it interactive. Fans from all over the world were invited to audition to play Alex and act alongside Hollywood professionals. Four thousand people put themselves forward, and a total of twenty-six different Alexes were cast in the lead role. More than fifty other audience members were also able to play Alex on his Facebook timeline.

So, not only did the narrative become scalable but the casting did, too. It was inclusive and adaptable – sending a positive message about the brand to the target millennial audience. The Toshiba Portégé Ultrabook with Intel inside was seamlessly integrated into the storyline, as Alex used it on a daily basis to chronicle his ever-changing appearance.

The project won accolades from both sides of the industry – including three Cannes Lions Grand Prix (Film, Content and Entertainment, Cyber) and a Daytime Emmy, proving itself as successful as a piece of entertainment as it was a piece of advertising. (One of the running jokes on our jury was that the ultimate accolade was a Cannes-Cannes – a film festival and a Lions win . . . but at second best, an Emmy or Bafta would do – and Bartle Bogle Hegarty was very pleased to win a Lions and a Bafta for the film *Home*.)

The IP of *The Beauty Inside* has since grown. In 2015 an award-winning South Korean film was made based on the premise (*Byuti Insaideu*), and there are plans to create a US feature based on the concept in 2018. The agency has credits on the movie and drama series, and the brand has part ownership of the IP with the option to include its product where compliant.

It's great how the IP of *The Beauty Inside* has scaled across territories and platforms, and it is a rare scripted format that travels with such momentum. As a benchmark, comedy drama *In Treatment* is the world's biggest scripted travelling format of the last seven years, with a mere twelve adaptations, and this is down to the small cast and single set which makes it so easy to produce. *The Beauty Inside*, though, has already been a web series and a Korean movie, and now a US feature and a Korean TV series are planned.

Another piece of advertising that became a long-form piece of entertainment was Pepsi's *Uncle Drew* campaign. It starred NBA's Kyrie Irving as an old man with incredible basketball talents and played out from 2012 to 2015 as a short-form digital series, winning a Silver Lion in 2013. This year it's been made into a full-length feature film, *Uncle Drew*, with Pepsi's original IP at its heart.

A less successful (but still brave) attempt to scale up an ad was Geico's *Cavemen* series. What began life as a series of award-winning commercials, featuring Neanderthal-like cavemen in a modern setting, was commissioned as a TV series for ABC in 2007. The show had the same writer as the ad, but the cast was different, the storyline didn't work and the context which served a thirty-second spot so well never actually translated to a TV series. It was pulled from the US network after only six episodes.

Kids know best

The IP around children's content behaves in a similar way to scripted content, in that the scalability of a kids' format is much more likely to be a tape sale than a fresh localized version. Animation lends itself to being dubbed into multiple languages, and it's true that kids under twelve like the same things the world over.

Peppa Pig has been on-air since 2004 and has travelled to over 180 countries, while *Paw Patrol* has been transmitted in more than 160 countries since 2004. The TV IP for kids' shows has tremendous licensing opportunities via books, games, merchandise and clothing.

Another kids' show, *RAD Lands*, for Chipotle from CAA Marketing, won a Bronze Entertainment Lion in 2017. Chipotle is no stranger to branded content. It has had a winning formula creating top-notch animation shorts accompanied by powerful music tracks. In 2012 it did *Back to the Start*, which won the first Cannes Lions Branded Content Grand Prix; they went on to create *The Scarecrow*, which won both a Cannes Lions Grand Prix and an Emmy. In 2014 it delivered the episodic *Farmed and Dangerous*, a satirical four-part series on Hulu, which unfortunately never scaled beyond this transmission. In 2017 it also entered *A Love Story*, another music-led animated short that undoubtedly has the potential to be produced as a series or a feature.

RAD Lands is an unbranded six-part entertainment series for kids aged between six and eleven about the importance of better food being accessible to everyone. It features a combination of animation, live action, YouTube influencers and music from supercool artists, including Wayne Coyne from the band the Flaming Lips (no doubt an incentive for parents). The series includes live cooking demos, facts about real-life cultivation and the science of food. There is a ton of stuff going on – too many ingredients in this one dish to digest – but its potential led to it being awarded a Bronze Lion for TV and VOD: Fiction Series.

It's virtually impossible to advertise to children because of compliance legislation, but by creating an unbranded series with no logos or burritos Chipotle proved that it was a force of change in the industry. The high production values (the animation was by the same producers of US children's show *Yo Gabba Gabba!*), the ambition and the energy in this series made me believe that one or two elements had the power to grow into their own IP. Remember when *The Simpsons* was just a segment on *The Tracey Ullman Show*? My discerning six-year old son Ari watched all six episodes of *RAD Lands* and asked for more. And he got the take-out about sustainable food production.

RAD Lands was hampered by its distribution strategy – it was released for $4.99 on iTunes. In a universe where so much kids' content is available for free, five bucks is a big ask from audiences for an unknown content entity.

It will be interesting to see if and how Chipotle plans to grow the IP of this show. *RAD Lands* is already in partnership with Discovery Education for *RAD Lands in School* – a programme for elementary students that pairs the series' episodes with lesson plans and activities. There is scope to grow some of the show's elements and relocate them to TV, as a book or as localized versions in other territories.

Love at first bite

Although our Entertainment Lions jury were somewhat divided on *RAD Lands*, we were united in the selection of Gold Lions. We are all from different backgrounds (TV production, networks, ad agencies, brands, gaming, talent agencies), but after six days locked in a darkened room together we were on the same page when we chose the winners. Many of the contributing factors have been covered in this book – but a key differentiator was the potential for the best projects to have a life beyond their initial campaign.

One Source for Absolut from VML in South Africa was a dead cert. It is a sumptuous and scalable project featuring South African hip-hop star Khuli Chana. It is already a documentary series, an EP and a music video, and in theory has the potential to be re-enacted in other territories and seasons. But is it limited because it comes from a small territory in a global network? As Jason Xenopoulos explains in his chapter 'Advertising Ninjutsu and the Secret Art of Operating in the Shadows', being off the radar allowed Jason's company VML more freedom when it came to creating a branded entertainment solution. Inversely, because it didn't originate in London or New York, the project may never be scalable. Do the global headquarters of brands and agencies have the track record, business incentives or infrastructure to take a local project and scale it up to other territories . . . even when that project wins a Cannes Lion? Whoever heard of a global hit TV series coming from South Africa or Peru? A great idea can come from anyone and anywhere – and it's important that TV production companies and agency networks alike wake up to the idea of incubating great universal branded entertainment and disseminating it around the globe.

A Love Song Written by a Murderer was a supersmart entry from Circus Grey from another smaller territory, Peru, for the women's charity Vida Mujer. This followed on from 2015's campaign centred on a book, *Don't Die for Me*, featuring letters and apologies from men to their partners after episodes of domestic violence. This idea is in its own way scalable, developing and growing the same theme. The simplicity and power of this strand of IP could work in many other instances, but the concept could face similar geographical challenges as *One Source*.

The surprise entry for most of the jury was *From the Start*, from OgilvyOne, Athens. This is a Greek five-part webisode with a fantastical premise about a guy who doesn't believe in love falling for a girl that he sees in a dream every time he eats a piece of Lacta chocolate.

The trailer did not do the full series justice, and the few of us in the room who had watched all the episodes as part of the pre-judging process had a hard time convincing the rest of the gang that this was not just a schmaltzy soap opera. However, once they had viewed it the entire jury was converted by this magical modern fairy tale. It's a haunting, sensual and emotional story featuring an imperfect hero. It reminded me very much of a magical-realist short story by Gabriel García Márquez called 'Eyes of a Blue Dog'. A man and woman meet every night in their dreams where they say to one another: 'Eyes of a blue dog.' In the morning the woman remembers her dreams and devotes her entire life to finding the man. She walks around saying 'Eyes of a blue dog' and writing the phrase everywhere hoping he will recognize her. But the man always forgets the phrase when he wakes up.

The IP morphed with the life of the project, but the core message remained: the sweetness of chocolate correlates with the sweetness of falling in love. Back in 2010 Lacta created a branded content crowd-sourced film called *Love in Action*, and in 2013 they launched the short cinema film *Love in the End*, which won a Silver Entertainment Lion. The 2017 idea started as a TV spot with the tagline 'Every piece of Lacta chocolate is like falling in love, from the start.' It was developed into the web series on YouTube. It also had a VR experience where viewers could look around the main set on the island through the eyes of the hero. It was picked up by a Greek broadcaster, repackaged as a TV feature and shown on Valentine's Day. Without doubt, this charming gem of a series has the power and craft to be localized in other markets.

The golden age of cinema

Lo and Behold: Reveries of the Connected World was another Gold winner and a close contender for the Grand Prix. This is a documentary feature film directed by Werner Herzog funded by internet security company NetScout.

Although the film is 'brand-lite', it uses entertainment as a weapon for a niche target market of CEOs, tackling the need for internet security. NetScout and agency Pereira O'Dell handed over the editorial reins to Herzog and let him run with the idea.

It could have been risky, but using Herzog always meant that this project could be scaled. There was a guaranteed global arthouse audience, and the film was entered into the prestigious Sundance Film Festival where it was picked up by Magnolia Pictures. Magnolia paid back NetScout for their investment and went on to distribute and market the movie to multiple cinemas around the world before selling the project to Netflix. So NetScout ended up with its name on a global project that was essentially cost neutral – in fact, the general public were choosing to spend money to watch it! Go figure.

What's interesting is that the movie got sold. If it had been short-form and made for YouTube there would have been no market unless the idea was redeveloped. If it had been a two-part series there would be little scale. But, following the success of *The Lego Movie* brand-funded feature films can have immense global success. There is no doubt that cinema has enormous power. This is not simply down to the audiences in the theatres; it is also about the marketing and PR collateral that goes with a theatrical release.

The Grand Prix winner of Cannes 2017 Entertainment Lions was *Beyond Money* from MRM//McCann Spain, a short film for Santander Bank. It is very zeitgeist in the way it speaks to millennials about the value of experience over money, and it echoes the sci-fi trend of *Black Mirror*. The brand was integrated in a brave and subtle way, and the results in Spain were excellent; what it achieved there beyond the cinema was interesting. The trailer was viewed millions of times; the premiere, which featured Adriana Ugarte (the latest Almodóvar actress), attracted 12,500 people and was a PR hit. The out-of-home posters and the point-of-sale materials in banks were an amplification of the film itself.

Of all the entries in 2017, this film is the one I can most imagine having a robust lifespan beyond the campaign, perhaps as a series for Netflix, a feature film, a US remake, a book, a podcast . . . It's such a strong piece of genuine entertainment that goes way beyond its initial ambition and one that's likely to recoup its investment.

Tipping the scales

More and more brands and agencies are beginning to see the financial potential of branded content. Unilever founded U-Entertainment, Bartle Bogle Hegarty has Black Sheep Studios, and Dentsu has grown The Story Lab. They are investing in scalable projects in which they own part of the IP, so when the show travels they make a profit. Meanwhile, TV production companies are starting to see the benefit of working closely with agencies and are becoming increasingly willing to share their IP. The synergies between the two industries are growing.

There are still a number of obstacles in creating lasting IP, and many of them are inherent in the structure of the advertising business. Budgets may be released on an annual rather than longer-term basis. Autonomous local business units mean that global strategies are difficult to implement. And it's always much less risky to pay for that cup on the desk in an existing format such as *American Idol* than to create your own new talent show. It can be precarious, you might not get it right first time, and you'd be mistaken if you thought that a healthy return on investment is automatically guaranteed.

Partnerships can be precarious without trust. TV production companies, brands and agencies all differ in their cultures and business structures. So it's important that each party does what it does best and sticks to it: agencies and brands, we love your vision, your creativity and your commercial drive, we really enjoy collaborating with new partners in refreshing ways . . . but please trust us TV types to get on with what we know best, which is making long-form content for devoted audiences and selling it to broadcasters around the world.

I've already let rip about the limitations of scalability in scripted content. It's time for the industry to move into factual and entertainment. I can't wait to see the next *Big Brother*, *The Voice* or *The Price Is Right* co-owned by a brand. To date, there hasn't been a global branded entertainment reality series, game show or shiny-floor programme.

Even if there were any, I doubt that we'd ever see this genre of content winning at Cannes. As with the evolution of *Got Talent*, this type of IP takes years to grow and is unlikely to scoop an award at its first appearance. The best we can do is keep on experimenting, innovating, collaborating . . . and that kernel of a creative idea may turn into a global mega-hit.

ADVERTISING NINJUTSU AND THE SECRET ART OF OPERATING IN THE SHADOWS

Jason Xenopoulos, VML South Africa

When I was a child someone told me a story about a ninja. I have no idea whether or not it is a true story, but there was something so compelling about it that it has stayed with me ever since.

In feudal times Japan was ruled by a military elite. Shogun leaders, daimyo lords and samurai warriors together held sway over peasants and royals alike. Their power was unassailable. Like any ruling class they had their fair share of enemies ... but none was more feared than the ninja. These days most of us know that the outlandish stories of the ninja are more fiction than reality, but still these mythical shadow warriors continue to hold the public's imagination.

As a young boy the story that grabbed my attention was one in which a fearless ninja assassin went to almost inhuman lengths to neutralize his adversary. This particular legend concerned a powerful daimyo named Uesugi Kenshin who lived in the sixteenth century. Because of his powerful position Kenshin was untouchable. Surrounded night and day by samurai bodyguards, he was well-protected from all his enemies. All, that is, except for one. Cloaked in the darkness of a moonless night, a silent warrior infiltrated the castle walls and hid in the one place he knew Kenshin would eventually be alone – his toilet. Concealed in the stinking cesspool beneath Kenshin's latrine, the ninja patiently lay in wait. When the daimyo eventually and inevitably sat down on his toilet, the merciless assassin thrust his sword upwards – killing the warlord instantly.[1]

Despite the gruesome nature of this tale, when I think of ancient Japan I imagine a majestic landscape with mist hanging over craggy mountains, like an epic frame from a Kurosawa movie. I hear the sound of a bamboo flute trembling on the breeze and then, rising in the distance, the thunder of horses' hooves. Rumbling. Pounding. Making the earth shake as they charge towards me. This is a land of mystery and magic in which warriors face one another in fierce battles for honour and pride. But like all magic this ancient world has a dark side, too . . . and it is this duality that gives the legend of Uesugi Kenshin's death its uncanny allure.

Like feudal Japan, our modern media landscape is a hierarchy in which established players exert maximum influence. Global brands are our shoguns; CMOs and their marketing departments are the daimyos, and the samurai are the creative agencies that fight to help them gain share in an increasingly competitive marketplace. But, as in feudal Japan, there are also those who operate in the shadows, outside of the traditional channels, using their secret skills to find new and stealthier ways to reach their targets. Branded entertainment is one of these dark arts, and the creators of the work I will showcase in this chapter are its masters. Like all shadow warriors these 'ad ninja' hail from unlikely places. They are not the well-armoured samurai with glinting katana swords. They are not the daimyos or the shoguns or any part of the military elite. Instead they emerge, like their art, from the shadows.

A global battlefield

Unlike feudal Japan, however, today's war for consumers is fought on a global battlefield, with the most powerful dynasties emerging from the world's largest markets – places like the USA and the UK. But at 2017's Cannes Lions International Festival of Creativity we saw proof that ad ninja operate best when they are in the shadows. Of the thirteen Gold Lions awarded in the Entertainment category, five were won by smaller or less affluent markets – countries such as South Africa, Singapore, Greece, Spain and Peru.

As a jury we were impressed and surprised by this unexpected outcome. We wanted to understand the dynamics behind this phenomenon, so we reached out to some of the people involved in creating the winning work. These conversations resulted in a set of lessons that can be applied to the art of branded entertainment – not just in developing markets but all over the world.

Operating in the shadows

The first piece of work that I want to reference is Absolut's *One Source*. I can speak about this campaign with confidence because I was involved in creating it, which makes it a good starting point for me.

Back in 2015 Absolut Vodka was losing market share in South Africa. A proliferation of new brands had entered the market, and Absolut's relevance was waning. You see, after decades of 'coca-colonization' African consumers are tired of having global brands shoved down their throats. They want to be recognized for who they are and where they come from. This Afrocentrism has given rise to a cultural renaissance that is now sweeping across the continent. At VML South Africa we saw an opportunity for Absolut to increase its relevance by becoming a torchbearer for this emerging creative revolution. But to do that we needed to create an authentically African campaign. That may sound obvious, but for an iconic global brand like Absolut, whose ad campaigns had historically been developed in Europe and passed down to smaller markets, this would require a massive change in direction.

Up until that point virtually all the above-the-line (ATL) collateral used to advertise Absolut in Africa had been developed globally. Local campaign collateral had been limited to digital, experiential and other below-the-line channels. Undeterred, we proposed a fully integrated campaign called *Africa Is Absolut* (2015). Because the campaign was designed to reposition the brand, we planned to use a range of media, including above-the-line channels such as television and outdoor. That was our biggest mistake.

When we presented our first cut of the TV ad – a proudly African expression of the brand – the global team baulked. They wanted to be relevant to local consumers, but they could not get their heads around such a radical shift. We fought for the ad, but in the end we had to compromise. The campaign was still a bold departure for Absolut, but it didn't go quite as far as we had hoped. Resigned to this fact, we expected the rest of the campaign collateral to be watered down as well. But a strange thing happened. Once the above-the-line elements had been signed off no one from global seemed particularly concerned about what we were doing in any other media. The branded-content films that we made passed through approvals without a single change.

Over the years, working on several global brands, I have encountered this same phenomenon over and over again. Despite the industry's shift away from traditional media and towards digital, there tends to be far more latitude when it comes to developing online content. For some reason marketers are still more cautious in their approach to above-the-line elements than non-traditional elements such as branded content. In a world in which online content has the ability to generate more views than a TV ad this seems counter-intuitive . . . and yet the phenomenon exists. Branded content often flies under the radar. When did you last produce a TV ad that did not have an army of agency personnel or clients on set? Compare this with the small crew that produced your latest online film without much interference. One could argue that this has something to do with the relative amounts of money being spent, but while the budgets for online content are rising this blind spot persists.

When 2016 rolled around and a new brief for Absolut arrived at the agency, we decided to use this to our advantage. Rather than trying to reposition the brand using ATL media again, we embraced the power of branded entertainment instead. We partnered with local hip-hop star Khuli Chana to create a concept album called *One Source*. The pan-African musical collaboration celebrated Africa as the one source of all human creation. It featured ten artists, eight original tracks, a music video, a documentary series and live performances. The integrated campaign involved the audience every step of the way, turning *One Source* into a war cry for Africa's creative revolution.

One Source was a massive success for Absolut and for Khuli Chana. The album shot to number one on iTunes, driving a spike in sales and helping Absolut to reclaim its position as the biggest-selling premium vodka in Africa. Despite the breadth of content that we created, and despite its radically Africanized aesthetic, we experienced almost no push-back from global. In fact, by the time the campaign won Gold at Cannes Lions the global-marketing team had become its biggest supporter. *One Source* is clear and definitive proof that branded entertainment can operate in the shadows, circumventing many of the restrictions levied on traditional advertising. This is why I call it the ninjutsu of advertising. But *One Source* is also a clear example of how much additional cover can be created for ad ninja who operate in smaller markets.

Had we tried to create a piece of mainstream pop culture like this in the USA or western Europe, chances are that we would have faced far more resistance. In a high-profile market, failure on this scale wouldn't just be costly, it would create massive reputational damage, too. Smaller markets limit a global brand's exposure to risk, and so, theoretically, they offer agencies a correlative amount of creative freedom. Unfortunately this does not always translate into braver clients. In my experience the biggest barrier to doing good work in a small market like South Africa is a lack of courage on the part of marketers. But if you can convince your local client to take the risk on a piece of branded content, chances are high that you will be able to slide it past their global counterparts. The irony is that this isn't true when it comes to ATL advertising. Global marketers are less likely to allow a small market to stray from the centre when producing ATL elements. It's simpler and cheaper for them to insist that small markets use global collateral. The intersection between non-traditional collateral (branded entertainment, for example) and the dynamics of a smaller market (such as South Africa) produces the greatest amount of cover for an ad ninja. It is at this unique juncture that you will find the area of deepest shadow.

With these personal experiences in hand I reached out to other people involved in producing Gold-Lion-winning work from smaller markets so that we could compare notes. I quickly discovered that many of the forces driving the success of branded entertainment in these smaller or less affluent markets can be applied to larger markets as well.

Media jujutsu

David Webster, Managing Partner and Chief Growth Officer for BBH Singapore, was part of the team that created Nike's *Unlimited*

Stadium. For those who haven't seen it *Unlimited Stadium* is a masterpiece of brand experience.

It is a high-tech running track designed in the shape of a Nike Lunar Epic footprint – only much bigger. It features a 200-metre running track lined with LED screens where runners can engage in a virtual race against avatars of themselves.'[2]

According to David, the Philippines (where *Unlimited Stadium* first made its debut) is a relatively small market for Nike, so the agency has to be innovative in the way it takes the brand to market. TV is still the biggest, most dominant medium across most of Asia Pacific, but budget limitations make it difficult for Nike to compete in this channel. In addition, agencies in the region often struggle to access the skills necessary to produce high-quality TV advertising for local markets. While this may be frustrating, these limitations create the perfect conditions for branded entertainment.

Experiential marketing has been successful for Nike Singapore – not only because it can produce experiential work to the desired quality but because the immersive nature of these experiences tends to create much deeper brand engagement. But the real marketing power behind an experience like *Unlimited Stadium* isn't the experience itself; it is the brand's ability to amplify that experience through earned media.

Twenty years ago – before Facebook, Twitter, Instagram and Snapchat – the impact of a live activation was limited by the number of people who could experience that activation first hand. Today, social media gives marketers the ability to amplify their actions, potentially turning a local stunt into a global media event. But creating a viral sensation isn't easy. You need to do something truly remarkable if you want people to remark on it. But when you are an iconic global brand like Nike you need to make sure that whatever you do is on-brand as well. *Unlimited Stadium* was a great way to achieve both of those objectives. As a world-first innovation *Unlimited Stadium* was newsworthy, ensuring its ability to generate mainstream PR. But by creating an experience that made ordinary people feel like professional athletes it also ensured its place in the Facebook and Instagram feeds of every individual who experienced it.

If branded entertainment really is a form of advertising ninjutsu, then it is this ability to harness the power of earned media that is its secret weapon. We can compare this special capability to jujutsu – a martial art famous for its capacity to redirect an opponent's force. Jujutsu formed the basis of the ninja's empty-handed fighting techniques in the same way that earned media provides branded entertainment with its ability to scale. In smaller markets, where it is difficult to justify the investment in bought media, branded entertainment's efficiency at amplifying reach through earned media is critical.

Sun Tzu and the importance of terrain

One of my personal favourites from Cannes Lions 2017 was the campaign for Lacta chocolate called *From the Start*. I spoke about this campaign in an earlier chapter, 'From Product Placement to Idea Placement', and it has been described in some detail by my co-authors ('The Battle of Time and the Fallacy of the Short Attention Span' and 'Back to Basics'), so I won't repeat the storyline here in any detail. The important point to stress, though, is that when I began watching the first episode of this five-part web series I was not expecting to be transported across space and time. In fact, to be honest, when I noticed that the entry was over an hour long I gritted my teeth and hoped it wouldn't be too painful. By the end I had tears of joy in my eyes and a clear sense that this was going to be a big winner. It was unlike any advertising or entertainment I had seen before. Combining the drama of a mainstream TV series with a clear product message, *From the Start* succeeded in transcending both the advertising and entertainment industries.

I spoke to Panos Sambrakos, the Executive Creative Director of OgilvyOne Worldwide in Athens, about their work. The agency describes its entry as 'a web series that tells the story of a man who doesn't believe in love falling for the girl he sees in a dream that he has each time he eats a piece of Lacta chocolate'. While that may sound like an ambitious plot line, it is beautifully executed with great visual storytelling and faultless performances.

When I spoke to Panos about *From the Start* he confirmed one of my personal theories about why a campaign like this emerged from an unexpected market such as Greece. All over the world audiences are drawn to local content. (Samantha Glynne explores this fact in some detail in her chapter 'Ideas That Scale'.) This appetite for local content is particularly true in smaller culturally diverse markets in which English (the entertainment industry's lingua franca) is not the mother tongue. While countries such as France, Germany and India produce excellent film and TV programmes, most of the world's biggest feature films and TV shows are still produced in English.[3] This Anglicized content is then broadcast around the world, and, while often subtitled or dubbed, the cultural references remain inherently North American or British. With the advent of streaming services, these giant entertainment titles are becoming increasingly accessible to all. But no matter how much of this high-quality entertainment is produced, local audiences continue to seek out relevant local content because people love stories that reflect their own experiences. This creates a great opportunity for brands to support local content – especially in smaller markets.

The ancient Chinese strategist and philosopher Sun Tzu dedicates an entire chapter in his seminal book *The Art of War* to 'terrain' and the associated strategies for dealing with it.[4] Shadow warriors consider Sun Tzu's work to be a major influence on their art and his strategies are applicable to ad ninja as well.[5] Knowledge and mastery of your terrain is a powerful weapon, and when operating in smaller markets you can use this local knowledge to outmanoeuvre bigger and stronger adversaries. In branded entertainment terms this can translate into a brand's ability to outperform a major international entertainment property on a fraction of the budget.

When creating branded content for a market like the USA or the UK you are competing with the world's biggest titles. Your movie will have to go head-to-head with the summer's Hollywood blockbuster or the latest HBO TV series. If you are producing music you will be competing with the likes of Ed Sheeran and Beyoncé, and if you are staging a live event you will have to contend with Tomorrowland, Coachella and Disney's Magic Kingdom. While the existence of these entertainment behemoths may be intimidating for creators of branded content in small markets, the one thing that these franchises lack is cultural relevance. That doesn't mean that local audiences won't support these global entertainment properties – of course they will, and they do – but they will hanker after more relevant content and experiences as well. *From the Start* may not be steeped in Greek cultural references, but the film is set in Greece and performed in Greek by local actors, and its exceedingly romantic storyline surely resonated with audiences who were still reeling from austerity and a damaged economy.

There are other benefits to producing branded entertainment in smaller markets. In the USA, getting Ryan Gosling, John Malkovich or David Beckham to appear in your branded film may be necessary to cut through the clutter, but in a small market local celebrities can provide real bang for your buck. In Spain, *Beyond Money*, a superslick seventeen-minute sci-fi film created by MRM//McCann for Santander Bank, used local celebrity power to draw a mainstream audience into cinemas across the country. This classy sci-fi thriller was directed by Kike Maíllo, a well-known Spanish director, and featured Adriana Ugarte, the star of the 2016 Pedro Almodóvar film *Julieta*. I have no idea what Santander Bank paid Ugarte, but I am fairly confident that it came nowhere near what a major A-lister like Emma Stone or Jennifer Lawrence would have cost. The irony, though, is that for Spanish audiences Adriana Ugarte is a bigger draw than her expensive Hollywood counterparts. *Beyond Money* reached an audience of 7.3 million people in its first week, demonstrating the power of local talent and highlighting an important strategy for anyone creating branded entertainment in smaller or less affluent markets.

But what I find most impressive about this Grand Prix winner isn't the quality of the film-making or even its highly innovative distribution strategy. For me the campaign's real success lies in the underlying meaning that it created for both the brand and its audiences.

The warrior's code

When I spoke to Miguel Bemfica, the Chief Creative Officer of MRM//McCann in Spain, I was blown away by the fact that the agency was involved in developing Santander's 1|2|3 Smart Account, an innovative new kind of bank account that helps young people with more than just their money by offering them assistance with a range of lifestyle services as well.[6]

According to the agency's Cannes Lions entry: 'Spanish millennials blame the economic crisis on the banks; 71% would rather go to the dentist than listen to commercial proposals made by a bank.'[7] By creating a new kind of bank account that offers not only financial benefits but also youth-oriented services and experiences, Santander was able to tap into the issues that are most important to young Spaniards. In my opinion it is this foundation of shared values that gives *Beyond Money* its real edge. This isn't just a film, it is an ideological statement about one of the most important social issues of our time. In a world of rampant consumerism, shining a light on the balance between money and experiences is highly relevant and deeply meaningful. As a jury, one of the primary reasons why we awarded this piece the Grand Prix is the fact that it didn't just shift the brand, it actually moved the entire financial-services category forward by getting people to question whether money is more important than experiences.[8]

I was reading *AdBusters* the other day, a magazine to which I remain loyal despite its vehemently anti-commercial ethos (or perhaps because of it), when I came across a piece from editor Kalle Lasn in which he says that thriving economies are built on values and culture.[9]

I don't always agree with Lasn's perspective on things, but I am a strong believer in the importance of purpose and the transcendent power of shared values. I also believe that smaller and less affluent markets (which invariably suffer from marginalized or disenfranchised cultures) are hungry for a sense of purpose, making shared values an excellent tactic for creators of branded content in these markets.

Based on my experience working on the *One Source* campaign I am convinced that 'meaning' is the most powerful differentiator of all. While the quality of the music and filmed entertainment that we created was key to the project's success, it was the resonance of the *One Source* ideology that elevated the campaign to the next level. *One Source* wasn't just a song, it wasn't just an ad, it was a war cry for Africa's creative revolution that inspired unity among Africans by reminding people that we all come from one source. It should be noted, however, that tapping into shared values is by no means the preserve only of marginalized or disenfranchised cultures. It is something that anyone who has the right intention can achieve, and it is one of the primary reasons why branded entertainment is so powerful. Seamlessly integrating your brand into an entertainment property (rather than simply making an ad) will provide you with a broader canvas on which to explore shared values, and it will give you a credible way to create meaning for your customers.

Over the centuries the mythical ninja may have become notorious for their treachery and deception, but like all warriors they followed a strict code. I believe that ad ninja should adhere to a code as well. There may be several tenets to this code, but for me the most critical one is that branded entertainment must always serve both the brand and the audience in equal measure. Creating meaning is one of the most powerful ways to achieve this difficult balance successfully.

The way of the warrior

Entertainment Lions 2017 clearly showed us that there are benefits to operating in the shadows. While many dream of creating global branded entertainment properties starring big-name celebrities there are actually significant advantages to working in smaller, less prominent markets. That said, we also discovered that many of the principles underlying these unexpected successes have broader application to the art of branded entertainment – not just in developing markets but all over the world.

Like the mythical ninja of ancient Japan, modern creators of branded entertainment thrive by doing things differently. They use the darkness to their advantage, turning the fact that many marketers still view online as less important than TV into an opportunity to push creative boundaries. They do not try to match strength with strength, preferring instead to use their branded entertainment properties to harness the power of earned media, thereby outmanoeuvring larger opponents with bigger media budgets. They understand the importance of terrain, leveraging their knowledge of local markets into strategic vantage points from which to outflank their global competitors. But, most importantly, they adhere to the warrior's code, remaining steadfast in their commitment to serving not only the brand but also the audience, striving to create value and meaning for both at every turn.

1. Szczepanski, Kallie, 'The Ninja of Japan', ThoughtCo, 16 July 2017, thoughtco. com/history-of-the-ninja-195811

2. Nudd, Tim, Adweek, 'How Nike Made Unlimited Stadium, the World's Coolest Running Track', 23 June 2017

3. Clarke, Steve, Variety, 'US, UK Are World's Top TV Exporters, Australia Shows Improvement', 24 February 24 http://variety.com/2016/tv/ global/u-s-u-k-tv-exporters-australia-1201713741/

4. McCallum, John S., Ivey Business Journal, 'In War and Business, It's the Terrain that Matters', January/February 2007 https://iveybusinessjournal. com/publication/in-war-and-business-its-the-terrain-that-matters/

5. Cummins, Anthony, 'The Japanese Ninja and Sun Tzu', https://www.sonshi. com/the-japanese-ninja--sun-tzu.html

6. ContagiousI/O, 'Insight & Strategy: Beyond Money', 28 July 2017 http://www. mccann.es/assets/contenidos/noticias/xrbOs_insight-strategy-beyond-money.pdf

7. Cannes Lions Archive http://www.canneslionsarchive.com/the-work/ entry/829581/beyond-money

8. Diaz, Ann-Christine, AdAge, 'A Sci-Fi Short by Santander Wins the Entertainment Lions Grand Prix', 21 June 2017 http://creativity-online.com/ work/santander-beyond-money/52099

9. Lasn, Kalle, AdBusters, 'Manifesto for World Revolution Pt. 6', January/ February 2016 https://www.adbusters.org/

THINK LIKE A MARKETER, BEHAVE LIKE AN ENTERTAINER, MOVE LIKE A TECH START-UP: A BEHIND-THE-SCENES LOOK AT THREE CANNES GRANDS PRIX

PJ Pereira, Pereira O'Dell

Like every great idea, it started with a single thought: *What if, in the near future, people could sell their memories to fill their bank accounts. What if we showed that future, just to remind our audience how memories are worth more than money?* That's something people would stop to watch. They knew it. That was probably the reason for the mischievous grin on my friend Miguel's face when he came to visit me in San Francisco.

It was late February, and he had an event in town, and – this was the official line, at least – he told me he was taking the opportunity to come by and say hello. As we talked I could see his excitement and curiosity growing the more we discussed the mysterious world of branded entertainment and how I had managed to get my Branded Entertainment Grand Prix produced a few years back. Being a smart veteran of the industry himself, he had already realized the way we had traditionally got advertisements done would never have allowed an idea like Intel's *The Beauty Inside* series to be created, sold, done.

He had been talking about the possibilities of attracting consumers instead of interrupting them with his team back in Madrid, where he ran the local office of MRM//McCann, and at that time my work for Intel was still one of the most famous projects in that field.

So he called.

If I wanted to have a chance to do more of those I needed more people, more agencies pushing different buttons and testing the gears of this strange, unknown machine. So for almost two hours we talked. I opened the process, explained the changes we had to make on the process, from the way we think, to the way we cast, approve, distribute, promote . . . and then he left.

A month later I was invited to speak at an event in San Sebastián, Spain, and reached out to him to return the visit. We had drinks at the fancy bar of the Hotel de Londres, and he told me that as soon as he had got back his people had presented him with an interesting idea about money not being the most important thing in the world, a bold move for their main account: Santander Bank. He immediately knew that was an entertainment idea not a regular advertisement.

'We're shooting it tomorrow,' he said. 'If it turns out OK I'll send it to you.'

I didn't hear from him for six more weeks, but then an email from him popped into my inbox. A link and a question: 'What do you think?' I was late for a meeting but decided to take a peep before showering, then finish at work. So I did. Pressed play.

For eighteen minutes I sat there. Right to the end. Then I told my wife, 'Miguel just took a Grand Prix out of my hands.' I had a smile on my face. I had heard that my agency's *Lo and Behold* was one of the front runners for the main prize in the category I was going to chair at Cannes a few months later. The thought of having to go on stage and award my own shop the top prize of the night was terrifying.

'Love it, Miguel! This is really good!' I wrote in an email later that day after watching it again with some people at the agency. I didn't tell him my prediction at that point. The judging process is too complex for that.

The next time we met was in Cannes. I had been sitting outside the judging room for about forty minutes waiting for the Grand Prix deliberations. *Lo and Behold* was indeed one of contenders under discussion, so the rules required me to step out and leave the decision to the other judges. When they called me back in, the jury, always so animated, was in sombre mood. Funeral quiet. There was a picture up on the screen: the poster for *Beyond Money*. I knew what it meant, so I grinned.

'That would have been my choice, too!'

It was as if I had dragged death itself out of their throats. In an instant we were all laughing and popping champagne to celebrate the long week of work and everything we had learned and accomplished together. We left an hour later, and that's when I saw Miguel for the third time that year.

He took my call, and I told him to meet me at my hotel. I had something important to tell him. Some of the judges agreed to help with the prank. We told him he got a Bronze.

Miguel was so happy; this was the agency's first Lion ever!

We waited, let it sink in, let him enjoy the glory of a shiny cat. Then we told him we had elevated it to Silver, and his wide smile got even wider. We hugged; he screamed. Then we dropped the news that we'd upped it to a Gold. He was already jumping, holding back his tears, when someone finally asked if that was enough, if he was satisfied with it.

'Of course,' he replied, happy and bouncing like a ballerina who's just learned to balance her entire body on her little toes.

So they said: 'Maybe we should give the Grand Prix to someone else then.'

He went quiet.

Then tried so say something.

Stuttered.

'Yes,' we said. 'You got your well-deserved freaking Grand Prix!'

At that point he became one of the very few people ever to have won a Grand Prix Lion at Cannes. And I gave him a long hug that felt so different I couldn't quite understand what it was I felt. Yes, there was happiness for a friend, and there was relief that it was him instead of me. But there was also a lingering feeling I now recognize as pride. Not the kind you have when you do something yourself but the joy I guess an elementary-school teacher must feel when one of her old students accomplishes something big in his or her life. Miguel had never been a student of mine. I had never even taught him much, only encouraged him to follow a path I was already on, but he did it quite spectacularly. There was no merit I could claim over his amazing creative win, yet I felt I had accomplished something, for sharing my backstage stories helped him realize his masterful deed.

This final chapter is an attempt to do that again, to share some stories and secrets very few know, which may help more amazing ideas to be produced. Starting with the 2017 Grand Prix Winner of the Branded Entertainment Lions competition: Santander Bank's *Beyond Money*.

The story of *Beyond Money*, Grand Prix 2017

Almost every chapter in this book makes some sort of reference to *Beyond Money*, which is only natural given that it was our pick for the big winner of the year. But this chapter is different. It's about the backstage, how it came to be. Because the secrets, the pitfalls and *eurekas* may be more meaningful than looking at the work once it's done.

When the project started to take shape, the Madrid team of MRM//McCann already had a budget approved, a classic advertising budget. That was good because they didn't have to run after the money but also dangerous since a project like that might require different levels of investment. Thankfully, the client at Santander had previously been on the agency side, and she knew how things are, how ideas grow. Maybe there was a chance. They went for it.

That's when things started to go down a different route. Starting with the first pitch. The presentation was rough, barely a short description of what the idea could be – no scripts of the kind an agency would present in a traditional situation, not least because writing a full script for a fifteen-minute piece would cost a lot of money, real screenwriters and weeks they didn't have but also because they wanted time to let the idea develop together with the client.

It didn't take much to get the leading bank in Spain behind the idea. Because of the economic troubles haunting Europe, younger generations had been growing increasingly uncomfortable with the image of what a bank was. The kind of idea MRM//McCann and Santander were cooking up, so subversive and bold, one that placed money in a secondary position in everyone's life, would clearly demonstrate which side the bank was on.

Very quickly they realized that there was already too much risk in doing something so new, so the team had to be made up of real pros, starting with the executive producer, Sara Muñoz, someone with years of experience in the movie business who was brought in by the agency as a freelance instead of using the regular ad team. She was to partner the agency folks, who would learn the craft as they went along for possible future projects. It was she who put them in touch with movie-production companies instead of shops that only made ads.

With a commercial, the next step would have been to look through the showreels of directors with experience of working on similar projects. But it wasn't a commercial, so they searched for directors who had been doing the most interesting work aimed at younger audiences. (Jason Xenopoulos also deals with elements of this story in his 'Advertising Ninjutsu' chapter, but let me go through some of the details again.) They put the project to three directors, all of whom really wanted it after reading the pitch. But one of them was clearly more interested in working hand in hand with the agency, and his approach was just as if he were another creative working there. Luckily the guy, Kike Maíllo, had previously directed the second-most-watched-online video among millennials in Spain, a science-fiction story called *Eva*. They reached out to him through a production company named Oxigeno and, after a short period of negotiation, signed him up. No triple bidding, not long treatments . . . that project required vision and partnership. They had theirs.

It was only at that point that Rami Aboukhair, President of the bank, saw the idea for the first time. Luckily for the team, Mr Aboukhair liked it but had one request. He would only do it if they had a celebrity that would bring credibility to the project. That would cost more, but it was OK, since the celebrity would also bring an audience they would otherwise have to buy.

Wise move, Señor Aboukhair.

This request from the top freed up a little bit of extra cash and brought in Adriana Ugarte, star of Spanish director Pedro Almodóvar's 2016 movie *Julieta*. In return, she brought her friends to the project: Bárbara Goenaga, Will Shephard and Miguel Fernandez.

They had six weeks in total from idea to launch. No time to

test, to overthink, to overdo. It was them, their instincts, vision and accountability. It had to be great, otherwise there wouldn't be another one.

And they did it just right.

The entire film was shot in three days and launched on 18 April 2017.

In just two weeks following the release Santander recorded the fastest sign-up rate in the 160 years of the bank's history, reaching 35% of its annual business goal.

Hearing that story straight from Miguel's mouth, it was interesting to notice how the process started with all the marketing discipline our industry is used to, from the goals to the budgets and production rigour, but once the main direction was set they were quickly able to change to the way a proper entertainment company behaves. They brought in the right talent – artists used to being worth their audience's time – and were flexible to adjust to reality along the way. Which makes the project a shining example of what I see as the mantra of our time: 'Think like a marketer, behave like an entertainer, move like a tech start-up.'

Beyond Money was a remarkable winner, and the jury was very happy to be able to celebrate it on stage in front of the thousands of people in the audience at the Palais des Festivals as well as online. What very few people know is that to qualify as the big winner of the year an idea doesn't just have to be better than all others, it also has to motivate the jury to give it that honour. In 2014 and 2015, for example, the juries decided that there wasn't one piece that would qualify for a Grand Prix, which makes the recognition of MRM//McCann and Santander even more notable.

In 2016 the honour went to a *New York Times* project that combined virtual reality and journalism to create an immersive way for readers to be present in the stories. Definitely a feat anyone interested in storytelling should take the time to appreciate. A great way to apply marketing discipline, entertainment value and tech vision into a single execution. However, because it was produced by a publishing company some marketers have dismissed it as not being part of the branded entertainment world. Therefore, to avoid the pitfall and already feeling guilty for leaving aside such an amazing piece of work, I have decided to skip that year and go straight to the backstage of the next big winner. (I have skipped the *NYT* piece here, but you shouldn't. Get your VR goggles on, and go and try it out.)

The story of *The Beauty Inside*, Grand Prix 2013

You've read about *The Beauty Inside* series and its predecessor *The Inside Experience* in Marcelo's chapter 'The Battle of Time and the Fallacy of the Short Attention Span'. What you don't know is how one led to the other. A hint: it was an act of near panic.

Both are from my agency and are very likely responsible for my being picked as president of the jury in 2017. It was also what sparked in me the realization that the way agencies and clients operate together should be different. The whole thing started with a call. My old client from McDonald's, Johan Jervoe, today Global CMO at UBS Bank, had just moved to Intel and needed some help with its partner marketing programmes, in particular the relationship with Toshiba. The two brands weren't doing very well with younger buyers, and we convinced them to surprise the audience with a multi-year programme where they would combine youth-driven film content with social media features. We called them 'social films' and made them all around the idea that it is what is inside that matters for Intel and featured the hottest Toshiba computer that season. That would help position the brands as being more than up to date with the technology but would also present them as true innovators that were expanding the boundaries of Hollywood.

One of the pillars of this strategy was to break the way the money is spent. Traditionally, brands have been investing their marketing dollars mostly on media – 80–90% – then what's left goes on the production of whatever the audience will see. We convinced them that in this on-demand world the hardest working dollars were actually the ones people could see on-screen and moved the investment to a remarkable 60% media, 40% production. That configuration meant that the entire campaign could keep the same budget as an ordinary partnership campaign, but the new allocation of money allowed us to get the level of production that would attract an audience, including *Disturbia* director D.J. Caruso and star of the US remake of *Shameless* Emmy Rossum. We were working on the first season of a thriller called *The Inside Experience*, in which a girl wakes up in an unknown room and needs help from the internet to get out, when we got a call.

It was 6.30 p.m., at the end of a long day before a big presentation, and the client wanted to tell us that everything else was fine but that their legal department wanted to make sure the main character would not at any point be afraid for her life or fear any sort of physical violence. When I arrived at the office the entire team was in panic. How could we produce a thriller if the protagonist isn't afraid?

Next morning at 9 a.m. we presented the idea the way we believed it should be: scary, with a character terrified for her life and what the villain would do to her. If they didn't want a thriller, they shouldn't do a thriller. They should switch genre. We then presented a few other ideas under the same strategy, although with a less subversive angle. One of those ideas was the story of a man named Alex, who wakes up every day in a different body. Same house, same life but looking completely different. He used his Toshiba notebook to record his different looks just for fun and enjoyed a life of first dates – until he falls in love but is unable to pursue a proper relationship. This series was to be called *The Beauty Inside*, and the client immediately fell in love with the story and the character. After a lot of debate we decided to proceed with the thriller for its shock value, then do Alex's story the following year. We did, and because of the success of the first round, this time we counted on an even better split of the budget: 50:50 between production and media.

This series was even more successful. Despite being launched during the London Olympics and all its fanfare, this love story by two tech companies featuring Topher Grace and Mary Elizabeth Winstead amassed hundreds of millions of views and was the most watched piece of branded content of 2012. The next year it won not only the Branded Entertainment Grand Prix at Cannes but also the Film and Cyber Grands Prix (Cyber is a now-extinct category for digital ideas). It also garnered a Daytime Emmy against regular television programming – an unheard-of feat for a piece of marketing. In 2013, as you have read in Samantha Glynne's chapter 'Ideas That Scale', it was made into a movie then a television series in South Korea, and now it's being transformed into a Hollywood movie and a new TV series in Asia.

The story of *Back to the Start*, Grand Prix 2012

The year before *The Beauty Inside* I wasn't that happy. In fact, I was jealous. The Branded Entertainment category gave its Grand Prix to an idea that took the USA by storm with its poignant story that was launched during the Grammys that year. An ad made by the marketing arm of a talent agency, CAA, a regular winner in the branded entertainment awards circuit, featuring a cute, sad then uplifting story of a farmer who gives in to industrialized farming only to change his mind and go back to where he had been at the start. Beautifully executed, that spot is still one of the boldest moves ever done by a food or beverage brand in recent years, especially considering that the advertiser, Mexican-food chain Chipotle, is not a big TV spender and, well . . . there are few positions more expensive than thirty seconds during the most important music awards on television: the Grammys.

The brilliance of the initiative, as the industry quickly realized, was that they used the event's massive audience to attract critical mass then continued the spectacle mostly online; a path multiple brands have taken before, even more after, but none with the same effect that Chipotle did that year. After all, not only was it over two-and-a-half-minutes long instead of the usual thirty seconds but it also featured a magical cover version of Coldplay's 'The Scientist' by Willie Nelson, an iconic defender of the American farmer. If you haven't heard it yet you should stop reading this and do so now.

This ambitious project has haunted my nightmares ever since. How did those bastards manage to pull it off? 'Oh, they are a talent agency; they have all the talent to hand . . .' I answered myself with soothing ego-salving excuses. Because I was to write this chapter, however, I felt I needed to go deeper than my jealousy had allowed up to now. So I called them.

What I found left me humbled and inspired.

It had begun as part of their customer-relationship programme. They had the steps, the mechanics, the process for how they would engage people, reward them – and they had a story. A little piece of online content to reward their most loyal customers. The tale of this little pig farmer who turned his farm over to industry only to regret it later and bring it back to how it used to be. Small, sustainable, romantic. The catch: at that point, there was no Coldplay, no Willie Nelson, just a massive customer-relationship-management programme architected to close the gap between the brand and its most passionate audience by celebrating the very principles that made Chipotle one of the most successful food companies of the past decade.

The script evolved into a storyboard, just as it was expected to. From there, it was animated in the lovely geometrical yet huggable style created by Nexus Studios, and only when they were finishing the edit was the music brought in. First they tried a scratch track and were . . . meh? Not there yet. Then days searching for different songs – old ones, new ones – until someone stumbled upon Coldplay's 'The Scientist'.

It was magic. Lyrics and story matched. The melancholy of the lost past, the decision to go back. 'Nobody said it was easy . . .' goes the song. They played them together. It was perfect. Suddenly the animation about the brand principles was something bigger. It had the weight of pop culture. It was a message not an advertisement. Something people could embrace, make theirs, seek out.

Then, as sometimes happens when an idea strikes such brilliance, someone in the room decided to push it further. 'How about we don't use the Coldplay version? What if we try someone closer to the country-music universe like . . .'

Willie Nelson! An icon. A legend. A . . . foolish dream, they thought. But they tried anyway.

Finally, they were ready to flex the talent-management muscles of mothership CAA. They called both Willie Nelson, who is represented by the agency, and Coldplay, who aren't, and got both parties enthusiastic enough about the project that Willie wanted to record the song and Coldplay's Chris Martin liked the idea of a country-music icon covering it – to the point where one would only participate if the other was on board, too. And from all that love was born one of the sweetest pieces of branded entertainment ever produced.

Immediately the little video got the entire organization excited. 'That's what we stand for!' they claimed in the hallways. To such an extent that the humble CRM video that was planned for online distribution among their main customers evolved into a TV spot and stole a quintuple slot in one of the most prestigious media seconds of the year, the Grammy's, when Chipotle ran the piece in its entire two and a half minutes of glory.

From that burst of pride to a 20% increase in revenue that year was just a natural consequence, one that started a tradition of investing in branded entertainment that Chipotle has been keeping alive ever since.

Those stories have a few things in common

The title of this chapter serves as a unifier of the three backstage stories. The creators behind each idea have all 'thought like marketers', in the sense that they applied the necessary discipline to pinpoint the specific goals the creative endeavour had to achieve. Then they 'behaved like entertainers' to make sure consumers' time spent was worth the expense of employing top talent to bring their audiences with them. And they 'moved like tech start-ups', dodging obstacles along the way instead of operating under a single production plan that doesn't really work when you are breaking new ground.

There are a few lessons that might shed some light on the practices that allowed those top-level directives to happen:

1. **Shift the money**
   Consumers have got used to seeing the money on-screen for their entertainment. If brands want to compete for the audience's time they have to shift a good amount of cash in that direction, too. The good news is that media spend is less

critical for initiatives of this calibre, so the overall budget may be kept the same as long as the person in charge on the brand side has enough power to move money between media and production. Unfortunately in most companies that is not easy unless the project is backed by someone very high up the food chain.

2. **Not just a part but the whole thing**

    Big rule-breaking content doesn't happen if it has to split the money with other executions in the same initiative. *The Beauty Inside* wasn't part of a campaign, it was the campaign. *Beyond Money* wasn't supporting a bunch of TV spots; it was supported by traditional ads to bring its own audience. Even *Back to the Start*, which was born as part of a CRM initiative, eventually grew into becoming the centre of everything. Looking back, we may be witnessing the evolution of marketing from being TV-centric to being content- or entertainment-centric, where other executions may exist but are there to support the core, the piece everyone wants to see.

3. **Bring in the pros**

    If you want to compete against one of the most glamorous industries in the world you need to bring in the glamour, too, and that means the artists, the headliners, as the CEO of Santander insisted. That may even be a good way to justify to the CFOs why the move towards a more balanced production–media ratio.

4. **Pick artists who fall genuinely in love with the idea**

    As Carol Goll mentioned in her chapter 'What's in It for the Stars?' there are two ways of bringing big names to a project: you either pay them for the 'embarrassment' of doing an ad (that's how some of them think) or you make them want to play the character. This requires a balancing act between the interests of the brand, the audience and the stars, but that's how any form of entertainment is produced anyway. In order to play that game you have to be ready to stay flexible and adjust to that balance, to change the script to get the right star, to move money around your original budget to afford the right star when he or she finally agrees to join the initiative.

5. **Collaborate with the artists**

   There is a significant difference between hiring a spokesperson to perform a script in an advertisement and bringing in an artist to work on an entertainment project. The first is doing it for the money; the second, for the money as well as to satisfy their artistic objectives. It would be a wasted opportunity to keep that person outside the process just because a script has been approved or a concept has already been locked. Staying flexible and less controlling is essential for all the creative juices to flow. That's true for directors, actors, writers, editors . . . My advice is you stay focused on making sure your core message is protected, clear and evident in the premise and the early moments of the execution (in case some people only watch the beginning), then stay out of the way.

6. **Keep the teams small and nimble**

   Committees may work on tried-and-tested paths where following best practices can help ensure success, but in vision-driven projects there's nothing worse. Entertainment is a vision-driven world. It's fed by the passion a single person pours into it and how he or she infects the rest of the crew with that passion. In TV series it's the showrunner; in movies the director. You need a single voice of command if you expect to create a true sense of what Tomoya Suzuki called 'artistic integrity' in the chapter 'Back to Basics' and want the audience to respect what you are doing. If you can't, branded entertainment is not for you. And if you're unsure I recommend you revisit Jason Xenopoulos's chapter 'Advertising Ninjutsu and the Secret Art of Operating in the Shadows' and think about his ninjas a bit more.

7. **Include the brand in the premise**

   Consider the three projects featured in the chapter. They are as much PR plays as they are content ideas – as Monica Chun established in 'The News It Creates' and exactly how Jason Xenopoulos and Pelle Sjoenell proposed in 'From Product Placement to Idea Placement'. They all have examples of projects that worked even for people who didn't watch them, who only *heard* about the story of the farmer who went back to basics or the man who had a different body every day but remained the same inside. That's the big secret. If you make it impossible to talk about the idea without the brand, yet make it interesting enough to generate some buzz, you have something special in your hands.

8. **Be ready to go beyond**

There is so much opportunity in this new landscape. As Samantha Glynne mentioned in 'Ideas That Scale', ad series and short films can be turned into movies and television series that would always be credited as having been borne out of an advertisement for Brand A or Brand B. But brands aren't very good on exploiting these opportunities. Some can't make money out of them; others have legal departments that aren't prepared to risk the sort of unpredictability of an entertainment negotiation. Being ready to let an idea fly beyond the original execution demands flexible rights with few ties to the past. Of course, brands can negotiate first rights of refusal or that no competitors get involved in future incarnations, but chances are higher if the rights remain with the agencies and production companies in charge, who are more nimble when it comes to this sort of operation. Besides, in a world where marketing partners keep getting squeezed into smaller and smaller contracts in terms of finance, this may be a good way to create a bonus for ideas that are truly remarkable.

9. **Be mindful of time**

Marcelo Pascoa hit the bullseye in his chapter 'The Battle of Time and the Fallacy of the Short Attention Span'. Consumers are ready to spend massive amounts of continuous attention on content they love. Anyone who has ever marathoned a series knows this. But just because

we can, doesn't mean we should. When you think of consumers' time as their investment, you need to be careful
with each cent you are asking them to invest. Some ideas
can sustain one hour of pleasure, some two minutes and
there are those not worth more than six seconds. They can
all be wonderful until right before they become too long.
That is one of the most difficult decisions brands will have
to make when taking decisions about their entertainment
initiatives. Because there will always be the creator who
wants it longer, the boss who reads that no one spends more
than two minutes watching a video online, and all sorts of
gurus of best practice to impose their generic rules. Don't
listen, or do but then make decisions not based on those
rules but on what the idea wants to be.

Daring to enter this new and exciting territory is not for everyone.
It will require philosophical debates, budgetary decisions and artistic
risks; it will stretch the teams and force decisions that might have
unpredictable consequences further down the project line. But if
you assemble a great team of talented people all equally committed
to giving a return on the money the brand is investing and the time
consumers will spend, and if you learn from the ones who came
before you – as Miguel at MRM//McCann did when he started to ask
questions – you are likely to become a pioneer in the discipline that is
going to transform marketing for ever.

There is still time.

ABOUT THE AUTHORS

Monica Chun is EVP/Chief Operating Officer at PMK•BNC, a global, full-service PR and marketing firm that specializes in entertainment and pop culture and was recently voted number two on the *New York Observer*'s 'Power 50'. PMK•BNC delivers inspired communications and marketing strategies for brands as well as a who's who of the entertainment world. Their clients include over 400 of the most respected talent, influencers, content creators and brand innovators, including Kate Hudson, Cameron Diaz, Carrie Underwood, Sean Combs, Pepsi, Audi, Samsung, American Express and T-Mobile. Monica is an award-winning strategic-marketing professional with over twenty years of agency experience in brand strategy, influencer marketing, entertainment outreach, experiential marketing, sponsorship and promotions as well as insights and analytics. Monica has a proven track record of success creating and implementing marketing programmes that drive innovation for various Fortune 500 brands.

Jules Daly is President of RSA Films and producer/executive producer of numerous movies and TV series, including *The Grey, Daybreak, The A-Team* and *Shanghai Noon*.

Ricardo Dias is currently Vice-President Marketing for Middle Americas, at Anheuser-Busch InBev, having previously served as Global Vice-President, Consumer Connections, in New York. Ricardo has been named a 'Media Maven' by *Advertising Age*, a 'Branding Power Player' by *Billboard* and has been inducted into the AAF Hall of Achievement, the industry's premier award for outstanding advertising leaders.

Samantha Glynne is Global Vice-President of Branded Entertainment at the TV production giant FremantleMedia. She is based in London but drives branded entertainment activities for FremantleMedia around the world, working with regional commercial and digital teams to deliver brand strategy. She also leads key relationships with brands and agencies to maximize advertiser engagement on TV and digital platforms. Prior to this role she was Managing Partner at Publicis Entertainment in London and Paris and worked as Head of Branded Content at All3Media.

Carol Goll is a partner and Head of Global Branded Entertainment at ICM Partners. Since joining ICM in 2008 Goll has built one of the most coveted brand and talent endorsement divisions in the entertainment industry, structuring lucrative deals and building brands for A-list talent in film, TV, sports and music. Known for her creative and entrepreneurial edge, Ms Goll also founded ICM Partners' corporate-representation business, which provides strategic-entertainment-marketing counsel and development of cutting-edge campaigns for high-end luxury, automotive and fashion brands, leveraging all areas of the business to deliver the highest impact of success. Ms Goll has been recognized by *Advertising Age*, *Billboard* and *Adweek* as a top entertainment marketer for brands and by *Variety* as one of the top women in the industry making an impact. Prior to ICM she was an executive at Mercedes-Benz USA for close to fourteen years, leading the company into its first global forays outside of traditional automotive marketing/communications. She repositioned the brand as a competitor in the luxury goods and entertainment industries while delivering profitable return on investment. Ms Goll negotiated the brand's top alliances, including the global initiative Mercedes-Benz Fashion Week, which *Adweek* deemed 'a brand buzz surefire marketing decision'. Ms Goll has a BA in Journalism and an MA in Marketing Communications from Michigan State University.

Gabor Harrach is a New York-based TV and digital media producer, documentary film-maker and former head of the Entertainment, Editorial and Culture Departments at Red Bull Media House. He currently consults with global brands in content marketing. Trained at the Yale School of Drama as a theatrical producer and at the CBS Broadcast Center in New

York as a TV producer, Gabor's path to content marketing went from the theatre through investigative television journalism and documentary film-making to overseeing the development and production of entire portfolios of brand-produced content.

Marissa Nance is a managing director at OMD. She has been with Omnicom for over two decades and with OMD since its inception. There she has honed her skillset of developing, negotiating and executing entertainment-based media strategies across any medium. Her expertise includes original content development and production, storyline and product integrations, promotional extensions and custom 360 media platforms.

Toan Nguyen started as an intern at Jung von Matt and became the youngest strategy director in the company's history. He is now named equity partner at Jung von Matt/SPORTS, Germany's most awarded sports marketing agency. He advises national and international federations, football clubs, sports brands and blue-chip companies and a few top athletes. Toan manages several eSports teams, including the German Mousesports clan, and he is also the lead strategist for many eSports sponsorships such as Mercedes-Benz, Pringles and Vodafone.

Luciana Olivares is CCO of Latina Media, one of the most important TV networks in Peru, having previously led the marketing strategy for BBVA, one of the most respected and loved brands in Peru, achieving important business goals and winning many prestigious national and international awards. She achieved two Cannes Lions in 2015 with *The Concert No One Was Waiting For* in the Branded Content and PR categories, and another Cannes Lion in 2016 with *The Mute Performance*. She has written three best-selling marketing books and is one of the top one hundred executives in Peru.

Marcelo Pascoa is the Global Head of Brand Marketing for Burger King. He started his career as a copywriter, working for agencies such as Grey and DDB. For five years he worked as a creative director at

New Content, where he led the creation and production of branded content projects for Unilever Brazil. In 2014 he moved to the client side as the Creative Excellence Director for Coca-Cola Brazil. He later moved to Atlanta, Georgia, USA, to become Coca-Cola's Global Creative Director. Both as a creative and as a client, his work has always focused on bringing advertising and entertainment together, in projects that have been recognized by several international awards, such as Cannes Lions, the Clios and the Effie Awards.

PJ Pereira is co-founder and Creative Chairman of Pereira O'Dell, where he has worked with brands such as MINI, Coca-Cola, LEGO, Google, Skype and Intel among others. In 2017 he had the honour to serve as the president of the jury of the Branded Entertainment Jury at the Cannes Lions Festival of Creativity, thirteen years after chairing the Cyber Lions jury, when, according to the festival, he was the youngest president in the history of Cannes Lions.

Misha Sher is Vice-President, Sport and Entertainment, at Mediacom, one of the world's largest media agency networks and part of WPP Group. An industry veteran with over fifteen years' experience, Misha has advised and worked alongside some of the most admired global brands, events, properties and talent in creating innovative partnerships that truly harness the power of sport and entertainment. Misha has been on juries for numerous national and international award shows, and his opinions have featured in some of the leading global publications, including the *New York Times*, the *Wall Street Journal*, *Fortune*, CNN, CMO, *Adweek*, *Campaign* and *SportBusiness International*.

Pelle Sjoenell is Worldwide Chief Creative Officer of Bartle Bogle Hegarty (BBH). He founded BBH in Hollywood in 2010 to harness the creative power at the intersection of advertising, technology and entertainment. He also co-founded the Creative Studio, a joint venture merging the marketing insights of BBH with Scooter Braun Projects, the architects of modern pop culture and influence.

Tomoya Suzuki is founder and CEO of STORIES®, a joint venture between Hakuhodo DY and SEGA. With offices in Tokyo and Los Angeles, it produces film and TV based on Japanese IP, commercials and branded entertainment. STORIES® represents more than forty creators from Hollywood and Japan with backgrounds in filmed entertainment and expertise in branded content. It has produced over two hundred branded content and music videos, including J.W. Marriott's *Two Bellmen* and Namie Amuro's 'Anything'. Tomoya has created the Subaru branded entertainment campaign *Your Story With*, with sixty episodes of ninety-second story-based commercials and regular TV dramas based on the spot as well as a hit novel based on the commercials. He's currently partnered with Marc Platt (*La La Land*) to develop and produce *Shinobi* and the producers of *The Walking Dead* on *Altered Beast* for film and TV adaptations by Hollywood. He is a graduate of the USC Peter Stark Producing Program. WelcometoSTORIES.com

Jason Xenopoulos is the Global Chief Vision Officer of VML and Chief Creative Officer of VML, EMEA. Jason has written and directed feature films, directed award-winning TV commercials and started and managed successful businesses – including VML South Africa. Under Jason's leadership, VML South Africa won a host of international awards and was named Entertainment Agency of the Year in the Cannes Lions Global Creativity Report 2017.

INDEX OF WORKS CITED

SOME AUTHORS WE HAVE PUBLISHED

James Agee • Bella Akhmadulina • Tariq Ali • Kenneth Allsop • Alfred Andersch
Guillaume Apollinaire • Machado de Assis • Miguel Angel Asturias • Duke of Bedford
Oliver Bernard • Thomas Blackburn • Jane Bowles • Paul Bowles • Richard Bradford
Ilse, Countess von Bredow • Lenny Bruce • Finn Carling • Blaise Cendrars • Marc Chagall
Giorgio de Chirico • Uno Chiyo • Hugo Claus • Jean Cocteau • Albert Cohen
Colette • Ithell Colquhoun • Richard Corson • Benedetto Croce • Margaret Crosland
e.e. cummings • Stig Dalager • Salvador Dalí • Osamu Dazai • Anita Desai
Charles Dickens • Bernard Diederich • Fabián Dobles • William Donaldson
Autran Dourado • Yuri Druzhnikov • Lawrence Durrell • Isabelle Eberhardt
Sergei Eisenstein • Shusaku Endo • Erté • Knut Faldbakken • Ida Fink
Wolfgang George Fischer • Nicholas Freeling • Philip Freund • Carlo Emilio Gadda
Rhea Galanaki • Salvador Garmendia • Michel Gauquelin • André Gide
Natalia Ginzburg • Jean Giono • Geoffrey Gorer • William Goyen • Julien Gracq
Sue Grafton • Robert Graves • Angela Green • Julien Green • George Grosz
Barbara Hardy • H.D. • Rayner Heppenstall • David Herbert • Gustaw Herling
Hermann Hesse • Shere Hite • Stewart Home • Abdullah Hussein • King Hussein of Jordan
Ruth Inglis • Grace Ingoldby • Yasushi Inoue • Hans Henny Jahnn • Karl Jaspers
Takeshi Kaiko • Jaan Kaplinski • Anna Kavan • Yasunuri Kawabata • Nikos Kazantzakis
Orhan Kemal • Christer Kihlman • James Kirkup • Paul Klee • James Laughlin
Patricia Laurent • Violette Leduc • Lee Seung-U • Vernon Lee • József Lengyel
Robert Liddell • Francisco García Lorca • Moura Lympany • Thomas Mann
Dacia Maraini • Marcel Marceau • André Maurois • Henri Michaux • Henry Miller
Miranda Miller • Marga Minco • Yukio Mishima • Quim Monzó • Margaret Morris
Angus Wolfe Murray • Atle Næss • Gérard de Nerval • Anaïs Nin • Yoko Ono
Uri Orlev • Wendy Owen • Arto Paasilinna • Marco Pallis • Oscar Parland
Boris Pasternak • Cesare Pavese • Milorad Pavic • Octavio Paz • Mervyn Peake
Carlos Pedretti • Dame Margery Perham • Graciliano Ramos • Jeremy Reed
Rodrigo Rey Rosa • Joseph Roth • Ken Russell • Marquis de Sade • Cora Sandel
Iván Sándor • George Santayana • May Sarton • Jean-Paul Sartre
Ferdinand de Saussure • Gerald Scarfe • Albert Schweitzer
George Bernard Shaw • Isaac Bashevis Singer • Patwant Singh • Edith Sitwell
Suzanne St Albans • Stevie Smith • C.P. Snow • Bengt Söderbergh
Vladimir Soloukhin • Natsume Soseki • Muriel Spark • Gertrude Stein • Bram Stoker
August Strindberg • Rabindranath Tagore • Tambimuttu • Elisabeth Russell Taylor
Emma Tennant • Anne Tibble • Roland Topor • Miloš Urban • Anne Valery
Peter Vansittart • José J. Veiga • Tarjei Vesaas • Noel Virtue • Max Weber
Edith Wharton • William Carlos Williams • Phyllis Willmott
G. Peter Winnington • Monique Wittig • A.B. Yehoshua • Marguerite Young
Fakhar Zaman • Alexander Zinoviev • Emile Zola

Peter Owen Publishers, Conway Hall, 25 Red Lion Square, London WC1R 4RL, UK
T + 44 (0)20 7061 6756 / E info@peterowen.com
www.peterowen.com / @PeterOwenPubs
Independent publishers since 1951